Understanding
LUIGI PIRANDELLO

UNDERSTANDING MODERN EUROPEAN AND LATIN AMERICAN LITERATURE

JAMES HARDIN, *Series Editor*

volumes on

Ingeborg Bachmann
Samuel Beckett
Thomas Bernhard
Johannes Bobrowski
Heinrich Böll
Italo Calvino
Albert Camus
Elias Canetti
Céline
José Donoso
Rainer Werner Fassbinder
Max Frisch
Federico García Lorca
Gabriel García Márquez

Juan Goytisolo
Günter Grass
Gerhart Hauptmann
Christoph Hein
Eugéne Ionesco
Milan Kundera
Primo Levi
Luigi Pirandello
Graciliano Ramos
Erich Maria Remarque
Jean-Paul Sartre
Claude Simon
Mario Vargas Llosa
Franz Werfel
Peter Weiss

UNDERSTANDING

LUIGI
PIRANDELLO

FIORA A. BASSANESE

UNIVERSITY OF SOUTH CAROLINA PRESS

Published in Columbia, South Carolina, by the
University of South Carolina Press

Manufactured in the United States of America

01 00 99 98 97   5 4 3 2 1

Library of Congress Cataloging-in-Publication Data

Bassanese, Fiora A.
  Understanding Luigi Pirandello / Fiora A. Bassanese.
    p. cm. — (Understanding modern European and Latin
American literature)
  Includes bibliographical references and index.
  ISBN 1–57003–081–2
  1. Pirandello, Luigi, 1867–1936—Criticism and
interpretation. I. Title. II. Series.
  PQ4835.I7Z53478 1996
  852'.912—dc20   96–25198

For my mother,

Adalgisa Furlan Bassanese

CONTENTS

Editor's Preface   viii

Preface   ix

Chronology   xi

Chapter 1   The International Provincial   1

Chapter 2   *The Late Mattia Pascal* and Goddess Luck   22

Chapter 3   *Right You Are (If You Think So)* and the Crisis of Reality   42

Chapter 4   Moscarda's Nose, or the Disintegration of the Individual   63

Chapter 5   Henry IV's Sane Madness   76

Chapter 6   The Theater Plays   97

Chapter 7   The Myths   121

Chapter 8   Other Works   136

Notes   157

Selected Bibliography   171

Index   189

EDITOR'S PREFACE

Understanding Modern European and Latin American Literature has been planned as a series of guides for undergraduate and graduate students and non-academic readers. Like the volumes in its companion series Understanding Contemporary American Literature, these books provide introductions to the lives and writings of prominent modern authors and explicates their most important works.

Modern literature makes special demands, and this is particularly true of foreign literature, in which the reader must contend not only with unfamiliar, often arcane artistic conventions and philosophical concepts, but also with the handicap of reading the literature in translation. It is a truism that the nuances of one language can be rendered in another only imperfectly (and this problem is especially acute in fiction), but the fact that the works of European and Latin American writers are situated in a historical and cultural setting quite different from our own can be as great a hindrance to the understanding of these works as the linguistic barrier. For this reason the UMELL series emphasizes the sociological and historical background of the writers treated. The peculiar philosophical and cultural traditions of a given culture may be particularly important for an understanding of certain authors, and these are taken up in the introductory chapter and also in the discussion of those works to which this information is relevant. Beyond this, the books treat the specifically literary aspects of the author under discussion and attempt to explain the complexities of contemporary literature lucidly. The books are conceived as introductions to the authors covered, not as comprehensive analyses. They do not provide detailed summaries of plot because they are meant to be used in conjunction with the books they treat, not as a substitute for study of the original works. The purpose of the books is to provide information and judicious literary assessment of the major works in the most compact, readable form. It is our hope that the UMELL series will help increase knowledge and understanding of European and Latin American cultures and will serve to make the literature of those cultures more accessible.

J.H.

PREFACE

Like the other volumes in this series, *Understanding Luigi Pirandello* was not conceived for an audience of specialists in Italian Studies or theater, but for a general, informed readership who knows little or nothing about the author, his culture, or his works. This book is also primarily intended for an English-speaking audience that cannot read the material in the original language but depends on the availability of translations to experience the fictional world of Pirandello in print or in performance. For this reason I gave limited attention to the complex issue of the writer's stylistics and to his contribution to literary language, instead favoring the fostering of a better grasp of his conceptual framework, themes, and innovative discourse. The discussion of specific texts has been limited, necessarily, by their availablity in an English-language version and by their publicly recognised significance in Pirandello's overall production.

While this volume generally follows a temporal chronology, the chapters are not organized according to publication or performance dates but follow a thematic arrangement highlighting two genres: the novel and drama. For the study of some writers this structure might pose a problem, but less so for that of Pirandello, who demonstrated extraordinary consistency in his motifs and outlook throughout the five decades of his prolific literary career. The first chapters in this book also highlight the cultural environment that formed the man and his works. Particular attention is paid to the importance of Pirandello's Sicilian roots in inspiring many of the settings and plots for numerous stories, novels, and dramas, but the writer's relationship to the significant cultural movements of his day, in a broader Italian and European context, is also discussed. Four chapters focus primarily on one central work, such as the novel *The Late Mattia Pascal* or the celebrated play *Henry IV,* but also treat related fiction or drama. One section each is devoted to the playwright's two trilogies: the theater plays, centering on *Six Characters in Search of an Author,* and the myths, produced in the last years of his long career. The last chapter offers a review of the nature and disposition of Pirandello's fictional universe by briefly examining other works not previously discussed. Much has been said about Pirandello's writing,and much more remains to be done. I hope that *Understanding Luigi Pirandello* will inspire readers to go beyond its introductory limits and examine some of the excellent resources cited in the Selected Bibliography.

The complete bibliography on Luigi Pirandello includes hundreds of books and thousands of articles in dozens of languages. Given the intended audience of this study, the Selected Bibliography concentrates on English-language sources. Only a handful of works in Italian are cited; these include secondary sources scholars generally recognize as historically or critically significant additions to Pirandello studies. Scholarly articles appearing singly in literary, drama, and psychology journals are more suited to a specialized, rather than a general, readership, and therefore have not been included. Still, I wish to acknowledge a debt of gratitude to the many fine journal publications and scholarly works in languages other than English that I have consulted through the years. These have enriched my understanding of Pirandello and, in their own way, contributed to this volume. While not included in the Selected Bibliography, a few such titles appear in the notes.

Finally, I would like to thank some individuals and institutions that have helped me in the preparation of this work: first of all, Professor James Hardin and the editors at the University of South Carolina Press for their unending patience; my own institution, the University of Massachusetts at Boston, for supporting this research with a special summer faculty grant; two former deans of the College of Arts and Sciences, Richard Freeland and Louis Esposito, for their personal and professional support and respect for my work; and a particular thanks to Louis Esposito for giving me a scholar's greatest gift, time, so that the project could finally come to fruition. My appreciation also goes to the staffs of two libraries where I spent many fruitful hours, repeatedly requesting their generous assistance: the Widener Library at Harvard University and the Healey Library at the University of Massachusetts—Boston. Furthermore, a debt is owed to the hundreds of students to whom I have taught Luigi Pirandello in both English and Italian: by teaching them, I too learned. Finally, a particularly warm note of appreciation goes to Professor Amy Millstone and Professor Nancy Harrowitz for being there throughout the long gestation and delivery of this book.

CHRONOLOGY

1867	Luigi Pirandello, the first son of Stefano and Caterina Ricci-Gramitto, born on June 28 in Girgenti, Sicily. A wealthy businessman, the father is involved in sulphur mining.
1880–1887	Family moves temporarily to Palermo, largest city on the island. Luigi enrolled in classical lyceum, then university. Later transfers to the University of Rome, then to the University of Bonn, Germany.
1889	Publishes his first book, a volume of poetry: *Mal giocondo* (Joyful Ill).
1891	Receives doctorate with a thesis in linguistics on the dialect of Girgenti. Continues to publish poetry.
1894	Residing in Rome, Pirandello takes part in the capital's traditional intellectual circles, collaborating in literary journals and befriending key cultural figures such as Luigi Capuana, theoretician of *Verismo*. Marries Maria Antonietta Portulano, daughter of Stefano Pirandello's business partner. The couple will have three children. Publishes first collection of short stories.
1897	Accepts teaching position in Italian literature and stylistics at the Istituto Superiore di Magistero, a woman's teaching college. Will resign from post in 1922.
1901–1912	Focuses on writing fiction. Publishes half dozen volumes of short stories and five novels, including the celebrated *The Late Mattia Pascal* (1904).
1903	Bankruptcy of Pirandello-Portulano mining concern. Pirandello experiences major economic setbacks. Wife suffers a severe breakdown.
1906	Joins the prestigious publishing house Treves.
1908	Publishes the literary essay *On Humor*. Start of polemical rapport with critic-philosopher Benedetto Croce.
1910	Begins theatrical collaboration with producer Nino Martoglio, who stages two one-act plays: *The Vise* and *Sicilian Limes*.
1915	Composes first Sicilian play for impresario Angelo Musco. Several dialect productions follow. Wife's illness worsens after sons enlist in World War I.

1916–1917	Premieres of the famous plays *Liolà, Right You Are (If You Think So),* and *The Pleasure of Honesty.* Pirandello is a modest success in Italian theater world.
1918	First edition of *Maschere Nude* (Naked Masks), a theater anthology, appears.
1919	Antonietta Portulano Pirandello confined to a nursing home where she dies four decades later.
1921	Riotous Rome premiere of *Six Characters in Search of an Author,* Pirandello's recognized masterpiece, followed in 1922–23 by successful runs in London, New York, and Paris.
1922	Premiere of *Henry IV.* Adriano Tilgher publishes seminal study of theater, forming basis of serious Pirandello criticism. First edition of *Novelle per un anno* (Short Stories for a Year), the collection of Pirandello's short fiction, offered by his new publisher, Bemporad.
1923	Pitoëff production of *Six Characters* makes Pirandello an international celebrity. Pirandello begins feverish activity in theater.
1924	Adheres to Fascism with public declaration during Matteotti Affair.
1925–1928	Assumes position of artistic director of newly formed repertory company Teatro D'Arte di Roma. Undertakes new role as director. Hires Marta Abba as company's leading lady. She will become his closest confidante. Publishes last novel, *One, No One and One Hundred Thousand* (1926). Writes ceaselessly for theater. Commences constant international travel, residing primarily in Berlin or Paris from 1928 to 1933. First play of myth trilogy, *The New Colony,* staged in 1928.
1929	Named to Italian Academy by Benito Mussolini, effectively becoming member of cultural establishment.
1934	Awarded Nobel Prize for Literature.
1936	Dies suddenly on December 10. Unfinished, his last play, *The Mountain Giants,* the myth of art, was posthumously staged in June 1937.
1956–1960	Mondadori Publishers issues complete works in six volumes.

Understanding
LUIGI PIRANDELLO

CHAPTER ONE

The International Provincial

At a death vigil a pensive Pirandellian character muses on the passage of time, the hurtling transformations of modern history, and the equally rapid alterations wrought to lives and psyches. "Four generations of lights, four," the character declares, "oil, kerosene, gas and electricity, all in sixty years' time . . . are too many, you know? It ruins your sight, and your head too; oh, the head too, a little."[1] Such lights, the protagonist concludes, merely illuminate externals: "Does it help us see better inside? No." During Luigi Pirandello's sixty-nine years on earth, revolutions in scientific technology, social institutions, and cultural thought provoked substantive changes that could easily ruin the head and affect the sight without illuminating the interiority. Incessantly venturing beyond the easily viewed surfaces, Pirandello spent a lifetime and thousands upon thousands of pages in attempting to "see better inside." Having personally experienced the displacements caused by the technological shift from oil to electricity, the cultural shift from romanticism to surrealism, and the psycholgical shift from ontological certainty to the Freudian subconscious, the author reveals their impact on the heart and mind in the questioning, reflective, tragicomic, and enlightening creations born of his vigorous imagination.

Luigi Pirandello was born into an economically depressed region where even oil lamps were a luxury, in a newly formed nation whose unity was constantly challenged by its geography and history. An island, Sicily stood apart from continental Italy in many of its customs and social habits and in its worldview. Its natural beauty contrasted sharply with the burdens of daily life, forming an inherent dichotomy that the writer would exploit in his pessimistic and paradoxical fictional universe. Pirandello's Sicily was a patriarchal land of ancient taboos, restrictive behavioral codes, and onerous proprieties that fueled the strong passions, sudden violence, and frustration of its inhabitants. During his lifetime the island was still an anachronism mired in feudal remains: a land where the Mafia operated as a sociopolitical force protected by a conspiracy of silence that naturally reticent Sicilians could easily comprehend and respect; a land where the misery of peasants and mine workers occasionally exploded into violence and insurrection; a land where honor and family were venerated and inextricably entwined. The Catholic church fostered tradition and the status quo with the backing of a landed gentry in decline and a conservative middle class on the rise while the poor barely survived in their fatalism, superstitious faith, and timeless reality. Eventually life would take the provincial Luigi Pirandello from Girgenti to Rome, then to Paris, Berlin, London, New York, and beyond. He would travel the great temporal, spatial, artistic, and psychological distances separating oil from electricity, regional naturalism from Hollywood film scripts, and Sicilian donkey carts from the automobile.

A poor, parched corner of southern Sicily, the windswept town of Girgenti was an unlikely birthplace for one of Italy's literary icons and its greatest modern playwright, yet Luigi Pirandello understood his land's vital role in his life and imagination. Sicily is Pirandello's literary microcosm for the universal condition of humanity. Its sun-drenched earth, distant shimmering sea, ancient ruins, roadside shrines, dangerous sulpher mines, crumbling palaces, and populous slums are an ideal universe to house his prolific inventions. "I am a child of Chaos and not only allegorically,"[2] the author declares in a well-known biographical sketch, emphasizing the mythic proportions of this particular place and time. In point of fact the family's country house was situated in an area locals called Chaos, a name dating back to ancient Greek colonists. The author came into the world there,"one June night falling like a firefly under a great solitary pine," a premature child born during a cholera epidemic into a world marked by disease and death. Notwithstanding the writer's disclaimer, his birth at Chaos is also a key element in the creation of his personal mythology and an allegorical sign for his creative universe, one dominated by the belief in an incomprehensible and unmanageable world where disorder and chance—chaos, the void—reign supreme.

Pirandello was born into a prosperous family on June 28, 1867, a few short years after Italian political unification was achieved. Stefano Pirandello and Caterina Ricci-Gramitto were drawn together by their shared patriotic zeal, a heroic enthusiasm whose ashes their son was to depict in his only historical novel, *I vecchi e i giovani* (1913, *The Old and the Young*). The Ricci-Gramittos were Sicilian separatists: anti-Bourbon and anticlerical patriots who, after participating in the failed political revolt of 1848, suffered years of exile and the confiscation of their property. Twelve years later three of Caterina's brothers joined the forces of Giuseppe Garibaldi (1807–1882), the military hero of Italian unification. They met Stefano Pirandello among the ranks of idealistic Sicilian volunteers. It was during a visit to his comrades-in-arms that Stefano proposed to Caterina and decided to settle in Girgenti, today called Agrigento, entering the lucrative if perilous mining business. Luigi was the second of six surviving children and the couple's first son. Born into a household, and a young state, that was hopeful and confident in its romantic ideals of progress, equality, and national pride, Pirandello found himself entering adulthood in a country in decline. In his view the years following the *Risorgimento,* or rebirth of Italy, witnessed the collapse of the moral values espoused by the patriots and the triumph of hypocrisy, corruption, and mediocrity. A bitter sense of loss and emptiness followed, which Pirandello calls "the bankruptcy of patriotism." This loss was particularly hard-felt in the deep south, where political union rapidly developed into a form of internal colonialism. The government favored the more industrially developed north, leading to exploitation and political repression, a situation that only deepened the skepticism and despondency shared by many Sicilians and reflected in Pirandello's writing.

Growing up in this atmosphere of disillusionment, the boy Luigi showed a particularly sensitive and introspective temperament far better suited to intellectual pursuits than to the combative life of an entrepreneur such as his despotic and choleric father, a man capable of challenging the local Mafia bosses. Demonstrating little aptitude for commercial studies during his first year at a technical institute, the adolescent Pirandello was permitted to pursue a humanistic education at the classical lyceum in Palermo, Sicily's largest city. Throughout his student years Pirandello voraciously consumed books and knowledge, pushing himself mercilessly, which resulted in regular bouts of ill health. His dark, self-conscious, and skeptical worldview was formed early on. At the age of nineteen Luigi wrote his sister that life was like "an enormous puppet show without connection or rationale," a suggestive image that would recur in his creative and personal writing. Pirandello eventually enrolled at the University of Palermo in both law (soon abandoned) and the humanities, then transferred briefly to Rome. Following an academic disagreement, he went to Bonn, Germany, where he completed his studies after presenting a thesis on the dialect of his native Girgenti; he received the doctorate in philology in 1891. Even in the stimulating and international atmosphere of a German university, Pirandello nurtured his attachment to his insular origins.

During his student years the fledgling writer experienced his first sentimental attachments—including a long but ill-fated engagement to an older cousin—flirted briefly with socialism, and discovered the pleasures of literature. Like many a sensitive young man of the nineteenth century, Pirandello composed poetry, publishing his first collection, *Mal giocondo* (Joyful Ill), in 1889. In Bonn this Italian steeped in classical culture came to love the masterpieces of German literature, translating Goethe's *Roman Elegies* and imitating them in his own *Elegie renane* (1895, Rhenish Elegies), a work inspired by both his readings and a tender infatuation with a charming local girl, Jenny Schulz-Lander, who was also the muse of the springlike rhymes of *Pasqua di Gea* (1894, The Easter of Gaea, or Earth)[3]. Although Pirandello was invited to stay in Bonn as a lecturer, poor health and his own proclivities called him home. Determined to continue his studies and pursue his literary interests, Pirandello went to Rome, then the hub of Italian intellectual life. Sicily would never again be the writer's home, but it remained central to his life: he would return there to heal, to vacation, and to find a wife. More important, Sicily was always the significant locus of his imagination, a place destined to continuously provide the seeds for Pirandello's fertile fantasy, producing the innumerable characters, plots, and situations of his works.

With a monthly allowance from his father, Pirandello settled permanently in the capital. He quickly began collaborating with literary and artistic journals and, befriending influential men of letters, took part in Rome's traditional intellectual circles. Pirandello was determined to have a voice in current intellectual debates while shedding the image of transplanted provincial. Building on the intellectual curiosity stimulated by his sojourn in Germany, the writer explored the works of international thinkers and artists and found himself particularly drawn, like many of his generation, to the philosophies of Friedrich Nietzsche (1844–1900) and Henri Bergson (1859–1941) and their disciples. The perception of individual and social crisis Pirandello experienced throughout his life became the focus of his analyses, as he sought to understand the historical reasons for contemporary humanity's existential plight and the failure of ideologies to respond to this massive crisis of identity. In the rapidly changing landscape of the early twentieth century, Pirandello perceived the widening hegemony of capitalism, industrialization, and science as detrimental to personal needs. Caught in these shifts, individuals suffered from the effects of humanity's rapid displacement from a traditional and comforting position at the center of the universe to a state of epistemological uncertainty. Moreover, Pirandello believed that the codes and obligations of bourgeois Western society repressed natural impulses by surrounding the individual with roles, taboos, and the forced dissimulations of respectability, effectively hiding the inner self. Pirandello found that the function of intellectuals such as himself was being revised and diminished: artists and thinkers could no longer provide satisfactory answers to modern humanity's anguished queries or perform as messengers of belief systems as they had in the past. One of the first writers to recognize the dissolution of the institutions and certainties of nineteenth-century Europe, Pirandello depicted a world in serious disarray, where the new models for progress were unable to recreate the lost order that had been preserved for centuries by humanity's persistent belief in reason, religion, logic, and coherence. In these early years of his creative development, Pirandello was caught between the push of positivism, which focused on facts and advocated the primacy of reason, and the pull of unfulfilled spiritual aspirations and of the subterranean mysteries of the human psyche. In time Pirandello would demolish the legacy of naturalism and positivism in his works. Eventually he would find all the "isms" of his day wanting, including idealism, intuitionism, nationalism, rationalism, and Fascism. But as the old standards were disintegrating, no certainties appeared to replace them, and no new norms were being created.

During those first years in Rome, Pirandello established enduring friendships with some of the nation's leading literati, most notably his fellow Sicilian Luigi Capuana (1839–1915), renowned theoretician of verismo, the Italian form of naturalism. Pirandello's arrival in the capital also marked the point of departure for his extensive creative output, which includes numerous essays and reviews, hundreds of short stories, seven novels, several volumes of poetry, and more than forty works for the theater. Notwithstanding his evolving cosmopolitanism, the pull of Pirandello's regional roots was always strong. His first published story, "Capannetta" (1884, Little Hut), clearly displays Pirandello's indebtedness to the Sicilian masters of verismo, who represented the realities and local color of their region. Subtitled a "Sicilian Sketch," this first tale freely bases its depiction of the misery of peasant life on the works of Giovanni Verga (1840–1922), the acknowledged master of verismo. But as his narrative skills developed, Pirandello gradually distanced himself from the conventions of naturalism, in seach of more imaginative and reflective writing.

Soon after having established himself in Rome, Pirandello readily agreed to an arranged marriage with a young woman he barely knew, the daughter of his father's business associate. Although Luigi proclaimed rebellious attitudes toward social institutions, such as anticlericalism, he also manifested a markedly traditional side that relished the role of petit bourgeois pater familias. This duality is indicative of the coexisting tensions ever present in Pirandello's personality. He was a man noted for great warmth as well as for petulance and simmering resentments who could blend intellectual daring and extreme personal restraint. Passionate by nature, he was correct to a fault, even prudish, in his demeanor. Pirandello himself was well aware of the multifaceted nature of his personality, which he sought to communicate to his intended. The letters to his fiancée describe a dualistic "little me" and "Big Me" who constantly do battle and split the future bridegroom in two, personifying the antagonistic drives in his life. The "Big Me" is directed toward solitude, study, and achievement: the contemplative life of the serious intellectual. The "little me" is drawn to the comfortable security of marriage and family life: so-called normalcy. In these epistolary reflections for his fiancée, Pirandello anticipates one of his major literary themes: the doubling of the self.[4] However, such rigorous self-analysis was unlikely to seduce the future Mrs. Pirandello.

Motherless since birth and convent bred, Antonietta Portulano was a southern Italian girl of restricted education and life experience, yet Luigi, blind to her limitations, proposed to mold her into his "ideal" woman. This naive Pygmalion soon discovered that his beautiful wife neither shared nor understood his intellectual interests, resented his literary associations, and preferred to center her existence round familial and maternal duties. Antonietta never learned to appreciate the creative and intellectual dimension that engaged her husband. Indeed, she came to despise his writing as an exhibitionist act and never read any of his publications. The first years of their marriage were not unhappy, however, and the couple had three children and a comfortable life financed by the Pirandello mining interests in Sicily. Besides producing a steady stream of reviews, articles, and fiction, in 1897 Pirandello also accepted a post at the women's Istituto Superiore di Magistero, or teachers' college, in Rome, to provide better for his growing family. Yet there was a cheerless quality to the writer's life. On the surface he was a most proper and dapper professional who dressed exclusively in grey and exuded a law-abiding, family-oriented, bourgeois persona, but the surface disguised a deep-seated nihilism.

The impossibility of achieving authentic communication, either in marriage or in any other human relationship, became a core idea in Pirandello's expanding literary production. In seeking to represent the lack of dialogue and the hopelessness of establishing avenues of reciprocal exchange with others, the author developed a literature filled with an evergrowing sense of alienation. His characters' state of solitude is further exacerbated by social reality, wherein community is founded on impositions, expectations, and dehumanizing regulations. Pirandello perceived life as a fluid element constantly evolving and changing. Custom, institutions, and societal roles remained stagnant and stultifying, imprisoning the individual in their forms. These abstractions became all too concrete for Pirandello in 1903. By then the dilettante author had two novels, three poetry collections, a failed literary journal, and a play to his name. He was a modest success. That year, however, disaster struck: the family's sulphur mine flooded, followed by complete financial ruin, including the loss of his wife's handsome cash dowry. Suddenly impoverished, Pirandello thought of suicide. Antonietta, more fragile then her husband, experienced her first major nervous collapse, retreating to her bed and into her agitated mind for several months. Sitting at the bedside of his stricken spouse, Pirandello wrote his narrative masterpiece, *Il fu Mattia Pascal* (1904, *The Late Mattia Pascal*), a serio-comic tale of personal and social exclusion.

After his financial setback Pirandello was forced to publish, tutor, and teach to survive. His critical activities as a reviewer, scholar, and essayist are chronologically parallel to his creative production and illuminate it. Two erudite volumes focusing on aesthetics and literary analysis appeared in 1908, affording important insights into the writer's artistic vision and conceptualization of the role of literature: *L'umorismo* (*On Humor*) and *Arte e Scienza* (Art and Science). Their publication resulted in Pirandello's promotion from lecturer to chair in Italian language and stylistics at the Magistero. More important for Pirandello studies, these texts detail the author's thoughts on writing and the creative process. Pirandello's works deal with theoretical issues such as the rapport between art and inspiration, the use of language, and the function of rhetoric. Pirandello viewed his art as a spontaneous and honest expression of human feeling, communicated in a language that is natural, based on current usage, and capable of voicing the writer's creative impulse. The author firmly speaks in favor of a literary language that expresses human experience, thus countering the rhetorical embellishments of much contemporary Italian literature in the wake of Gabriele D'Annunzio (1863–1938), the country's most popular turn-of-the-century artist. Whereas D'Annunzio saw the writer as a refined aesthete, a Nietzschean superman, or an orphic seer, Pirandello rejected the underlying artificiality and arrogance of such images. According to Pirandello, humor is the ideal instrument for expressing the paradoxical nature of reality and denouncing the absurdity and pain of the human condition.

Pirandello did not develop his ideas in an intellectual vacuum. A lifelong insatiable reader, the author drew from a wide assortment of philosophical, literary, historical, cultural, and even theosophic sources. Several French thinkers figure prominently in his critical reflections on the nature of art, life, and consciousness. The aesthetic theories of Gabriel Séailles, for one, strongly influence the discussion in *On Humor*. Séailles suggests that the creative process consists of both a reasoning plane and a feeling capable of arousing images that give form and expression to an idea, thereby creating art.[5] The humorist, Pirandello argues, experiences first an awareness of opposites, then reflects upon it, eliciting a feeling of opposites which is at the heart of humoristic art. Alfred Binet's *Les Altérations de la Personnalité* (1892, The Alterations of Personality), a work that focuses on scientific experiments in pathological psychology, introduced Pirandello to issues of consciousness and psychological relativism. After reading Binet (1857–1911), Pirandello was better prepared to formulate his own insights: the unity of the self can be reduced to temporal aggregates; the personality consists of a collection of continuously combining and recombining elements, in constant flux. Pirandello's repeatedly expressed belief that awareness, feeling, and reflection are all essential to the artistic process reflects his time's growing fascination with psychological issues that range from the development of psychoanalyis to scientific research into pathologies, as well as parapsychology. Finally, Pirandello borrows his concept of the fluidity, essential evanescence, and changeability of life and emotion from Bergson, who also suggests that reason, or intellect, is used to fix life by proposing immutable forms that necessarily stem its flow. Reality, Bergson argues, cannot be grasped by the intellect because the universe is constantly changing while mental concepts are fixed. Pirandello would artistically render such fixed forms as roles, masks, and social definitions that suffocate individual authenticity and freedom.

Pirandello's increasing visibility in some of Italy's established national periodicals and the publication of *The Late Mattia Pascal* opened the doors to a prestigious publisher for his fiction: Treves. But this success was not evidence of any general acknowledgment of his contributions to a new sensibility or style. For the most part Pirandello's contemporaries viewed him as a second-generation naturalist, another regional writer in the Sicilian mold who specialized in objective renderings of southern village life or drawing-room society. Worse still for his literary reputation, in 1908 Pirandello entered into a permanently antagonistic relationship with Italy's celebrated philosopher-critic Benedetto Croce (1866–1952), the luminary of official culture. Responding in part to Pirandello's open hostility toward his own aesthetic system, Croce criticized the essay *On Humor* on grounds of lax critical thinking and stylistic impropriety. But the dissension between the two reached deep into their personal definitions of art and artists. Whereas the idealist Croce saw a work of art as the product of intuition and lyricism, not reason or thought, the humorist Pirandello emphasized the primacy of reflection and the contribution of intelligence to the creative process. Croce's insistence on logical classifications inevitably clashed with Pirandello's accent on relativity, fragmentation, and the irrational. The Sicilian writer found philosophical and aesthetic systems highly incompatible with his view of art because they categorized and immobilized the flow of life and avoided its messy complexities. Whereas Pirandello stressed the artistic union of passion and thought, Croce could only see Pirandello's work as a hybrid, neither art nor philosophy. In the 1920 edition of *On Humor,* Pirandello responded to Croce by demanding a new direction in Italian literature that would free it of aestheticism, sentimentality, artificiality, and rhetorical excess: a literature in which consciousness and intelligence would play a key role.

Unfortunately for Pirandello's public image, these intellectual quarrels with Croce influenced critics and reviewers, who stereotyped the writer, placing him into two neat, albeit somewhat oppositional, authorial categories: naturalist or rationalizing sophist.

These years of intense intellectual activity accompanied years of cohabitation, punctuated by separations and reconciliations, with a depressed, morbidly jealous wife. In her paranoia Antonietta formed the image of an unfaithful, irresponsible husband, thus nurturing Pirandello's thoughts on the multiplicity of the human personality and his views on the subjective nature of reality. After her breakdown Antonietta found it extremely difficult to accept her marriage with any semblance of equanimity, repeatedly accusing her husband of fantastic infidelities and betrayals.[6] As his wife's mental health declined, Pirandello, often unwelcome in his own home, was forced to rent bachelor's quarters at semiregular intervals. But the man was unable to let go of his crazed wife. Matters worsened during the war years: family life deteriorated rapidly after both sons, Stefano and Fausto, enlisted in the Italian army in World War I. Pirandello was blamed for Stefano's continued internment in a prison camp and for Fausto's enlistment. Antonietta went on to accuse her spouse of incest with his beloved daughter and of attempted murder; convinced he wished to poison her, she regularly had her food tasted. The situation came to a head when daughter Lietta, the only child left at home, attempted suicide in 1918, having become the victim of her mother's increasing paranoia. The following year, with the support of his children, Pirandello had Antonietta institutionalized, effectively transforming him into a married bachelor. She would survive her husband by several decades. Notwithstanding these traumatic personal events—or perhaps because of them— Pirandello discovered his dramatic potential in the years of the Great War and its aftermath. "Mine," he would say, "is a theater of war."[7]

Pirandello became a committed dramatist relatively late in life. Just as Luigi Capuana had persuaded his young protegé to try the narrative genre, another Sicilian friend, Nino Martoglio (1870–1921), playwright and theatrical producer, convinced a middle-aged Pirandello to reattempt the theater. At Martoglio's insistence Pirandello dusted off a half-forgotten play, *La morsa* (*The Vise*), written in 1898, and quickly composed *Lumie di Sicilia* (*Sicilian Limes*), drawn from the plot of a published short story. These two one-acters, premiering in late 1910, launched Pirandello's career in the theater, which he would never abandon. Martoglio also introduced Pirandello to Angelo Musco (1872–1937), a successful actor-impresario who specialized in popular Sicilian theater. Prevailed upon to compose a piece in dialect for Musco's talents and repertory company, Pirandello turned out *Pensaci, Giacomino!* (Think It Over, Giacomino!), also derived from an older short story. The play proved a success at its 1916 premiere in Rome. That same year *Liolà* was produced by Musco, followed in 1917 by *Il berretto a sonagli* (*Cap and Bells*) and *La giara* (*The Jar*), all written in Sicilian and set in the world of Pirandello's birth. Like his early novels and tales Pirandello's first plays were influenced by his regional roots. In 1917 the playwright also presented one of his most-celebrated works, *Così è (se vi pare)* (*Right You Are [If You Think So]*), situated in the other sphere of Pirandello's existence: a middle-class home. Other "bourgeois" dramas soon followed, leading critics to compare Pirandello to another brilliant dramatist of ideas, the Norwegian Henrik Ibsen (1828–1906).

At first glance Pirandello's Sicilian plays show clear evidence of naturalist traits: the delving into slice-of-life situations; the employment of popular or colloquial language, including dialect, to denote precisely the setting; the introduction of realistic production values to concretize situations, such as having barking dogs in a country scene at night or demanding accuracy in costumes, props, and furnishings; the manipulation of the characters' physical appearance to imply physiological and pathological predispositions; and the use of the stage to present a "case study." But such naturalist elements merely serve Pirandello as familiar pathways leading the audience to his unique depiction of a universal human condition of needless suffering, social alienation, suffocating roles, and painful self-awareness. Pirandello's chosen milieu, the insular environment of Sicily, serves to amplify the dramatist's themes by placing them in a land of conflicting extremes, emphatic emotions, and imperative behavioral codes. Pirandello's literary Sicily is equally real and emblematic. While his Sicilian character is a realistic rendering in the naturalist vein, he is also a symbol for universal man in search of meaning in a chaotic, irrational world. Thus the fictional representation of the restricted and restricting atmosphere surrounding Girgenti becomes Pirandello's metahistorical stage for the spectacle of life: a privileged space where the physical meets the metaphysical, where facts meet illusion, where paradox reigns. Pirandello's Sicily of the imagination maintains contact with the existing realities of Sicilian life but offers a dialectical actuality of its own through the interplay of fact and fantasy, joy and pessimism. Glimpses of this dual world of light and darkness are caught in the differing tonalities of *Liolà* and *Cap and Bells.*

The illustrious Marxist theoretician and cultural commentator Antonio Gramsci (1891–1937) considered the dialect plays Pirandello's greatest achievement. Enchanted by an early production of *Liolà,* Gramsci's review of the piece underscores the life-affirming components of the Sicilian setting: its sunniness, pagan spirit, and peasant earthiness. These elements, Gramsci notes, connect Pirandello's comedy to the theater of pagan Magna Grecia, the ancient Greek colonial era in Sicily, with its tradition of pastorals, idylls, and dionysian frenzy. Gramsci is equally taken with the "truth" of Pirandello's characters, who do not behave like intellectuals masquerading as peasants but "like historically and regionally real Sicilian folk."[8] According to the Marxist thinker, the title character embodies the moral and physical robustness of pagan life, just as his three boys resemble primitive little satyrs imbued with dance and song.[9] Thinking along similar lines, Pirandello scholar Anne Paolucci considers Liolà a pagan divinity inebriated by the strong Sicilian sun; he is a fusion of Pan and Dionysius, the gods of song, love, and drink, who have been lowered into a Christian world of religion and morality.[10] In Walter Starkie's view Liolà is a rustic relative of the traditional Spanish archetype Don Juan, the eternal *burlador*. Other scholars interpret the character as the figuration of the romantic poet, free-spirited and defiant of social impositions. For Eric Bentley *Liolà* "is Pirandello on holiday,"[11] taking a break from his typical gravity and pensiveness. Offering a contemporary feminist point of view, Susan Bassnet-McGuire reads the play as "a tasteless example of reactionary male chauvinism."[12] Intriguingly, these contrastive views of *Liolà* are all justified by the text, which contains the germs for many interpretations, in keeping with its Pirandellian genesis.

Following a typical pattern of cross-fertilization, the outline of *Liolà*'s plot was drawn from an episode of *The Late Mattia Pascal*. It was Pirandello's habit to recycle material from one work or genre to another. The dramatic action revolves around two standard Sicilian motifs: property and seduction. Liolà is a handsome, self-sufficient, joyful peasant with a talent for song and wooing. As a result he has three sons by three women. Ardent but equally accountable, Liolà and his self-sacrificing mother have taken in the boys, who are being taught to sing, dance, and work. The stage action begins with the discovery that a fourth woman, Tuzza, is pregnant by the prolific hero. This time the peasant Lothario is willing to do his duty and save her honor by offering marriage. The unexpected occurs when Tuzza, spurred on by her greedy mother, rejects Liolà in favor of a more profitable, if illegitimate, union. Tuzza and Zia Croce plan to use the girl's pregnancy to ingratiate themselves with their wealthy relation, Zio Simone, who has no heir to receive his accumulated wealth—his *roba*. Simone is old, rich, unpleasant, and childless—a situation he alone attributes to his young wife. Consequently he physically abuses Mita, blaming her for his deficiencies. Simone is delighted to enter into a public deception with Tuzza: the child will be declared his, thus providing him with an heir and offering public proof of his questionable virility. The materialistic Tuzza will profit from

Simone's generosity, as the mother of his acknowledged heir. Catching wind of this conspiracy, Liolà proposes a second deception to poor Mita, the real victim of her husband's craving. He will help her supply Simone with a "legitimate" heir the same way Tuzza supplied him with an illegitimate one. Reluctantly the battered wife agrees. As befits a comedy, all's well that ends well: the guilty are punished, and the virtuous are victorious. Tuzza will lose honor and riches; Mita will maintain status and security; Simone will have his "legitimate" heir; and Liolà may well add a fourth mouth to his joyous progeny. In the end, Liolà's fertile mind and body have not only shaped a new life but also a new reality, a transformed situation for all concerned.

Read in a positive fashion, Liolà embodies instinct and nature outside the hypocrisy of society. The creature of a pagan sin-free world, he brings a joyous exuberance with him that is the source of his seductiveness. He is a lover of life, as well as of women: he fruitfully amasses children (all sons) and happily nests with his brood of chirping "goldfinches" as indisputable corroboration of his essence as earth father. A nonconformist, the singing peasant is outside the control of society: he is immune to the weighty impositions of property and conventions. Unfettered by institutions, materialism, or public morality, he is one of Pirandello's few happy men. On the surface *Liolà* is a farcical romp modeled on the *beffa,* or trick, a comic topos found throughout medieval and Renaissance tales and theater. An impotent and wealthy old man, Simone figures as an archetypal caricature, the ideal victim of the extended practical joke about to be played on him by the intelligent trickster, Liolà. Logically the two male characters are drawn antithetically as befits antagonists. While Liolà is young and charming, Simone is aged and nasty. One is as fruitful as the birds of the air, the other infertile. The former is blissfully poor, the latter obsessed with property. Paternity promises to even the score a bit for Simone. Tuzza's child initially represents fulfillment, so the old man is more than content to accept her dishonest falsification to obtain his cherished heir. Liolà's counterplot, a careful balancing of reality and appearances, is also dependent on deception and illusion.

In many ways Liolà is a dangerously transgressive character who challenges social institutions, values, and expectations. Indeed, transgression is the major source of happiness in this play: it gives birth to the hero's joie de vivre just as it produces a happy ending for both Mita and Simone, the newly expectant "parents." But transgression has a price—there is a dark side to this charming comedy. As a lover Liolà had approached Tuzza instinctively. But the second-act seduction of Mita is another matter: it is based on a rational manipulation of morality. Liolà offers Mita a paradoxical ethical proposition: as the faithful wife she can only remain in her rightful place by producing a legitimate heir of superior value to the illegitimate one offered by Tuzza. Plainly stated, Mita can save her marriage and preserve her honor only by committing adultery. Liolà's logic amounts to sophism with a pinch of revenge, albeit undertaken with the best of intentions to protect Mita. Simone's young wife illustrates the precarious status of women in a patriarchal society. Defined by her gender, Mita's function is procreation; her blameless childlessness devalues her. Ironically, it is through infidelity that she regains the position of honored wife, a status dependent on the appearance (but not necessarily the reality) of sexual virtue.

Other illusions and deceptions drive *Liolà*'s dramatic action. In her greed Tuzza emerges as both villain and victim of her envious choices. At play's end she is the dishonored object of general censure for having lost the characteristics expected of unmarried Sicilian women: virginity, reputation, integrity. However, her attempt to stab Liolà in the third-act finale is easily thwarted, maintaining the play's sunny tone. Tuzza's violent reaction simply does not have the narrative power to transform the story line from a blithe comedy into a naturalist slice-of-life drama. *Liolà* ends in song, not sorrow. Mita's impending maternity affords a socially suitable and dramatically appropriate denouement to the stage action. Mita's pregnancy is legitimized by Simone's illusions: the aging husband insists on his biological paternity against all insinuations and evidence to the contrary. As Paolucci has noted, the deception practiced on Simone is transformed into an act of faith: like many Pirandellian characters he has come to see his desire, an illusion, as reality. The appearance of paternity is accepted by all as a new social contract; it will count more than the biological facts for both the old man and the community. Elsewhere in the Sicilian plays the issue of willed illusion appears with less gratifying results.

In *Cap and Bells,* Pirandello offers a seriocomic Sicilian tale of adultery, jealousy, and honor. The action builds around the relationship of two provincial couples: the well-to-do Fioricas and the poor Ciampas. An extremely jealous and somewhat hysterical woman, Beatrice Fiorica is certain her husband is pursuing an affair with the beautiful Nina Ciampa. However, the wronged wife has no proof to support this conviction. Instigated by neighbors—one of numerous instances of societal interference in Pirandello's work—Beatrice is willing to confront public ignominy to validate her belief, thus taking revenge on the straying spouse. Impetuous, Beatrice does not reflect on the possible consequences of her actions and calls in the law. The presumed lovers are discovered together (but not in flagrante delicto) and arrested, and a scandal erupts. Up to this point the dramatic action unfolds in patterns long familiar to audiences of turn-of-the-century European theater, which was saturated with stories of adulterous triangles and their consequences. Pirandello compounds this impression of familiarity by mounting the two-act drama in an equally conventional setting: the richly furnished drawing room of Fiorica's provincial home. The unconventional touch in *Cap and Bells* is provided by its central character: the Fioricas' clerk, Ciampa, one of numerous Pirandellian eccentrics.

Ciampa is not an ignorant peasant but a sophisticated thinker who suddenly finds his entire world at risk because of Beatrice's lack of thought.[13] Through the years Ciampa has managed to construct a fragile existential equilibrium for himself in a difficult situation. Seemingly aware of his beloved wife's infidelity with his employer, he conceals it by wearing the mask of the ever vigilant Sicilian husband. Quite literally Ciampa locks his Nina in, pocketing the key. Tacitly he understands the needs of this young woman married to an older, poor, and unattractive man—an understanding that is never openly stated or directly acknowledged but is clearly implied in the dialogue. Appearances are thus served and the respectability of the couple is preserved even in their own eyes. Ciampa has elevated the appearance of fidelity to a public fact. Beatrice threatens to destroy that appearance by demanding the truth. As is often the case in Pirandello's fictional universe, the truth is not necessarily knowable or even desirable.

In this petty provincial town the consequences of Beatrice's exposure are deadly serious. As a public figure Fiorica (who never appears on stage) will be discredited; the entire extended family will be touched with scandal and dishonor; Beatrice herself will be forced into the confined life of a separated wife. Under the unwritten rules of Sicilian mores, the consequences are all the more catastrophic for Ciampa: the stain to family honor must be avenged at all costs. Far more cognizant of the situation than his unwitting opponent Beatrice, Ciampa finds himself shouldering the heavy burden of public opinion. In the second act a remedy is sought to repair the damage done. Although the arrested couple, caught conversing, will be freed, Ciampa knows that this legal action will not save face. In the public eye he will be condemned on the basis of appearances alone, becoming one of the most dreaded of Sicilian laughingstocks: a cuckold. And the strict code of sexual morality exacts reparation: the betrayed husband is forced to kill to clear his name and regain honor, or he will be marked for life as a coward. With his quick mind Ciampa perceives an ingenious, if fantastic, alternative to his dilemma. In a twisted form of poetic justice, the source of the scandal, Beatrice, will break the deadlock by retracting her allegations and submitting to corrective measures to preserve both marriages and avoid dishonor. Having acted madly, she must be declared mad. The avowals of the crazed are notoriously undependable. Ciampa's solution is immediately embraced by the

Fiorica camp. In the end the wronged wife is forced to enter a sanatorium to "cure" her insane jealousy while the adulterous pair and the complacent husband are seemingly spared. In *Cap and Bells* the only irrefutable reality is appearances.

Through his own solitude and pain Ciampa experiences the predicament of the self-aware individual in a collectivity where self-affirmation and authentic honesty are repeatedly blocked. Like many Pirandellian characters Ciampa dreams of flight to another reality, far from the impositions and falsifying masks given him by a society that forces individuals into its preexisting molds and demands the construction of a conformist persona, no matter how counterfeit. Painfully analytical, Ciampa formulates theories to explain man's rapport with his fellows. To render the contrasts between truth and deceptions, reality and appearances, personal needs and social demands, the philosophical clerk has created whimsical abstractions and constructs to deal with the problematics of being and consciousness. As he explains to Beatrice, each person acts as a mechanism that runs on three cords which can be separately wound, producing social interaction: the serious, the civil, and the crazy. Each cord has its particular function and tone: the civil facilitates communal living through civilized behavior; the serious serves to explain and clarify, ordering life and the mind; once the serious fails, one is left with the crazy cord, the explosion that accompanies the loss of reason and control. Attempting to operate within the civil chord, Ciampa, like Beatrice, nevertheless totters on the brink of crazed behavior when he sees his control mechanisms collapsing as scandal overtakes him. Alarmed, he recognizes that his carefully constructed social self, his *pupo,* is at risk of annihilation.

Ciampa's consciously created self is embodied in the peculiarly Sicilian figure of the *pupo,* a sculpted marionette that often represents the heroic feats and adventures of medieval knights and their ladies.[14] Significantly for this context, the *pupo* is an actor of the puppet stage, a constructed imitation of man imitating life. All, Ciampa declares, have their self-created *pupo.* Each and every such human marionette demands respect, not for his inner self, which remains hidden to all, but for "the role he must perform on the outside." The *pupo* is the civil self, man's public identity, which must be defended. Revealing the unsatisfactory and frustrating self that the individual *pupo* conceals would destroy it and the persona. With no misgivings Beatrice has taken Ciampa's *pupo,* his good name, and trampled it, destroying the public man, a self-conscious pretense. What remains are the naked puppets of an adulterer, a whore, and a cuckold—social categories that can only falsify each individual's human complexity. Liberated by her feigned madness to expose her truth, Beatrice is carted off. She departs the stage in a frenzy, bleating like a billy goat, signaling to Ciampa that, in her eyes at least, he is undoubtedly a cuckold.[15] He, in turn, is exultant in his victory: his *pupo* has been preserved, but at great cost. He is last seen, collapsed in a chair, laughing horribly with rage, pleasure, and despair: a histrionic comment on the absurdity of it all. At play's end the crazy cord has taken charge.

Ciampa's self-constructed *pupo* is one of many forms of mask building in Pirandello's fictional universe. The dramatist's title for his collected plays, *Naked Masks,* underscores his awareness of the centrality of role-playing in the construction of human identity. But, just as the authenticity of the public mask is always in question, so too all manifestations of identity, assumed or imposed, are suspect. German theater critic Renate Matthaei considers Ciampa's entire physical appearance a disguise, from his piercing spectacled eyes to his messy hair and ill-fitting petit bourgeois apparel. This masking attitude necessarily brings into question the sincerity of all the character's responses. Is Ciampa's desperation in act 2 a ruse or sincere emotion? Is his verbal construction of a new *pupo,* the avenging husband, just as false and expedient as Beatrice's new *pupa,* the madwoman? Whatever the answer, the constructed persona will prevail, preserving the fiction of respectability for them all. In *Cap and Bells,* as elsewhere, Pirandello argues that illusions about the self and reality are constantly manufactured to give significance and order to one's world. As frequently occurs with Pirandellian characters, however, Ciampa's ability to reflect upon himself and human existence leads him to the inevitable conclusion that man cannot live without his masks. The Sicilian setting allows the playwright to project his paradoxical insights onto an environment where behavioral excesses are known to flourish.

Following the success of the Sicilian plays, the theater became the focus of Pirandello's substantial creative energies. Although his first decade as a playwright met with mixed reviews, a growing number of Italy's finest producers staged his works with some of Italy's best actors. Play followed play, totaling more than forty in all. In 1918 an anthology of Pirandello's theatrical works was published with the suggestive title "Naked Masks," which would be retained for all future compilations. However, like the proverbial prophet, the playwright was not immediately recognized in his own land. For example, *Liolà* was quickly pulled from the repertoire in Turin on grounds of obscenity, following hostile demonstrations organized by groups of young Catholic agitators. At its Roman premiere *Sei personaggi in cerca d'autore* (1921, *Six Characters in Search of an Author*), Pirandello's most celebrated play, was a notorious fiasco. Members of the audience loudly booed the drama with repeated cries of

and regional color. The royal family and Mussolini
the height of his international fame, Pirandello went
Arte throughout Europe, from London to Prague. In
rformed in South America.

Teatro d'Arte managed to survive, Pirandello's life
en his demanding roles as playwright, artistic direc-
ducer, he immersed himself in the study of stagecraft,
wn as a difficult but good director, Pirandello sought
in his performers. He believed in the transformation
ter portrayed, which he "wears" like a costume or, in
. Pirandello did not conceive of acting as a metamor-
are not "possessed" by their roles offstage but
y inhabit them on the boards. For Pirandello the char-
dominate the role, a perception that would be realized
ater plays. This was in marked contrast to current
s of both sexes held sway over playhouses as well as
ejected the star system in favor of the cohesion of a
e play, not the players, were the focal point of his
a solidly prepared and seasoned troupe of actors,
inated the prompter, whose presence fostered depen-
rs to prepare shabbily. From several contemporary
andello himself was a gifted natural actor, who would
ng dramatic readings of his plays and play-act their
f his direction. Eventually, however, the financially
as dissolved. Pirandello's dream of a national theater
se of the lack of firm state support for the project,
s Pirandello's enthusiasm for Fascism waned.

rs were intense: more plays, constant travel, cinematic
acclaim and honors. He mockingly referred to himself
age,"[19] in search of a suitable and welcoming new home
lodgings in international hotels. At odds with members
ultural elite and increasingly upset at the criticism re-
thor retreated from official culture and resided abroad,
is. Important honors accrued. In 1929 Pirandello was
d Italian Academy; the Nobel Prize for Literature fol-
were lonely and unhappy years for the man behind the
ionate, if platonic, attachment to Marta Abba was sorely
arations, brought on by increasing professional commit-
continued fondness for Abba, the writer's relationship

"mad house!"; the author and his daughter were mobbed by the exiting crowd
and had to be rescued. Acclaim came later, in Milan, Paris, London, Berlin, and
New York. As early as 1923 Manhattan's Fulton Theater offered a "Pirandello
Season" with the author in attendance. That same year *Six Characters* was staged
in Paris by the Pitoëff company, a theatrical event Malcolm Bradbury proclaims
"the most famous premiere of the age of Dada and Surrealism, establishing
Pirandello as the major influence on the subsequent history of French theatre
right through to the present."[16] After his Parisian triumph Pirandello's plays
quickly entered the standard repertory of European companies. In Germany the
internationally renowned director Max Reinhardt (1873–1943) acquired the
rights to Pirandello's entire theatrical output. *Six Characters* was translated
into twenty-five languages between 1922 and 1925. Pirandello had become
fashionable and much in demand, a situation the playwright relished, for fame
had come late to him.

The initial rejection of *Six Characters* can be attributed to the play's avant-
garde staging and its definitive break with the conventions of realistic theater
and bourgeois drama to which the conservative Italian audience had long been
accustomed. Nevertheless Pirandello's experimentalism gradually altered the
state of Italian theater in his day, displacing verismo, the rhetorical aestheticism of D'Annunzio and his imitators, and bourgeois melodrama. After
Pirandello European theater would veer from naturalist realism in favor of artistic and dramatic self-consciousness. Pirandello's theater plays are forerunners
of later experiments with the medium itself, including the theater of the absurd,
happenings, and performance art. Reworking the format of the play within a
play, *Six Characters* and its two companion pieces, *Ciascuno a suo modo* (1924,
Each in His Own Way) and *Questa sera si recita a soggetto* (1930, *Tonight We
Improvise*), expose the nature of theater itself to scrutiny, disrupting and re-
creating its illusions, showing its devices and innermost workings, such as the
ploys used to involve the audience and foster a participatory experience.

By 1922 Pirandello was successful enough to resign his professorship, a
professional responsibility he discharged dutifully but did not enjoy. Free to
pursue his own interests, he dedicated himself to his writing and to the world of
theater. The man from Girgenti became an international traveler, attending performances of his plays throughout Europe and the Americas. His rise to
prominence in the Italian cultural establishment pleased him but also made him
more vulnerable to critical scrutiny and attack. Often literary scholars and theatrical critics categorized Pirandello's works as being excessively cerebral and
insufficiently poetic. This critical perception of the author gave birth to the
notion of *Pirandellismo,* which represented the writer as an intellectual obscu-

rantist, an abstract theoretician, or a ratiocinative ironist, who delights in confusing his readers and audiences with denials of the existence of either objective reality or truth, with declarations on the impossibility of knowing, and with monologues on the comparability of being and appearance. Other critics, such as Piero Gobetti, appreciated the dramatic use of thought in the plays. It was Gobetti who dubbed Luigi Pirandello "the poet of dialectic," a dramatist capable of entering into the spirit of his characters and capturing their contradictions and complexities through the analysis of their tortuous anguish.[17] Pirandello himself held that thought, no matter how abstract, was transformed into drama and passion on stage, breaking down the long-standing distinction between intellect and emotion. Indeed Pirandello builds dramatic tension by representing the conflict between feeling and ideas in the consciousness of his protagonists. For this reason there is a constant presence of "philosophizing" characters, such as Ciampa, who are obsessed by their need to expound, discuss, and analyze their thoughts. These persistently analytical protagonists of Pirandello's dramas project the need to understand a chaotic world where identity and meaning are ever-changing. Pirandello himself was a thinker, not a philosopher: his basic ideas were stimulating but not new. One of the most significant negators of the existence of a unified and knowable self, the author ironically discovered a multiplicity of unknown Pirandellos appearing in reviews and articles. In a letter dated July 30, 1935, the author, sounding like one of his own characters, laments the alien quality of the identities assigned him by others: "The world of international literary criticism has been crowded for a long time with numerous Pirandellos—lame, deformed, all head and no heart, erratic, gruff, insane, and obscure—in whom, no matter how hard I try, I cannot recognize myself, not even in the slightest degree."[18]

Despite the many misrepresentations of his thought and craft, Pirandello did acknowledge one literary critic who captured the essence of his creative universe admirably: Adriano Tilgher. In 1922 Tilgher published a seminal study of Pirandellian theater which suggests that the dramas revolve around the theme of the fundamental dualism of Life and Form; the former is fluid movement and change, while the latter seeks to give Life a structure and order, thus suppressing it. This synthetic formula satisfied Pirandello intellectually and he adopted it in plays such as *Diana e la Tuda* (1926, *Diana and Tuda*), although the artistic results were less than satisfactory. Tilgher's antithesis echoed some of Pirandello's preexisting thoughts on psychological and aesthetic problems such as the struggle between the individual and his social masks or between nature and society. Tilgher's formula also sharpened Pirandello's reflections on the significance of art: in its immutability and order art contrasts with the

with his three children was strained, and family life was often fraught with more irritation than joy. At the time of his death, December 10, 1936, Luigi Pirandello was a national cultural icon, but he went to his final resting place as he desired: naked except for a shroud, on a pauper's hearse. Without ceremony or accompaniment he was quietly cremated, eulogized by neither church nor state. Coming full circle, Pirandello's ashes were eventually immured at Chaos, back in the Sicily of his birth. His prolific literary output lives on.

Pirandello's works belong to the European cultural movement known as Modernism. Spanning the late nineteenth and early twentieth centuries, Modernism gave voice to the profound sense of crisis all writers experienced when confronting the purpose of literary discourse in a chaotic universe that had diluted language to serve the needs of mass culture and debased it to a vehicle for advertising, business, science, and bureaucracy. The modernist author faced a world in which confident faith in reason and empirical reality had shattered but no framework for collective belief had been reconstituted. In such a world, what could be communicated by authors to their audience? Pirandello's response was to bear witness to the crisis of literature and, by extension, to the crisis of man in society by analyzing, decomposing, fragmenting, demystifying, and unmasking man himself. In a celebrated passage from *Miti e coscienza del decadentismo italiano* (1960, Myths and Consciousness of Italian Decadentism), Carlo Salinari indicates Pirandello as "the consciousness/conscience of crisis,"[21] the writer who best interprets the instability of his era, the defeatism of modern humanity, and the existential anguish faced when confronting a world no longer understood. Certainly Pirandello's art is one of the first treatments of the fragmentation of both personal identity and reality, as captured in the symbolic use of mirrors and masks in his works. The self, the inner consciousness, emerges as the new subject of artistic endeavor. In fact, Pirandello's fiction and drama question the possibility of objective reality, moving incrementally toward greater and greater subjectivism. As a humorist, Pirandello sought to penetrate the masks of illusory self-constructions in order to discover the naked self and expose it. Acting on Ciampa's "crazed cord," human passions occasionally burst forth in crises, confrontations, jealousies, and violence—excessive (re)actions which have been criticized as being too operatic or melodramatic but which are decidedly Sicilian and quintessentially human. At his darkest Pirandello is a writer of anguish, estrangement, and gratuitous pain whose pessimistic vision of life can include endless oppression, everywhere and for everyone. Yet, this same author used his pen to denounce human suffering, injustice, and injuries and to paint the sunny delights of Liolà's joyous song in a vast, multifaceted tableau of life.

CHAPTER TWO

The Late Mattia Pascal and Goddess Luck

At the outset of his career as a novelist and narrator, Luigi Pirandello found reviewers defining, even dismissing, him as a naturalist in the mold of Sicilian verismo, a writer who specialized in slice-of-life tales with a strong regional component. But even the most dismissive critics noted a certain unsettling tone in his fiction that did not quite fit the anticipated pattern. Pirandello's distinguishing quality derives from his fascination with the incongruous and the unexpected, in sharp contrast to the models advanced by the scientifically oriented naturalist school, which focused on the centrality of physical and social determinants in shaping the individual. Given Pirandello's lifelong fascination with issues of identity, self-consciousness, relativity, and illusion, it is not surprising that he would differ from the devotees of naturalist writing, who advocated authorial dispassion, the introduction of scientific laws into literature, and the accurate and realistic representation of human phenomena.

The positivist movement had taken hold in Italy in the 1860s, the time of Pirandello's birth, and dominated philosophical debate well into the 1880s, thus informing his intellectual development. The movement's postulates included an unshakable belief in science's ability to generate progress. Optimistically the positivist viewed science as being the salvation of humanity by liberating it from superstition, poverty, and disease through the unstoppable march of progress. As befits a movement founded on scientific thought, positivism stressed the significance of concrete reality, demonstrable facts, and evidence. Its assumption that knowledge is based exclusively on sense perception led to an a priori rejection of all metaphysics. Positivist doctrines were far reaching, greatly impacting even the literary arena with the evolution of naturalist style.

In his early critical works Luigi Capuana, Pirandello's mentor, had elaborated the aesthetics of Italian naturalism, known as verismo. Its basic tenet was the direct portrayal of *il vero,* or truth; more specifically, the term refers to the literary representation of subject matter drawn directly from contemporary life, actual events, and news items. In verismo the literary text functions as a "human document," possessing both artistic beauty and scientific truth. More than providing a mere snapshot, or moment, of reality, the naturalist writer, employing the modern analytical methods of scientific reasoning, carefully studied, ordered, and observed the background, events, and motivational forces surrounding the human document. To allow the facts to speak for themselves, the writer was expected to suppress the authorial voice and viewpoint. Verismo impeded subjective intrusions by requiring "impersonality," effectively excluding the writer from his or her text.

One of the fundamental aspects of verismo is its emphasis on regionalism. Creating naturalist human documents drawn from the lives of peasants, fishermen, miners, shopkeepers, and even feudal aristocrats provided a varied, picturesque, and previously unexplored literary territory characterized by explosive passions. Among the Italian naturalists Sicilian writers in particular were a visible force. If Capuana was the recognized theoretician of verismo, its greatest writer was another Sicilian, Giovanni Verga. Verga adapted the theories developed by Capuana to his own vision of the cultural issues of the day. Positivist scientific doctrines, such as Darwin's theory of evolution, supplied Verga with a key to formulating the defining motif of his regional stories: the concept of the vanquished—men conquered by hardship, history, existence itself. In his fiction the miserable reality of the Sicilian masses, depicted as the victims of a futile struggle for survival, expands into a pessimistic view of all human history. In Verga's works mankind succumbs to economic and political oppression fueled by class differences and self-interest. To express his Sicilian milieu, Verga created a new Italian literary language. Integrating regional expressions, proverbs, local sayings, and dialectical syntax, Verga sought to capture a particular reality in the most expressive and accurate linguistic medium possible, outside of the dialect itself. A variation on the standard vernacular, Verga's prose directly imitates the cadences of Sicilian speech.

Often considered the twentieth-century successor to Giovanni Verga's literary legacy, Luigi Pirandello himself acknowledged a great debt to the master of verismo. In a lecture delivered to the Italian Academy in 1931, Pirandello provoked the cultural establishment by acclaiming Verga's unsung literary contributions, then overshadowed by the popularity of flashier wordsmiths. In this speech Verga is praised for his artistic integrity, always being on the side of "a style of things," or substance, in marked contrast to the "style of words" practiced in current Italian writing. If Verga represents honest and beneficial writing, the unnamed but clearly referenced Gabriele D'Annunzio uses language as beautiful artifice: sonorous but largely decorative and, as Pirandello clearly implies, false, superficial, and dishonest. This couched public attack on D'Annunzio, a living legend and a Fascist idol, operates as an implicit recognition that Pirandello's own literary roots are grounded in verismo. Although he clearly places himself among the concrete writers of "things," Pirandello nevertheless defies any easy categorization as a canonical practitioner of verismo.

Early in his writing career Pirandello freely accepted two fundamental naturalist tenets: art was tied to life, and literary language should imitate the speech of the environment depicted. And, as has been repeatedly noted by scholars, Pirandellian narrative owes verismo its "realistic tension." His fictions are founded on the keen observation of reality, from which he draws his numerous characters and situations. Pirandello was concerned, however, about the limitations naturalist conventions imposed on writers. In the critical essay *On Humor,* for example, Pirandello questions the doctrine that moral phenomena are as subject to deterministic laws as are physical phenomena. He also challenges naturalism's belief in its ability to reproduce reality on the basis of the certainties contained in factual knowledge. Indeed, by this point, 1908, Pirandello had already formed the opinion that reality was varied and eternally changing, accompanied by equally varied and continuously changing human perceptions. But even the fiction written in the 1890s—offering Pirandello at his most objective—contains strikingly nonrealistic modulations. As in the works of his mentors Verga and Capuana, Pirandello's early fiction draws a pessimistic portrait of human life stifled by social conventions and imbued with a tragic sense of fatalism. Unlike his fellow realists, however, Pirandello added elements of irony and paradox to his narrative. If Verga proposed characters who struggle for survival against immeasurable odds, Pirandello introduced protagonists who feel themselves living, with resulting consequences for the narrative point of view and stylistic tone. The unexpected intrudes upon Pirandello's characters, who cannot control life but are subject to it. In the end, in creating his own human documents, interiority (human self-consciousness), not externality (the "facts"), would most intrigue the budding writer.

Pirandello's first narratives are modeled after the aesthetic canons of verismo: objective presentations of events, detailed descriptions, an impersonal narrator composing a "photograph" of a specific environment. The regional setting is framed by the use of local color, such as the introduction of folklore and superstitious practices, the depiction of costume and customs, and the discussion of prevailing belief systems and prejudices. Linguistically Pirandello favored spontaneous expression based on current usage with a considerable infusion of dialogue, but he discarded verismo's studiously cultivated approach to dialect. He considered it artificial to translate regionalisms and dialect structures into Italian, because such a language is invented, not spoken. On similar grounds Pirandello rejected the purely literary form of Italian that had prevailed for centuries in canonical creative writing. When Pirandello did employ dialectal expressions or popular forms of speech, they served comic, ironic, and mimetic functions, going beyond the mere verbal representation of regional speech suggested by verismo.

At first glance Pirandello's novel *L'esclusa* (1908, *The Outcast*) appears to be a companion piece to the major works of the Sicilian naturalists: Verga's *I Malavoglia* (1881, *The House by the Medlar Tree*) and *Mastro Don Gesualdo* (1889), Capuana's *Il Marchese di Roccaverdina* (1901, *The Marquis of Roccaverdina*), and Luigi De Roberto's *I Viceré* (1894, *The Viceroys*). Undertaken at Capuana's insistence, composed in 1893–1894 with the working title "Marta Ajala," serialized by the newspaper *La Tribuna* in 1901, and revised for publication by Treves in 1908, *The Outcast* seems to justify the generally held opinion that Pirandello was a product of Sicilian verismo. The novel's plot is quite similar to the story line of Capuana's *Ribrezzo* (1885, Revulsion): an attractive wife is wrongly accused of adultery by her husband, becomes a social outcast, and is abandoned to her own devices. Eventually she commits the act for which she was unjustly blamed, validating her social leprosy. This basic intrigue, founded on the themes of adultery and marital misunderstanding, is recurrent in naturalist fiction. Intended to criticize the tyrannical prejudices of a closed provincial environment that suffocates the individual with its notions of propriety, honor, and male supremacy, the topic points to a failure in social morality, which has hardened into exterior forms that no longer denote deep-seated beliefs. Pirandello's adherence to naturalist themes is reinforced by the novel's stylistic choices: employment of an "objective" third-person narration, a linear plot development, chronological sequencing of events, and authorial detachment. In *The Outcast,* however, naturalist social commentary eventually gives way to Pirandellian paradox. The punished but innocent wife demonstrates her courageous independence, regaining a measure of self-respect through her work, only to return to a newly contrite husband *after* submitting to the other man. The unconsummated affair causes pain and degradation to the woman and her entire family when it is merely supposition, a figment of the public imagination, rather than a fact. When it becomes a fact, her adultery is forgiven. The wife experiences rejection when innocent, then acceptance when guilty. It is a twisted, totally unexpected, conclusion to the narrative action, which points to Pirandello's underlying feeling for the ironic or, to borrow his term, for the "humorous" element in literature.

The Outcast is set in a provincial Sicilian town whose inhabitants and locales are clearly delineated by the author. The chosen setting, with its confined spaces and equally confining mentality, is a suitable backdrop to stage the story of Marta Ajala, the novel's protagonist. Descriptive passages capture the environment surrounding the woman, as Pirandello employs the commonplace realist device of projecting the nature of places and persons through a description of their physical attributes. The Sicilian quality of Marta's life is presented in all its suffocating weight, personal restrictions, codified narrow-mindedness, and familial tyranny; an analysis of the protagonist's surroundings and contacts is an essential element in facilitating the understanding of her particular "human document." Marta Ajala belongs to the town's middle class, with its ingrained prejudices, pettiness, and incessant rumormongering. Following paternal dictates, she has married into the dismal and unfeeling Pentagora family, whose males seem to possess a genetic predisposition for selecting adulterous wives, making the attractive Marta immediately suspect. It is chance, however, not biological fate, that leads to Rocco Pentagora's discovery of his wife's "adultery." He finds her surreptitiously reading an unsolicited letter received from Alvignani, a man of considerable talent, status, and power. Nor is it the first missive of their epistolary exchange. It is not romance Marta seeks from the persuasive Alvignani, but the intellectual stimulation long denied her by marriage. Convinced of Marta's guilt, given the family legacy, her husband quickly banishes her. Discarding his wife like a soiled plaything, Rocco reproduces his father's rejection of an unfaithful wife, Rocco's own mother. Returning under her own father's patriarchal roof dishonored and pregnant, Marta Ajala experiences a series of exclusions: from her father's love, from motherhood, from her paternal home, from her teaching position, from her town. Condemnations and rejections are heaped upon the faithful wife, whose only sin lay in her attraction to the rhetorical advances of Alvignani, a virtuoso of words. Her child is stillborn; her father punishes her by entombing himself in local prejudices and a back room, only to die in debt; her students and colleagues torment her. The mere accusation of adultery, however unsubstantiated and denied, has become fact for all but Marta. Ostracized, penniless, and morally responsible for her newly widowed mother and unweddable sister, Marta Ajala moves to Palermo to start afresh.

At the conclusion of the first section of this bipartite novel, Marta Ajala could be considered one of the legions of naturalist heroines victimized by their environment and unable to fend for themselves as women. Or she could pass for one of Verga's vanquished men. However, the second section of Pirandello's novel and the further development of Marta's psychological profile alter the assumptions born of these naturalist premises in unforeseen ways.[1] Although the protagonist's sense of innocence permits her to continue in the struggle to overcome adversity, Marta finds her situation worsening incrementally. Trapped by social prejudice, she is also ensnared by her own thoughts, unable, like so many Pirandellian characters, to communicate her inner being to others. According to her own perception, Marta has behaved properly within the limits of the patriarchal code. She has demonstrated total faithfulness to Pentagora, an unloved but honored husband, yet she is unjustly excluded from social participation. Unable to voice her anger and dismay at the impossibility of projecting her inner self to the world, Ajala is forced ever deeper into the recesses of her psyche. She is imprisoned in the fracture between her guiltless self-image and her adulterous public image. On the road to destitution in Palermo, Marta Ajala is aided by her unwitting nemesis, Alvignani. She is grateful, but, more important, she begins to view herself as his property: his by virtue of public opinion and society's certainty of their guilt. Gradually Marta allows the imaginary yet publicly acknowledged seduction to become fact. By all accounts save her own she has been Alvignani's mistress. In her mind, however, she convinces herself that the external perceptions are destined to become reality. Therefore, she merely accedes to this publicly constructed image, making its illusions her reality. But even in the adulterous relationship with Alvignani, there is no communion of either mind or body. In her sexual remoteness Marta maintains a state of existential solitude and is no longer comforted by the knowledge of her innocence.

Throughout the novel the doubling of Marta Ajala—personally innocent yet publicly adulterous—is reinforced by Pirandello's consistent employment of a bipartite structure. The text itself constantly mirrors the two-fold image of Marta. The two sections of the book present two locales, two unreasonable patriarchs, two cast-off wives, two teaching posts, two dangerous lovers, two pregnancies, two parental deaths, two truths. At the deathbed of Rocco Pentagora's adulterous mother Marta sees her potential fate duplicated in that of her dying mother-in-law. Ironically it is during this vigil that Marta reconciles with her repentant husband. After a bout of typhoid Rocco has drawn near to death himself, shattering his arrogant certainty, just as Marta's social death shattered her integral self-image. Rocco can now understand and forgive what he formerly rejected and condemned. The spousal reconciliation anticipates a paradoxically circular conclusion to Marta's tale: she will be returned to the Pentagora house, to her former social status, to her reputation, to motherhood. The irony is, of course, that the expected child is not Pentagora's and that the actual transgression has been confessed. Marta the sinner is more welcome than the virtuous cast-off wife. The protagonist will be reintegrated socially, but Marta's psyche must now deal with her newly disintegrated self-image, with the fact that her attempts at self-sufficiency were illusory, and with the pained knowledge that she must don the mask of social convention to survive. The individual has no valid independence or authenticity in Pirandello's world.

Thus, while the surfaces of *The Outcast* clearly suggest narrative themes, devices, and models borrowed from naturalism, as critic Carlo Salinari has noted, even Pirandello's earliest works began turning nineteenth-century myths and ideals inside out. [2]

A character such as Marta Ajala, found guilty in her innocence and innocent in her guilt, embodies the disjunction between inner consciousness and outer perception, a core concept driving Pirandello's creative world. The clearest statement of this and other aesthetic and artistic ideas formulated by the writer is to be found in his most ambitious theoretical essay, *On Humor*. Pirandello's exploration of the nature, history, and artistic figures of humor is, at first glance, a scholarly publication replete with historical, philosophical, and literary definitions, examples, and analyses. On closer inspection, however, the essay emerges as a Pirandellian poetics in which the writer defines his own voice within a study of the psycho-artistic mindset that produces humorist writers. Humor,[3] according to Pirandello's extensive discussion, is essentially a quality of expression composed of three elements: the *avvertimento del contrario*—the perception of the opposite, or the awareness of incongruity; the special activity of reflection; and the *sentimento del contrario*—the feeling or sense of the opposite which elicits a response in the perceiver based on the conflict between surface realities and deeper meanings.

In the development of his theory Pirandello sought to integrate the creative and rational processes, which are generally considered separate activities by philosophers and theoreticians. This integration is accomplished through humoristic reflection. Not to be confused with conscious thought or meditation, Pirandellian reflection is a spontaneous impulse that accompanies the entire parabola of the creative process, from conceptualization through development. After the first step of awareness reflection steps in to function as a dynamic assessor that judges, analyzes, dissembles, and disrupts the images received by evoking associations through contraries, or oppositions, so that the images are presented in dualistic conflict. It is from this process of reflective deconstruction that the sense of the opposite emerges. For example, humor alone perceives the comic within the tragic and the tragic within the comic. In practical terms this means that the humorist, searching for the hidden sense of the opposite, takes apart, or deconstructs, all emotions, thoughts, or perceptions as they are received. For such a writer the feeling for the incongruous is never just an amusing game: it demands active participation. A humorist may laugh at his subjects, but he also understands them, displaying compassion and indulgence. By exposing self-contradictory situations and the weaknesses of his protagonists, such a writer is sympathetic, not disdainful. In the artist, Pirandello asserts, "reflection is almost a form of feeling."[4]

The three terms that express the humoristic experience also serve to distinguish humor from other related forms, such as comedy, irony, and satire. For example, unlike humor, irony can be pitiless, showing no sympathy for its subject; the comic never moves beyond the realization of the opposite, remaining at the level of awareness; satire is wholly intellectual, eliciting no feeling. Unlike the practitioners of nineteenth-century romantic irony discussed by Pirandello in his essay, the humorists are neither detached nor condescending toward their created worlds. They must take their creations seriously. While comic writers laugh at their subject matter and satirists display mockery, the situation of the humorists is different: they can concurrently perceive the duality of tragicomedy and the serious underpinnings of a funny situation or character because they have gone beyond mere awareness to the heart of the matter. To attain humor, the surface images must be plumbed to discover their hidden depths, and the writer must develop a participatory attitude toward the characters.

In *On Humor* Pirandello offers a sample of the humoristic process in action by proposing the image of an incongruous old woman. She cuts a ridiculous figure: her hair is dyed and pomaded; her face is clumsily and excessively made up, while her figure is inappropriately attired in youthful dress. The first impression is risible: she is the walking contradiction of society's image—its stereotype—of a proper old lady. It is this incongruity that elicits laughter. This is equivalent to the first step in the humoristic process, at the level of comedy: the awareness of the opposite. Humoristic reflection is triggered when the cause for such a ludicrous appearance is sought. Once we are informed that the lady has dolled herself up to erase the passing years and hold on to the love of a younger husband, the initial comic impression is modified. The altered perception produces a feeling of pity and sadness based on understanding rather than on surface impressions: the feeling of the opposite. Humor is predicated on this shift in the viewer's perception of an experience. The humorist burrows to discover the masked reality. Reflection fosters compassion and responds to what is universally human by weighing existential factors and their impact on the individual. In the humoristic shift from the awareness of the incongruous to the feeling for it, a profound change occurs at the level of consciousness and perception, one that revises initial reactions. In Pirandello's theatrical masterpiece, *Enrico IV* (*Henry IV*), first produced in 1922, the protagonist recalls the physical traits of the old woman of *On Humor*. Middle-aged, he appears in medieval dress, sackcloth worn over imperial vestments, with rouged cheeks and badly dyed graying hair to feign a lost youth. Absurd in normal circumstances, he is tragic in his own situation. Henry's figure does not, cannot, elicit laughter for long because he is known to be mad. In the scrambled mind of madness, paradox can be normal and is accepted as such. In the mind of the viewer, Henry's comic appearance is touched with empathy and pathos when understanding dawns.

The second, expanded edition of *On Humor* (1920) was whimsically dedicated "To Mattia Pascal, librarian, God rest him!" With a touch of unusual levity, Pirandello had presented his scholarly opus to one of his most celebrated creations, whose fictional life story often illustrates the humoristic theories elucidated in the critical essay. While the humorist writer searches for paradox, Mattia Pascal lives it. Pirandello's third novel, *Il fu Mattia Pascal* (1904, *The Late Mattia Pascal*) moves from a nineteenth-century preoccupation with historical and cultural forces oppressing individuals to the development of psychological situations, interiority, and issues of personality that indicate a thoroughly modern perspective. Both the novel's style and its contents announce a definitive break with the norms of naturalism. From the impersonal narrator of verismo, Pirandello has moved on to the subjective use of first person. *The Late Mattia Pascal* functions as fictional autobiography and private confession, interior monologue and personal memorial: it is a work whose stylistic devices make it declaratively subjective as the protagonist, creating a monologic apologia for the self, indulges in regular bouts of compulsive self-explanation. Through the direct narration of his astonishing adventures into the labyrinth of identity and anarchy, Pascal opens his consciousness for all to see. The first-person narrative also makes the improbable adventures more credible, as Mattia Pascal is both a participant in the action and a witness to past events. In the role of retrospective narrator, Mattia has gained some insight into the movements of the character—his earlier self—infusing his story with indulgent mockery, amused skepticism, and witticisms. Pascal, in possession of one good eye and a wandering one, embodies the idea of humoristic art that deforms the natural appearance of things. Throughout the novel chance events, incongruous incidents, and unpredictable happenings occur with astonishing regularity. The determinism of positivist doctrine has made way for the realm of Goddess Luck, with its games of chance and illusion, roles and identities, life and death. But it is Mattia Pascal's own consciousness that represents him and his tale. He is the prism through which events and characters are refracted, according to the vagaries of his perceptions and the deformations of his cross-eyed vision.

Invited by the prestigious literary journal *La Nuova Antologia* (The New Anthology) to submit a novel for publication in serialized form, Pirandello created a plot that would epitomize his humoristic interpretation of the crisis of modern humanity. Appearing between April and June in 1904, *The Late Mattia Pascal* is quintessential Pirandello: a blend of comedy, paradox, surprise, anguish, and realism. The first section of Pascal's life story adheres to the conventions of narrative realism by recounting the protagonist's background, family history, education, community ties, social options, and so on in an orderly chronological fashion. After a happy and reckless childhood and youth—comically described—Mattia Pascal is thrust into responsible adulthood by his unfortunate union with the lovely and pregnant Romilda.[5] The bride soon resents their poverty and becomes quite the unattractive shrew, egged on in her complaints by the widow Pescatore, her cronish mother. Unhappily married, harassed by his mother-in-law, distraught at the dual loss of his beloved mother and baby, Mattia runs off in despair, contemplating both suicide and emigration. Selecting neither of the two remedies, the protagonist casually alights in Monte Carlo with his mother's funeral money, seeking a temporary reprieve from his woes at the gaming tables. There Fortune smiles upon him, and he wins a tidy sum at the roulette wheel. Mattia Pascal has entered the magical realm of chance.

On the train reuniting him with his wife and unhappiness, Pascal happens to read about his own death in the local paper. He has been mistakenly identified as the decomposed body of a drowned suicide. This fortuitous turn of events is the coveted opportunity for a better life, or so Pascal believes. By dying Mattia has come into great expectations. Taking on a new identity, a new appearance, and a new lifestyle with his winnings, he transforms himself into Adriano Meis, wanderer. After considerable travel Mattia, now Adriano, decides to settle in Rome, taking a room in the Paleari household. The lonely wanderer, particularly taken with the delicate, sweet, and sensitive Adriana Paleari and hungry for fellowship, is gradually drawn into the lives of the household. Through these new relationships and in reaction to a series of unrelated events, such as the theft of money from his room and the encounter with a "ghost" from his Monte Carlo days, the "new" man discovers that he has no valid identity.

Lacking any documents and, thus, any legal right to exist in society, Adriano Meis is a nonperson. Without social credentials and official papers, Meis cannot marry, own a dog, or file a police report. Similarly, without a past and without human ties, Mattia/Adriano's freedom is meaningless. Having sought authenticity by erasing his social identity, Pascal has become a shadow man instead. To exist once again, Mattia destroys his other self, Adriano Meis, by simulating a suicide in the Tiber River. He then returns home, where at least his social identity is fixed. There he discovers that Romilda has remarried and started a new family. It is life's final joke on the twice-dead protagonist. The only viable solution for all concerned is that Mattia remain legally defunct, nonexistent for the law but quite real for the community and himself. Such a compromise permits a paradoxical rebirth and offers Pascal a shadowy but acceptable modus morendi in his new identity as the *late* Mattia Pascal, the living dead man who places flowers on his own grave. Thus Mattia Adriano Meis Pascal is given a third life, affording some reintegration into the social fabric but also the autonomy of its posthumous character. It is typical of Pirandellian humor that the returning prodigal "husband" cannot resume his place, since it has been occupied. Therefore, having acquired a new mask as the living but late Mattia Pascal, he continues to play dead, at least for the law of the land.

Pascal's story contains several archetypal elements drawn from cultural sources. Italian critic Arcangelo Leone De Castris notes that a new drama of everyman, a humorous epiphany of a diminutive Ulysses, takes shape out of Pascal's grotesque situation.[6] Indeed, Mattia embarks on a voyage of self-discovery which is both moral, like everyman's, and spatial, as he travels from his old self to a new self-consciousness, from his self-contained hamlet to the unknown countries and cities of Europe. Like Ulysses he too eventually returns home, but not until his encounters shape him into the self-reflective man who narrates his story to the world. In some ways *The Late Mattia Pascal* is a modernist bildungsroman, a traditional narrative genre which details the psychological development of the main character, with a focus on growth and process, as he explores the unknown world through personal experiences and travel. The *Bildung* novel's emphasis is on leaving childhood, exploring the world, and learning lessons, with the intent of producing rational, responsible citizens and members of society. In typical "Pirandellian" fashion the author reverses the goals. The returning Pascal is not integrated within the social fabric, although he has certainly learned from his experiences. He returns not to the family embrace and social responsibility as Ulysses to Ithaca, but to a "new" life in death, to a marginal position as a legally defunct observer, a material shadow man. Pascal's greatest journey was not to the metropolises of Europe but into the movements of his psyche, continually structuring and restructuring itself.

Pascal's voyage is made all the more engaging by the narrator's distinctive personality. Clever, bright, sensitive, and exuberant, he weaves a tale which can be delightfully comedic or somberly pathetic.[7] In a book-length study of the novel, Italian scholar Enzo Lauretta[8] has pointed out that its divisions correlate to stylistic differences in tone. The balletic choreography of the first chapters depict Pascal's early life in small-town Miragno, a blend of idyllic, grotesque, and comic registers. The sixth of the eighteen chapters recounts Pascal's Monte Carlo adventure, with echoes of the intense gambling scenes found in the work of the Russian novelist Fyodor Dostoyevsky (1821–1881). The brief existence of Adriano Meis follows through chapter 16, as the narrative tone shifts again to capture the protagonist's tormented sense of precariousness and absurdity. The pathos and gravity of this long section are relieved by the inclusion of comic vignettes and character studies; it also sounds several farcical notes, such as the agitated séance scene held in Meis's room. The novel's final chapters present the narrator's bitter conclusions and Pascal's defeatism but also his paradoxical rebirth to humor. These differing stylistic registers are held together by Pascal's narrative consciousness, but the shifting tones also indicate a key Pirandellian theme developed in the novel: fragmentation. *The Late Mattia Pascal* is the account of a fragmented individual with an uncertain identity. As Lauretta notes, the young Mattia is as different from the self-aware narrator as he is unlike Adriano Meis. The shifting tones of the narrative clearly correspond to the shifting identity of the hero, thus reflecting Pirandello's developing belief in a multifaceted, ever changing personality.

The first section of *The Late Mattia Pascal* is replete with amusing vignettes and comic characterizations. Caricatures abound, such as the family administrator Malagna. Known as "the mole" who undermines the Pascal fortune, he is depicted as a decomposing body. Being the figuration of unctuous dishonesty, he is more slime than human: "all of him slipped," moving downwards, from his eyebrows to his enormous drooping paunch, which "slipped almost all the way to the ground" over his short legs. True to her name, Mattia's aunt Scolastica is brusque, pragmatic, and dictatorial, a stereotypical "shrewish old maid, with her pair of ferret's eyes, dark and proud." A second old maid rooms with the Paleari household. Silvia Caporale is a piano teacher and a medium; sexually frustrated and alcoholic, she embodies dissipation and eccentricity with her sad doll's eyes "in a face as vulgar and ugly as a carnival mask," endowed with a handsome mustache and the lump of an enflamed nose. Pirandello's use of comic sketches and grotesques is a continuation of the Italian traditions of *macchiette* (comic characters) and the *bozzetto* (brief sketches), which are traditionally employed to alleviate narrative tension, provide comic relief, and develop local color.

In the Miragno episodes the character Pascal is only partially aware of himself and his identity. The narrating Pascal recognizes that his younger self is undisciplined, idle, naive, careless, eccentric, and impetuous, lacking seriousness of purpose and thought. But the young Mattia is also amusing, kind, generous, loving. From the high spirits and irresponsibility of this identity, the protagonist moves on to the weightiness of familial duties. As irrepressible sport gives way to chagrin, Pascal is forced into his social roles as husband, provider, father, worker, failure. Within this first section there is a qualitative shift in the nature of Mattia's life from carefree and comfortable childhood to the poverty and degradation of his marriage. An accompanying change occurs in his perceptions. The first shift in awareness takes place in a seriocomic episode in the chapter suggestively titled "Maturazione," to be understood as both ripening and maturing.

Tormented by his "witch" of a mother-in-law, Mattia is even more aggrieved by the mistreatment dealt his adored mother. Like an unexpected answer to his prayers, Aunt Scolastica sweeps into the house in the guise of an avenging angel. The widow Pescatore responds to this invasion by beating her bread dough in a provocatively synchronized fashion. When the Witch menacingly takes up her rollingpin, however, she is met with a headful of the pasty mess dumped by the irate angel, Scolastica. Mattia bursts into laughter at the sight of his furious mother-in-law covered in dough, only to be manhandled by the woman, whose reaction is hilariously grotesque. Bruised and bloodied, Pascal observes the widow Pescatore rolling hysterically on the kitchen floor, as the pregnant Romilda retches nearby. It is one of the lowest points in Pascal's married life. As literary critic Gregory L. Lucente has ably shown, Mattia's reaction to his latest misfortune defies all expectations: he laughs.[9] A humorist has been born. Mattia Pascal has learned to see the tragicomic aspects of life inseparably, finding himself both inside and outside the events he narrates. Pascal has become the knowing subject of his reflections and the experiencing object of his narration. It is a double-gaze symbolized by the mirror, one of Pirandello's preferred devices:

> I may say that, from that day on, I have made a habit of laughing at all my misfortunes and torments. At that moment I saw myself as an actor in a tragedy that could hardly have looked more comical. . . . My beard was all floury, my face scratched and wet—whether with blood or tears of laughter I didn't yet know. I went to the mirror to examine myself.[10]

Commingling tears and laughter are the outward sign of the humorist, indicating his perplexity when confronting the duality and uncertainty of reality. In a process repeated throughout the novel, Mattia Pascal continues to narrate events, only to decompose them with his reflective evaluations. While the mirrored gaze combines elements of narcissism with fundamental self-doubt, the mirror itself functions as an instrument for self-examination and as a vehicle for self-knowledge. Mirrors will reappear throughout Mattia Pascal's journey, as they do throughout Pirandello's fictional universe, as symbols of humanity's obsession to see itself living, as reminders of self-consciousness and as reflective turning points.

The actual turning point in Pascal's developing self-awareness, however, is purely random. As a desperate mourner, Mattia enters the realm of Goddess Luck, whose personification is the little ivory ball of the roulette wheel at Monte Carlo. Pascal readily joins the worshipers of chance who pray to "our cruel goddess" (51). As it moves, the little ball has the potential for destruction as well as for victory: it is inherently dual, and from this duality Pascal can emerge victorious, that is, financially secure, or he can meet annihilation like the gambler who shoots himself on the Casino's grounds. The chance reading of his own death notice is just another of Luck's gifts to Pascal: it presents him with unknown possibilities, freedom from the old, and the promise of the new. Yet the mistaken identification of the corpse indicates the fact that Mattia remains unknown even to his intimates: it is a specific instance of the general inability to know another, a sign of the book's underlying theme of human alienation. Ever the humorist, Pirandello builds Mattia's second chance at life on a mounting number of deaths: Mattia wins at Monte Carlo using his mother's funeral money; he breaks his fanatical attachment to the wheel of fortune after viewing the disfigured body of the suicidal gambler; the unknown drowned man identified as Mattia allows him to become Adriano Meis; it is a second imitative suicide, planned and false, that permits him to resurrect Pascal; there is even Max, an obliging ghost, in attendance at Anselmo Paleari's séances. Death is presented for its mystery, unpredictability, and absurdity throughout the novel's plot: as unknowable and unpredictable as life. Chance is the mover of Pascal's transformation.

It is "to obey Fortune and to fulfill [his] own personal need," that Pascal embarks on his journey into a new identity (83). In search of freedom, authenticity, and a new beginning, Mattia sets forth to create himself anew. Having discarded the suffocating role of provincial failure, he seeks an ideal construction that, unlike his previous identity, will prevail against life's storms. The persona of Adriano Meis emerges from a series of chance encounters, chance events, and chance decisions that Pascal gradually pieces together into the "imaginative construction of a life that had never really been lived" (92). Meis grows like a mosaic from pieces of foreign places, persons, and events until the completed picture becomes his identity. Having deconstructed his own experiences, memories, and knowledge, Mattia begins to fit the new role, living the part like an accomplished method actor. It is the mirror that introduces Pascal to his new identity, his second life. But the protagonist cannot immediately recognize himself in the image of the "monster" emerging from the reflecting glass. From an attractive, if cross-eyed, "Mattia," he has slowly pieced together "a German philosopher," complete with long hair, dark glasses, and broad-brimmed hat. Gazing upon the constructed image, Pascal can only experience dissociation: the reflected self does not confirm the substantiality and familiarity of his known being but bespeaks a dual, alienated identity. The wandering eye, however, remains to denote the continuing presence of Mattia Pascal in the newborn Adriano Meis. Pascal's gaze is fixed on his idiosyncractic signifier: the roving eye that "tended to gaze off in a different direction, on its own" (14). Observed as a pair, Pascal's two eyes are in opposition, connoting his dual personality and manifesting the "feeling of opposites" that this humoristic text seeks to project. On a psychological level Mattia's wandering eye colors his perceptions: it is a physical derangement that reflects the ontological derangement experienced as he attempts to live anew, endowed with the self-reflective and highly individualistic gaze of the humorist.

Like the good German philosopher he appears to be, Adriano Meis meditates on issues of epistemology and ontology. Excluded from human fellowship by the fear of discovery, he is a lonely man who finds his constructed identity the cause of profound soul-searching. As he journeys from place to place, an accidental tourist indeed, the protagonist's psyche travels inward, questioning his very being. His body, the spectacles, and the disheveled hair are all falsifications: "I seemed no longer to be I, it was as if I weren't touching myself" (107). This limbo existence, whose human contact is limited to strangers and a caged canary, becomes more death than life. To shake off inertia and doubt, Mattia/Adriano reexpresses his mania for living, that is, for significance—"I had to live, live, live!" (109)—and departs for the final destination in his voyage of discovery: Rome, a city ideally suited to receive a foreigner among foreigners. It is among the eccentric residents of the Paleari household that Mattia/Adriano plunges to the depths of his internal journey. Appropriately one of his guides into the mysteries of being is his landlord, the amateur philosopher-spiritualist Anselmo Paleari.

Sharing his library and metaphysics with the new tenant, Paleari introduces Meis to the world of theosophy, religious speculation based on mystical insights into the nature of God and the occult. On Paleari's eclectic book shelves science, philosophy, and history of thought sit side by side with psychic phenomena, the occult, the preternatural, and the metaphysical.[11] Beguiled by the mysterious, the eccentric landlord proposes two hermeneutical conceits to the fascinated Meis in order to explain the epistemological makeup of the human psyche and the ontological situation of humanity in the universe. Paleari's conceit for self-consciousness focuses on one of Pirandello's recurring metaphors: the puppet. In this case the puppet represents Orestes, the protagonist of Greek mythology dedicated to avenging the murder of his father, Agamemnon, by committing matricide. Intent upon revenge, Paleari explains, Orestes suddenly perceives a rip in the paper sky of his puppet stage. Now aware of himself "acting," Orestes stops, unable to proceed. Caught in the act of living, action suddenly becomes contemplation. Orestes gives way to Hamlet, the self-conscious embodiment of existential incongruity and psychological impotence. Paleari's conceit functions as a metaphor for the state of the modern individual, an absurdly self-aware puppet of life. Like the puppet, Adriano/Mattia also sees himself in the act of living, effectively blocking him from action, as the arbitrariness of his own construction takes hold. It is the fate of contemporary man, left with no absolutes in a mysterious and contingent universe, to be the observer of himself.

Paleari's second, related conceit proposes a systematic ontology, or philosophy of being, nicknamed lanternsophy. Its component elements reappear in varying configurations throughout Pirandello's fictional and dramatic production. Paleari explains that natural phenomena, from the earth to the trees and animals, are simply what they seem to be. Humanity, however, thinks and reflects on its being, tormented by the indicators of its existential insignificance. People are born with "a sad privilege: that of *feeling* ourselves alive" (162). Having stipulated the centrality of self-consciousness, Pirandello goes on to explore the function of human illusions. To counter impotence and existential despair, Paleari states, each of us constructs a personal light to brighten the darkness of mystery. The light flickers in a small lantern each individual carries to illuminate the darkness he or she neither knows nor controls. Beyond these small lights darkness looms, exerting its power. Large colored lanterns illuminate the darkness for an entire age, shining with humankind's shared illusions, opinions, and abstractions such as Truth, Honor, and Virtue. Naturally, like all lanterns, these large lights are also subject to extinction by the winds of history. The individual experience is thus repeated as a universal one. Paleari's conclusions, however, throw both Adriano and Pirandello's readers into the most daunting of paradoxes. What if darkness itself were an illusion? If mystery exists solely within us, not outside of us? If all reality is merely a construct of mind?

Paleari offers no definite answers, but his questions plague Meis, who is struggling to illuminate his own interior darkness. Issues of mystery and life are real to the protagonist, as he attempts to sort out the arcane forces that tyrannize him. Mattia Pascal suffers from the human malady of self-awareness or, to quote Paleari, "seeing" and "feeling ourselves live." Reasserting his need for authentic selfhood and freedom, the protagonist decides to eliminate the last vertiges of his former self: the roving eye. The physical blindness following his operation is accompanied by an equally profound lack of spiritual insight. Mattia does not fully comprehend his position psychically or socially as he is still blinded by his own illusions. At a séance held in his sickroom, Adriano explores the "astral plane" and discovers the depth of his feelings for the gentle Adriana, his namesake and soulmate. Yet this affection awakens the hero to the impossibilities of his position. After a biblical forty days of recovery to remove the mark of Mattia Pascal, the mirror informs him that the constructed face is just another mask. The straightened eye does not straighten out Adriano's life, which remains just as off-center as his gaze had been. The mirrored image confirms his alterity and exclusion.

Victim of a robbery he cannot report to the authorities, in love with a woman he cannot marry, Adriano Meis comes face to face with the fabricated nature of his identity. He also comes to appreciate the importance of social roles in defining people and making the connections to the world of others. Having believed in his escape into freedom, the dual hero Adriano/Mattia must confront the price of this presumed liberty: rootlessness and solitude. More important, he comes to realize the impossibility of escaping from oneself. Pascal learns that Adriano Meis is a mask, not an identity: the product of a schism, not a transformation. Underneath the mask Mattia Pascal continues to exist, unseen and unrecognized. Having severed his past, he can be a spectator of life but not a participant. Adriano Meis is an "out-law," outside of the law's reach but also outside of its security; he is excluded from all emotional fellowship and totally self-dependent and alone. He, like so many "unnatural" characters of gothic fiction, finds the constructed self a monster: Frankenstein and his creature inhabiting the same being. Progressing from an understandable impulse to escape to a thoughtful understanding of the absurdity of an anchorless existence, Pascal chooses subordination to the social ties which bind but also define the individual, as did the outcast Marta Ajala. Mattia Pascal is incapable of giving life to his alter ego: history and society do not accept undocumented illusions.

By the end of his adventure Pascal finds he has lost his sense of self. Neither Adriano nor Mattia, he cannot act because he has been stopped midstream by his awareness, like the blocked puppet Orestes. At the start of his experiment, Pascal felt powerful, seeing himself as the master of his own fate, the architect of his own soul. Being without a past, he considered himself pure potential, free to mold his future. His rebellion against social roles and expectations did not lead to wholeness, however, but to alienation, multiplicity, and fragmentation. Fiction imitates life when Mattia Pascal disposes of Adriano Meis through a simulated suicide by drowning, lifting his constructed mask from his identity. Other masks are less disposable; they oppress the individual, deform self-image, and alienate him or her from life as he or she understands it. The masks Mattia Pascal hoped to discard were social constructs: irresponsible spendthrift, impoverished rich man, bereaved father and son, improvident husband, and so on. Yet, these forms defined Pascal and offered a recognizable identity which the creation of Adriano Meis could not. The doubling of Mattia Pascal into two names, two lives, two men, recalls the dual image of Marta Ajala, innocent adulteress. Both Pirandellian protagonists seek to void the split, to return to a unified self-image. Neither actually succeeds. In the end Pascal/ Meis is not even two selves but a man and his shadow, experiencing the gradual annulment of his being. Coexisting simultaneously and naturally, the body (I) and shadow (non-I) nevertheless denote the juncture of concreteness and inconsistency. Mattia Pascal has found that decomposition is a far simpler process than re-creation. In his frantic attempt to erase falsifying definitions, Pascal sought his true self in its pristine purity. He gambled and lost, finding a shadow rather than a life at the hands of Goddess Luck.

Pascal's acts represent social anarchy, the rejection of tradition, convention, family, and duty, all of which imprison humankind but also provide context and some shelter against indeterminancy. Pascal's only certainty exists in his social identity, not in his ontological consistency: he knows his name, not his being. Unable to answer the ultimate questions of existence, incapable of shaping his destiny, tied to the numerous social and psychological roles imposed upon man, Pascal concludes his odyssey with the realization that total freedom from his social roles cannot be achieved. Pascal's narrative begins with an affirmation of fact: "One of the few things—perhaps the only one—that I know for certain is that my name is Mattia Pascal" (xi). By book's end he has become the "late" Mattia Pascal, whose name is etched on the tombstone he occasionally visits: as a social identifier the name itself is lost to him, transferred to a dead imposter. He remains society's outlaw, existing outside its order as a nonlife. Pascal's tale concludes at the cemetery, near "his" grave. Asked who he is, ever irreverent of conventions, he can only shrug and give a paradoxical nonresponse: "Ah, my dear friend. . . I am the late Mattia Pascal" (251). In some ways Pirandello's third novel is an ironic modernist revision of the parable of the prodigal son's dejectedly returning home after having sown his wild oats, only to find that "home" has disappeared.

As befits a living dead man, Mattia opts for a new role as philosophical sage. Pirandello's choice of Pascal as the surname for his first major protagonist is in itself allusive, merging as it does notions of reflection, existential flux, and universal mystery. Through Mattia the seventeenth-century French philosopher-scientist and student of man and spirituality Blaise Pascal meets Theophile Pascal, a nineteenth-century contributor to the Publications Théosophiques of Paris, who was a student of parapsychology, the discipline where mind meets mystery. They are ideal spiritual ancestors for a character in search of spiritual resurrection but caught in the intricacies of his own self-consciousness and subject to the inconsistencies of human life. In *On Humor,* Pirandello quotes a significant passage from Blaise Pascal, who observed "that there is no man who differs from another man more than he differs, with the passing of time, from himself" (136). The citation speaks directly to the Pirandellian concept of the fluidity of life, whose mobility and mutability exclude the development of a fixed personality. It also defines the nature of the character Mattia Pascal as he attempts to adapt to the vicissitudes of existence only to find himself metamorphosing physically and psychically.

As a living deadman, Mattia Pascal loses a legally definable self but finds some compensation in his birth as a literary protagonist. In real terms Pascal has abdicated existence by opting for a living death. But through writing the protagonist maintains being: in his pages *he is* in ways unavailable to living men. As an author Mattia Pascal controls his reality, builds a textual life, and expresses his inner self. If telling his story can be construed as a substitute for living it, writing nevertheless allows for ordering chaos, damming life's flow, and challenging the vagaries of chance. As a literary subject Pascal's new home is the written page. There he finds satisfaction in the construction of an identity that will not be imprisoned, altered, or dispersed. As a character of a written text Mattia Pascal achieves a wholeness unavailable to men. But even books have their limitations. Pascal composes his retrospective narrative in his former workplace, the chaotic, rat-infested Boccamazza library, aptly located in a deconsecrated church. In this allusive spatial image Pirandello humorously exposes his own uncertainties about the function of art in an age of crisis. Just as the church symbolizes the demise of religious belief, the library symbolizes the disintegration of cultural values. In the library Mattia is surrounded by the signs of culture, volumes upon volumes of books. But they remain jumbled, decaying, and unread by the citizenry. His manuscript will be added to the collection, abandoned to its fate and to the rats.

The Late Mattia Pascal was not without its detractors. Some critics considered the book a deviant naturalist novel because of its realistic narrative development. Others decried its implausibility by dismissing the plot as unlikely, given its abundance of coincidences, accidents, grotesque situations, and characters. Still others saw no more than escapist fare. Clearly taken aback by such criticism, Pirandello added a postscript, titled "A Warning on the Scruples of the Imagination," to the 1921 edition of the novel. In this afterward the author argues against the narrative necessity of imitating a logical order of events, as prescribed by naturalist conventions. The basis for the author's argument centers on the canonical concept of verisimilitude, fundamental to traditional realist literature. Rather than accepting the sway of verisimilitude, Pirandello altogether breaks with the notion that literature must appear true to life and comes out in favor of the creative imagination. On a deeper level his vision negates the possibility of logical order in a universe of senseless instability. Life, the author notes, is filled with contradictions, implausibilities, and the unexpected. To quote a banality, truth is indeed stranger than fiction, as the writer unquestionably proves by citing two factual newspaper accounts that seem to imitate plot elements of *The Late Mattia Pascal.* After demonstrating the insufficiencies of a realist structuring of personal experience, Pirandello goes on to justify the use of the fantastic in art. In his own words, "Life's absurdities don't have to seem believable, because they are real. As opposed to art's absurdities which, to seem real, have to be believable. Then when they are believable, they are no longer absurd" (256). In works such as *The Late Mattia Pascal,* Pirandellian naturalism becomes a self-conscious convention, self-destructing in a world dominated by irrelevance, illusion, and chance.

The Late Mattia Pascal remains a consummate elaboration of the Pirandellian world view, developing the author's oft-repeated themes of alterity, the fluidity of life, the difficulty of freedom and authenticity, and the imposition of societal roles on the individual. In both *The Outcast* and *The Late Mattia Pascal,* Pirandello shows the impossibility of creating a life that is concurrently authentic and self-affirming outside the confines of society and its institutions. Marta Ajala and Mattia Pascal inhabit a paradoxical condition, as self-conscious victims of their existential duality. But as a provocateur and rebel Pascal also embodies the contradictions of the humoristic character. Prone to reflection, caught in the morass of his own self-awareness, alienated yet seeking fellowship, stymied and frustrated, Pascal is one of the prototypical creations of twentieth-century European fiction. Like many a modernist character drawn in an age of crisis, Mattia Pascal, cut off from others and from himself, yet still attracted to life with its beauty and darkness, suffers his lonely agonies. Ever anxious to live, live, live!, even if only on paper.

CHAPTER THREE

Right You Are (If You Think So) and the Crisis of Reality

Through the years Luigi Pirandello's relationship with theater proved intense and conflicted. At the age of twelve Pirandello wrote a tragedy in five acts, titled *Barbaro* (Barbarian), which he directed, produced, and performed with siblings and friends. At the age of nineteen he composed an innovative play, now lost, conceived as a revised classical comedy, utilizing the pit as a stage and the audience as a chorus. When he was twenty-five, *L'epilogo,* later retitled *La Morsa* (1910, *The Vise*), was repeatedly rejected by theatrical managers in Rome. Indeed, Pirandello did not become known as a playwright until his forties, when in 1910 Nino Martoglio staged his first Sicilian plays. Nor did he become a celebrated dramatist until the international furor that occurred over *Six Characters in Search of an Author,* when he was a mature writer of fifty-four. Yet, at the time of his death, Pirandello, approaching his seventieth birthday, had a solid reputation as a director for the stage and an impressive record as a prolific, experimental dramatist with more than forty plays to his name. After his youthful enthusiasm to be a playwright met with rejection, Pirandello managed to repress his dramatic ambitions. In fact, possibly acting out of wounded pride, he publicly disdained the medium. The author, like many of his Sicilian characters, had prickly sensibilities and was easily roused. Nevertheless Pirandello was destined for the theater. Dramatic elements abound in his fiction, which overflows with lively dialogue, visual references, farcical or comic exchanges, and coup de théâtre. Similarly Pirandellian dramas are known for their abundant, even excessive, use of stage directions, adding a narrative element to the script.

Italian theater in Pirandello's day did not manifest the brilliance of the French stage, with its array of social dramas, romantic tableaus, and sophisticated farce, but did display a wide variety of themes, styles, and productions. Besides the ever popular French plays, works of native playwrights were performed along with those of the great nineteenth-century European dramatists Henrik Ibsen (1828–1906), August Strindberg (1849–1912), and Anton Chekhov (1860–1904), as well as those of other masters of psychological drama and the theater of ideas. When Pirandello composed *The Vise* in the early 1890s, naturalism was the dominant, if not exclusive, style for dramatic expression. In the theater verismo followed two popular currents with two linguistic registers. One direction favored regionalism by drawing on characters from the lower socioeconomic levels with an extensive use of local color. The other flowed toward realistic bourgeois drama by emphasizing the psychology of the protagonists within the confines of class interests. Linguistically the regional current tended toward a local dialect or a vernacular Italian, while the bourgeois drama was written primarily in an educated register. These two types of naturalist theater were, of course, not mutually exclusive. Pirandello's Sicilian plays, initially written in dialect for Martoglio and Musco, belong to the regionalist category, but they address powerful psychological issues involving a class component as well. By 1917 Pirandello had also made his mark in the bourgeois naturalist drama with a handful of drawing-room plays populated by the provincial middle class, which nevertheless exhibit a strong Sicilian flavor.

Literary historians have pointed out that these two currents indicate divisions betwen southern and northern Italian theater practice. In the south a tendency to choral works with numerous characters stresses community involvement in the dramatic action. The staging of religious processions, weddings, funerals, piazza or street scenes, and exterior public spaces often forms the backdrop for the depiction of blind passions, sensuality, violence, superstition, primitive conflicts, broken codes of honor, blood sport, and ancient feuds. Pirandello himself utilized such choral scenes in his plays, sometimes in a straightforward realistic fashion, as in the spectatcular *The Festival of Our Lord of the Ship,* which opened the first season of the Teatro d'Arte in 1925. The play brims with colorful and grotesque local characters set against a Sicilian town's annual religious procession with its plaster saints, priests, candles, fanaticism, and superstition but also its feasting, heightened emotions, and sensual frenzy, igniting in a final explosion. At other times Pirandellian local color functions as a theatrical device, as in *Tonight We Improvise* (1930), in which the Sicilianism of the staged religious procession is visually superimposed on a decadent cabaret scene redolent of Berlin nightlife in the Roaring '20s. On the other hand northern Italian drama, originating in a more-industrialized and -urbanized capitalist world, prefers the closed rooms of private or commercial life: middle-class drawing rooms or studys, working-class hovels, gray offices, pawnshops, and so forth. In these settings the daily struggle for survival is represented in the monotony of work, the conflicts of family members, and the drabness of the environment. Life is these spaces does not explode but implodes into stagnation and pettiness. Such theatrical settings do not yield melodrama but pathos.

The bourgeois theater of northern Italy produced good dramatists such as Giuseppe Giacosa, Gerolamo Rovetta, and Marco Praga, who depicted the middle and professional classes in their plays—the same classes that formed the majority of the theatergoing public. These playwrights stressed three essential themes of bourgeois life—money, love, and family—and touched upon related issues such as work, career, marriage, children, status, position, personal values, and public morality. A popular leitmotiv is the love triangle, often adulterous, and its connection to financial and ethical matters. Money is often the ruling passion of these bourgeois protagonists; therefore the dramatic action abounds in bankruptcies, scandals, suicides, marriages of convenience, dishonesty, betrayals, affairs, and moral degradation. Bored or ignored wives cheat on their workaholic husbands with the proverbial best friend; untended sons slip into gambling, bad women, bad marriages, or worse; beautiful daughters sell themselves to provide financial stability. Such themes also appear throughout Pirandello's dramatic production, from the adulterous and fatal love triangle of his first play, *The Vise,* which conforms to naturalist conventions, to the adulterous and fatal love triangle of his last completed play, *Non si sa come* (1934, *No One Knows How*), which was influenced by Freudian theories on dreams and the subconscious.

Other late-nineteenth-and early-twentieth-century theatrical vogues had far less impact on Pirandello's dramatic vision. In the early decades of the new century, Italians flocked to historical recreations of medieval and Renaissance epics, which provided easy escapism into the fantasy world of elaborate costume spectacle and heroic passions. These plays proved rich in grandiloquence but poor in staying power. Pirandello also rejected the direction taken by Gabriele D'Annunzio, arguably Italy's most popular writer prior to World War I. D'Annunzio's theatrical production exalts eroticism, perversions, violence, and glory in a lyrical, highly aestheticized language. His protagonists are heroic even in their negativity, with a proclivity for sonorously declaiming the Nietzschean superman's will to power. D'Annunzio's emphatic and melodramatic plays appealed to many of Italy's best actors, who, like great opera stars, tended to histrionic poses, languid gestures, and dramatic diction. Such interpretations did not appeal to Pirandello because of the posturing and artificiality. His preference went to colloquial forms of speech and a natural acting style that captured the character's attributes while respecting the textual word. Moreover it was the crisis of humanity, not its transfiguration, that interested the playwright. As Tom F. Driver has noted, "Pirandello stood, as it were, between realism, for which theater is imitation of life, and that later development for which theater is imitation of consciousness."[1]

During the war years, when he was achieving a measure of theatrical recognition, Pirandello found himself allied with a group of young, innovative dramatists.[2] For the first time he participated, however marginally, in an avant-garde movement whose intent was to shake the foundations of cultural tradition. The young playwrights of the Grottesco (Grotesque) wanted to reinvigorate and deprovincialize Italian theater by shedding its constricting naturalist skin and opening it to dreamscapes, parables, mystery, burlesque farce, visions, and fantasy. The Grottesco shepherded the use of multimedia productions and advocated the mixing of high and low styles, combining tragedy with comedy in their plays. In many ways Pirandello was already an antedated *grottesco,* given his theorization of humor as well as the seriocomedy of the Sicilian plays. The manifesto of the grotesque theater is a piece by Luigi Chiarelli (1880–1947) which premiered in 1916. From its title to its message, *La maschera e il volto* (The Mask and the Face) is clearly related to Pirandello's fictional, dramatic, and theoretical works.

Superficially *La maschera e il volto* masks as a standard bourgeois drama; however, Chiarelli's work subverts the formulas of the genre from the inside out. His tale of an adulterous triangle (husband, wife, best friend) is transformed into a farcical situation when the self-declared guardian of honor is logically enough suspected of murdering his unfaithful wife, although no crime has actually been commited. Paolo, the protagonist, is imprisoned in his public image (the mask) as a man of honor and an avenging husband. By negating his feelings for his wife, Paolo negates himself (the face) and becomes ridiculous in his own eyes. When the wife reappears to save Paolo from the pending murder charge, the couple must flee the country to avoid legal prosecution, not to mention the retribution exacted by a society bound to condemn them. To be free, the playwright suggests, one must escape the social order and its masks. Chiarelli's paradoxical reworking of the adulterous triangle caused quite a stir in cultural circles. Yet Pirandello's own rewriting of naturalist drama probes far deeper into character and social roles than does Chiarelli's grotesque play. One of the most successful challenges to the bourgeois world of naturalist drama, *Right You Are (If You Think So)* is nevertheless set in the familiar drawing room of naturalist plays. But *Right You Are* presents a dramatic situation which is both incredible and implausible, like so many of Pirandello's plots. The drama's hyperbolic world, with its far-fetched circumstances, provides glimpses into the universal condition of man, grotesque as it is.

Right You Are (If You Think So) debuted in 1917 to critical and public applause. Its positive reception was due in part to the audience's familiarity with the play's external structure, setting, and themes. There is nothing particularly innovative in the construction of *Right You Are*. The drama obeys naturalist theatrical conventions. There are three well-ordered acts, set in the familiar middle-class drawing room; a love triangle of sorts is at the core of the action; recognizable character types appear on stage. But Pirandello's external adherence to the canonical model contains the seeds of change, proposing alternative approaches to the question of reality and truth. If verismo had stressed the importance of "human documents," *Right You Are* parodies the possibility of documenting anything human. The heated search for proof, evidence, and logic in this grotesque opus challenges the positivist view that objective knowledge can provide answers, as the title immediately implies. Like many Pirandellian titles this one is provocative, somewhat enigmatic, and decidedly ironic. Cut in two, it offers the audience a contradictory perspective of the play. *Così è* has been translated as both "right you are" and "it is so"; a more casual interpretation might include "so it goes." An additional echo is subtly added if the indicative verb *è* is reconjugated as the exhortatory subjunctive *sia*. In Italian the familiar phrase *così sia* is rich in liturgical and metaphysical allusions, best rendered as "so be it." In any case the first part of Pirandello's title suggests actuality, certainty, and/or acquiescence. This element is placed in a syntactically oppositional stance with the parenthetical *(se vi pare),* which has been translated as "if you think so" and "if you think it is," but which can also mean "if it seems [so] to you," placing the addressee/audience in the Pirandellian position of evaluating perceptions and opinions, not facts. Indeed, the second titular element works as a corrective or rethinking of the first, placing both in doubt. As a trope the title of *Right You Are* establishes irresolution before the curtain rises; the audience has been alerted to a problematic situation with no exit in sight. In broader cultural terms the play's title suggests the shift from positivist belief in a knowable and recognizable universe based on fact and material evidence to the acknowledgment of a world of doubt and uncertainty emerging from the relativity and individuality of perceptions—Pirandello's world.

The plot of *Right You Are* amplifies the dichotomy of the play's title and its subversion of naturalist theater. The dramatic situation revolves around a family new to the provincial town where the action is set. Rather than offering the familiar adulterous love triangle of bourgeois drama, however, Pirandello creates an unusual family trio. A couple (Mr. and Mrs. Ponza) and the mother-in-law (Mrs. Frola) are inextricably joined in their own paradoxical love. As the locals view it, the family is odd, questionable, and abnormal, since it does not adhere to time-honored norms of human behavior and the assumed conventions of social interaction. The town elite is particularly intrigued by the arrivals' odd living arrangements and ungracious seclusion. For example, mother and daughter do not socialize, either with the townspeople or with each other; Mrs. Ponza, the wife, lives in drab and inconvenient popular housing on the outskirts of town while Mrs. Frola, the mother-in-law, resides in an elegant apartment in town; all three newcomers have demonstrated impropriety and rudeness by neither receiving visitors nor calling on their neighbors and social betters. In the eyes of all who matter, these strangers in town are behaving strangely indeed.

Gossip thrives on public curiosity; this curiosity is quickly transformed into importunity to the point of persecution. The locals demand the "facts" of the trio's lives. Cornered, both Mr. Ponza and his mother-in-law confuse the busybodies by giving differing versions of their arrangements and relationships. According to Ponza, his first wife died. Afterwards Mrs. Frola refused to acknowledge this death by insisting that the second Mrs. Ponza is her dead daughter. According to Mrs. Frola, Ponza had so obsessively loved her daughter that she was hospitalized after taking ill. Ponza was traumatized by the episode and now insists that his wife died and he subsequently remarried. Differing interpretations of reality, equally plausible, are provided by the two to defend themselves and their privacy. For at least one of them, this reality is an illusion that permits him or her to carry on. Yet questions continue to arise, going unanswered. Demanding the truth, the prying neighbors are presented two versions of the Ponza marriage from oppositional viewpoints. Questions rather than answers feed the public frenzy to know: is Mrs. Ponza the first or second wife? is Mrs. Frola her mother or a sweet but demented outsider? who is mad, the old woman or her son-in-law? The facts elude the curious. But facts in Pirandello are not solutions to human dilemmas. The documents which might give plausible answers and silence the townspeople are unattainable, lost in an earthquake that also decimated the population, thus eliminating any reliable witnesses to the actual events. The "truth" is irretrievable, as it often is in this writer's works. The answer exists in Mrs. Ponza—first or second?—who is called upon to untangle the skein of confusion in the final scene of the play. She enters, invisible behind her mourning veils, only to declare to the assembled busybodies who are destroying her family's precarious emotional equilibrium, "As for myself, I am whoever you believe me to be." The drama concludes with an ironic laugh, the playwright's final statement on the impossibility of knowing.

The oppositional nature of Pirandello's title is reiterated in the mood of the play itself. *Right You Are* is concurrently a tragedy and a comedy. For the bereaved, disturbed family, the action creates an unstable state of high anxiety. Their painfully constructed modus vivendi is endangered by the indifferent curiosity of the townspeople. To visualize their condition, the playwright has all three dress in the heavy black of traditional mourning. They are grieving figures of a tragic human experience who manage to maintain their equilibrium by their loving, if unorthodox, arrangement. Like many Pirandellian characters Mrs. Frola and the Ponzas are victims of social insensitivity and alienation, as well as of natural disaster. Suffering from a tragic fate, they are now subject to the violence of society. The townspeople have dehumanized them, invading their most intimate affections, their privacy, and their right to personal self-determination. Frustrated, meddling, demanding, arrogant, or merely intrigued, these local busybodies are the inhabitants of the bourgeois drawing room, the representatives of public opinion and social authority. The comic element of the play centers on the representation and interaction of the various characters that form this assembly of nosy neighbors. In their midst is Lamberto Laudisi, who baits the townspeople's insistent curiosity, mocks their belief systems, and concludes each of the three acts that compose the play with ringing laughter.

As has often been noted, the three acts of *Right You Are* correspond to the three stages in the conflict between the newcomers and the local truth seekers. The investigation of the trio is followed by a group confrontation that is concluded with the summoning of Mrs. Ponza and the anticipated resolution of the mystery. As Eric Bentley has pointed out, the comic action is repetitious. Change within the repitition functions to speed and magnify events, thus manicly accelerating the tempo while fraying the nerves of both the curious onlookers and the audience. At the same time, the behavior exhibited by Ponza and Frola on stage manifests growing evidence of their underlying hysteria or dementia. Technically the playwright is astutely building tension: he involves the audience in the psychological emotions born of the quest for truth by giving the play the tempo and architecture of a thriller—each act climaxing on a note of bafflement and suspense. By creating such a rhythm, Pirandello transforms the characters assembled in the Agazzi drawing room into projections of the audience. The busybodies pose the spectators' silent questions while voicing the frustrations concurrently experienced in the orchestra seats and on stage. Likewise the audience overturns its conclusions with each new revelation, as does the assembly. Like the characters on stage, the spectators seek to solve the riddle by rational conjecture, only to be taunted by the contradictions, multiple possibilities, red herrings, and dead ends posed by the unfolding story. In effect Pirandello seeks to erase the distinction between stage and audience by forcing public participation in the dramatic action. Like the assembled characters the spectators assume the roles of fact finder and inquisitioner, uncertain judge, and baffled jury. Doubt insinuates itself into the audience, demanding release, knowledge, certainty. None is forthcoming, for Pirandello poses enigmas, not solutions.

The determination of truth is made all the more difficult for the assembled inquisitors by the interference of appearances, which can easily be confused with reality. As Pirandello often does in his theater, the odd couple are paradoxically masked and identified by their outward aspects. In this fashion Mr. Ponza and Mrs. Frola can both embody and contradict public opinions and doubts. Both are in mourning, yet Ponza's burly blackness, ferocious expression, polite surliness, and dark complexion are familiar signs of evil and menace. By contrast Mrs. Frola's sweet grandmotherliness, neatness, white hair, and gentle smile infer a positive nature. These appearances evoke judgment in others or at least educe a psychological predisposition toward the images received. Thus the ladies are much taken with Frola, but taken aback by Ponza. Yet the mere mention of madness has the power to confuse onlookers by challenging initial sensory impressions, a bafflement made all the greater by Ponza's sudden shifts in temperament: well aware his histrionic skills have a disquieting impact on his audience, he swings from frenzied animal passion to polite composure before the assembled spectators. If not for the townspeople, Frola and Ponza are clearly acting for each other: each cultivates the erroneous image the other carries. As Ponza explains, he must simulate rage to persuade his mother-in-law of his derangement so as to protect her own fragile equilibrium. Within the play such scenes deliberately direct attention to individuals' artificial self-constructs, which fabricate identities and illusions. But the scenes also remind the audience of the nature of drama itself, which reconstructs reality through artifice and appearances.

The drawing room, with its "polite" society, becomes a torture chamber for Ponza and Frola, a site where they are hounded and martyred by public scrutiny. Their intimate secrets, personal disasters, and private pain are exposed to public view, adding to the blackness of their beings. The chosen setting for the dramatic action—the home of Ponza's superior, Counsellor Agazzi—is hardly accidental. Agazzi, the local commissioner, and the provincial prefect are all involved in ferreting out "the truth," so that order can be restored. They represent the arm of the state, the procedures of the bureaucracy, and the realm of legality—all of constituted order, which is being challenged by the irregularities, undocumented state, and unorthodoxy of the trio. In the end, however, the Ponza-Frola situation remains clouded in mystery. No satisfying revelation closes *Right You Are*. Having built up audience anticipation and demand, Pirandello does not solve the mystery, because the mystery itself is the solution. The appearance of Mrs. Ponza, the bearer of truth, provides no unraveling of facts for the tormenting and tormented curious. In her impenetrably veiled person, Mrs. Ponza proposes that truth cannot be found, at least not in the objective documents sought by the townspeople. In fact, she declares paradox to be true, contradiction to be reality. She is both the first and second Mrs. Ponza. She is Mrs. Frola's daughter. She is no one. The fact that this is an illogical contradiction is irrelevant, for each perception of Mrs. Ponza contains its own truth. The dramatic implications are clear: there can be no resolution of conflict, no conclusion to the mystery, no catharsis for either the busybodies or the audience.

As the "voice of truth," the veiled woman has no face and no documentable concreteness; she does not personify certainty, but unknowability. According to Anne Paolucci, this veiled figure is the embodiment of the dialectical process. Others have termed her an axiom become a character. John L. Styan views her as "the abortive truth" the townspeople have created for themselves. According to some, Mrs. Ponza is the embodiment of selfless love, a transfigured creature who sacrifices her individuality by making herself into the incarnation of the needs and illusions of those who love her. As Eric Bentley eloquently states: "She is the inner sanctum, the holy of holies. Her life being love, she has achieved complete self-sacrifice, she has no identity; she exists only in relationship, she is wife to the husband, daughter to the mother; she is what the husband thinks she is, she is what the mother thinks she is, she is what *you* think she is."[3] But the sacrifice of identity also denotes death to the self, an ontological suicide, to give life-affirming illusions to others.

The appearance of the enigmatic Mrs. Ponza serves to broaden the scope of the theatrical action far beyond the mere particulars of the family history and its riddles. The inconclusiveness of the veiled woman's declarations heightens rather than diminishes the tension experienced by all onlookers, including the audience, forcing them to go beyond the factual question of her specific identity to the greater question of human identity, that is, shifting the focus from an objective issue to a metaphysical one. Moreover, Mrs. Ponza's declaration that "there is a misfortune here, as you see, which must stay hidden: otherwise the remedy which our compassion has found cannot avail" further shifts the issue into an ethical dimension. The word for "compassion" employed in Italian is *pietà,* a far more allusive term that contains the religious meanings of mercy and piety but also the significance of the Latin *pietas,* which can refer to tenderness and love of family. The purposely constructed world of the Ponza family is a universe of conscious pretense, where individual illusions are fostered in the name of a greater truth than fact. Unlike the standard conflictual love triangle of bourgeois drama, the harmonious Ponza-Frola triangle is composed of merciful love and embraced illusions, which can never be explained through logic or scientific methodology. Their remedy is absurd and pitiable, but it shelters them from the pain of existence. Its fragility must be respected with compassion. While the busybodies constantly manifest dissonance, Mr. Ponza and his mother-in-law demonstrate affectionate solicitude for each other. The only relevant truth here is found in human terms, which take precedence over evidence or reason. Referring to this aspect of the play, Bentley proposes that its real principle is not the metaphysics of relativity but, simply, love your neighbor.

Pirandello's own designation of *Right You Are* as a parable confirms the presence of a moral lesson. Nonetheless literary critics repeatedly identify this piece as an exemplary case of *Pirandellismo,* the theatrical exposition of a proposition, as typically found in the writer's drama of ideas. The proposition is, of course, that truth cannot be known, since it differs according to individual perceptions. The importance of this idea is accentuated by the theatrical device of Laudisi's laughter at the close of each act; it peals forth in response to the word *verità* (truth). Depending on how Laudisi's role is performed, this laughter can indicate mockery, hysteria, absurdity, or humorist reaction. In part *Right You Are* is the dramatic enactment of the principle of subjective relativity and functions as an extensive elaboration of the themes of illusion and reality. The voice selected for the rational exposition of ideas in this play belongs to Lamberto Laudisi. As Counsellor Agazzi's brother-in-law, Laudisi seemingly belongs to the assembly of busybodies, but, through his continued challenges, questions, advocacy for the rights of privacy and his irreverent quips, he also acts as the voice of reason and awareness. As such Laudisi mediates between the two groups of characters and between the stage action and the audience.

Lamberto Laudisi is one of many Pirandellian characters who serve as spokesmen for the playwright's ideas. These designated *raisonneurs* (reasoners) are occasionally criticized for their self-consciousness and verbosity, but such characters introduce a dialectic movement into the text, easing the communication of complex meaning to the audience through the use of contextualized dialogue. In some plays these loquacious and intellectual characters, disappearing into the author's ideas and losing dramatic concreteness, risk sacrificing psychological depth to philosophical eloquence. But *raisonneurs* such as Laudisi can be existential questers, whose search proves painful, driven, alienating, and highly dramatic. In Pirandello's works reason can function as an intellectual screen for controlling submerged passions. Likewise thought can be experienced as anguish by intelligent characters longing for understanding, order, and meaning in a chaotic, absurd world.

In *Right You Are* Laudisi is the cerebral protagonist capable of daring friends, family, and gossips to define the truth, not only the one sought in the Ponza-Frola affair, but also their own inner truth. As he flippantly points out to the gathered assembly of the curious, identity is relative, and each individual is perceived differently by every other, resulting in several antithetical and contrasting images which may or may not relate to the individual's own self-assessment. Laudisi is voicing the Pirandellian dilemma of the multiplicity of the human personality. As the author would declare in the title of his final novel, the individual is one, none, and a hundred thousand. Given the multiplicity of the perceived self, the plausibility that only two possible solutions exist to the riddle of Mrs. Ponza is simplistic and naive. Her changing identity is multiplied many times over in the eyes of everyone who views her. Yet each view is an illusion; each different interpretation undermines all the others, and the veiled woman remains no one, at least no "one" definable and recognizable entity. Laudisi accepts the possibility of multiple realities, but he also respects whatever truth individuals assume for themselves. Unfortunately for the three members of the Ponza-Frola family, the town wishes to know exactly who they are, to delve into that oneness people believe they possess but do not. When Laudisi suggests to the assembly that truth is unknowable, his point is immediately discarded as a dreadful idea, not only in the opinion of the gathered group but in the name of the audience and readers of the play as well. Laudisi's moderate suggestion that "what other people see and feel" should be respected is also quickly discarded. Pirandello's *raisonneur* attempts to defend the Ponza family's right to privacy by declaring each individual's right to his or her own interpretations of reality. Laudisi is not heeded because the busybodies are intent on their right to know—a privilege more obvious to them than the individual's right to autonomy.

As the role is written, Lamberto Laudisi is neither a pundit nor a paladin: his character has a clearly comic function in the script. When staging *Right You Are* himself or selecting actors for the role of Laudisi, Pirandello assigned the part to the repertory member known as the *brillante,* who specialized in light comedy. Numerous critics have viewed Laudisi as a successor to the traditional clown figures of the improvisational Commedia dell'Arte, where physical comedy, gesture, expression, and boundless energy were demanded and embodied in a *maschera,* or mask, an archetypal identity with assigned traits and costumes, similar to the Punch and Judy of puppet theaters. It is an apt comparison, for Laudisi undergoes rapid shifts in tone, from sophisticated frivolity to sobriety, from mockery to jest to charm. These rapid alterations in characterization are a dramatization of Laudisi's point that each of us is a different person for each other, that human personality is neither unified nor constant, but a plural entity marked by flux and diversity. For that matter, the individual himself cannot totally know or control the different selves contained, notwithstanding the assertion that he or she is one for him-or herself. In short, man lives with a fiction of himself to give some semblance of order to an unstable and turbulent existence. This fundamental Pirandellian concept is dramatized in a central scene of *Right You Are*. In the middle of act 2, near the play's midpoint, Laudisi is alone with his thoughts, meditating on the frenzy to know the truth and get to the facts displayed by the family and neighbors. The scene takes place in Agazzi's study. Over the mantelpiece hangs a large, important mirror. Seeing his reflected image, Laudisi stops and addresses it. Man and image face each other, as the protagonist's gestures—touching his forehead, leveling a menacing finger, smiling—are repeated in the glass. The monologue is imbued with Pirandellian concepts:

> Between you and me, we get along very well, don't we! But the trouble is, others don't think of you just as I do; and that being the case, old man, what a fix you're in! As for me, I say that here, right in front of you, I can see myself with my eyes and touch myself with my fingers. But what are you for other people? What are you in their eyes? An image, my dear sir, just an image in the glass! They're all carrying just such a phantom around inside themselves, and here they are racking their brains about the phantoms in other people; and they think all that is quite another thing![4]

Like the unobtrusive butler who observes the scene, the audience witnesses Laudisi talking to himself in the mirror and wonders if he is mad. Deconstructing the episode further, one is forced to pose ontological questions. Who is the "I"? Who is the "you"? Is the "I" the man speaking or the reflected image? Is the image any less real than the man? Is there a man or only his phantom? The mirror does not answer, and Laudisi himself offers no conclusions concerning either the identity of the mad person in the Ponza affair or the question of his own identity. He merely offers the audience his self-awareness, materialized in the visible mirror image. The spectators experience the doubling of the self because it is enacted before their eyes, in the man and his mirror image. The question becomes which of them is more real or more true: Laudisi or his image? Mirrors are somewhat undependable sources of truth, for they deform reality. The mirror reflects the individual but also distorts: our reflected image is inevitably a perversion, whether it be the one in the glass or the image found in others or in ourselves. The confusion between self and reflection is at the heart of Pirandello's *teatro dello specchio* (theater of the mirror), which proposes drama as a means of projecting self-consciousness and subjecticity. In *Right You Are* the mirror becomes a stage prop and a signifier, a serviceable and a metaphorical object which is concurrently real and symbolic. As the looking glass is for Alice, the mirror is an entry into the world of the unknown where adventures are sure to follow. On stage it is a tangible presence for the audience as no fictional mirror can be for the reader of a text. Masks can also be theatrical ploys, objects through which the author and his characters construct identity, revealing as well as concealing. Pirandellian masks are multifaceted, both positive and negative, individually and socially constructed. Masks can be personae or fictions, social lies or disguises through which the individual defines him-or herself or is defined.[5]

In Pirandello's dramatic universe masks and mirrors are theatrical props, signs referring to deeper meanings, representations of ideas, and concepts become objects. Masks and mirrors are also the reigning images that define the author's world, appearing and reappearing throughout his vast literary production. As Pirandello himself declared, the mirror is essential to understanding the nature of his dramatic works:

> When a man lives, he lives and does not see himself. Well, put a mirror before him and make him see himself in the act of living, under the sway of his passions: either he remains astonished and dumbfounded at his own appearance, or else he turns away his eyes so as not to see himself, or else in disgust he spits at his image, or again clinches his fist to break it; and if he had been weeping, he can weep no more; if he had been laughing, he can laugh no more, and so on. In a word, there arises a crisis, and that crisis is my theater.[6]

The mirror is the instrument of self-knowledge, through which the individual can confront himself. The mask is the representation of both personal and social identity, the form worn to define the self. Not surprisingly, the collected plays of Luigi Pirandello are titled "Naked Masks," for his characters are stripped of their facades while gazing into that self-reflective mirror of consciousness. On stage Pirandello's characters uncover their painful humanity, their unmasked selves, to the world. In the bourgeois dramas this metaphysical pain overpowers the realistic surface of the texts.

Similar in tone and in the grotesque manipulation of naturalist drama, the plays *Il piacere dell'onestà* (1917, *The Pleasure of Honesty*) and *Il giuoco delle parti* (1918, *The Rules of the Game*) were written within months of *Right You*

Are.[7] Like the earlier drama they adhere to some of the conventions of naturalist theater. In both plays the settings are interior spaces—drawing rooms and dining rooms—where the games of bourgeois marriage are played out. Such enclosed spaces, with their elaborate furnishings, suggest a claustrophobic environment which can be more a prison than a home. Both plays focus on the traditional love triangle of husband, wife, and lover and stress issues of honor and respectability within the social and moral codes of the well-to-do. Like *Right You Are* both later dramas present cerebral protagonists who specialize in the analysis of situations, people, and themselves. As Pirandellian *raisonneurs,* Angelo Baldovino and Leone Gala soothe their existential suffering by rationalizing or by evading their relative self, or both. For these protagonists reason is both a comfort and a burden, for while it protects the *raisonneur,* it also blocks intimate communication with others. Like Laudisi, Baldovino and Gala are viewed as peculiar by the community of opinion. Their tendency to analyze renders them seemingly emotionless, unlike others, and they are often ridiculed, despised, or feared.

Angelo Baldovino, the central character of *The Pleasure of Honesty,* has led a somewhat decadent life and finds himself in terribly reduced circumstances. Given his current indigence, he becomes the ideal candidate for a financially advantageous marriage to Agata Renni, enamored mistress of Fabio Colli. In point of fact, it is not a husband who is sought, but a legitimate father for Renni's illegitimate child, because Fabio Colli is legally, if not sentimentally, attached to a wife. Baldovino is a philosopher of sorts, an educated man, someone people could respect and believe in. He therefore provides a plausible match for the beautiful Agata, a woman of character who would never marry a cad. Baldovino is rigorously logical and levelheaded about his future role. Upon accepting the position of husband in act 1, he insists on the maintainance of *onestà* (honesty) in the marriage—a word that indicates not only moral rectitude but also social respectability. Through marriage Baldovino will give his life another shape: "I enter this house and immediately I become what I have to become, what I can become: I construct myself."[8] Baldovino's new form is one of perfect respect, perfect honorability, perfect paternity with no room for pretense or fiction. It is, in Baldovino's view, a double wedding: he will marry both Agata and the concept of honesty. This infusion of self-imposed respectability will moderate the bitter errors of his past and make his new role less shabby.

The honest husband of a respectable wife: Baldovino seeks to be the abstraction he embraces. He will be the form lending the concept substance by taking on the roles Fabio Colli cannot assume because of his legal status. Indeed, Colli represents the dishonesty of a good person, who is quite willing to pay for the use of another man's honorable name to protect those he loves. In the ensuing months the role of honest man appears to transform Baldovino. His assumed duties are performed with the utmost seriousness so that all forms are observed and all social expectations met. Often his insistence on conforming to each and every propriety with unbending rigor causes great consternation among his intimates. One telling episode concerns the baptism of the newborn, whom he insists on naming for his own father, in keeping with the Baldovino family tradition, heedless of the ludicrous implications such a patronymic holds for the family and for Fabio Colli. Having assumed paternity, Baldovino carries his responsiblity to its logical conclusions. Given work by Colli, the protagonist has changed into a scrupulous, hardworking manager, as is to be expected of a respectable paterfamilias. Yet the personal cost is high. To embody "a pure abstract form," Baldovino must live outside of life in a quasi-Platonic world of ideas. He denies the emotional and instinctive part of his identity, which he terms the horrible and feared beast in himself: "this creature I freed myself from by chaining it here, in the conditions imposed by our agreement" (147). For others, particularly Colli and Agata's mother, Baldovino's presence is unsettling, since it forces them to maintain the same appearance of absolute honesty he personifies, counter to their predispositions and prior expectations.

In keeping with the thematics of bourgeois theater, money is a driving force in *The Pleasure of Honesty*'s dramatic action. Money is used first to obtain and, eventually, to eliminate Agata Renni's husband. Having fallen in love with his platonic wife, Baldovino's only defense against his overpowering feelings has been the maintainence of the self-imposed mask he wears to prevent the emergence of his most private being. But, grown tired of the high price of artificial honesty, Fabio Colli plans to deconstruct Baldovino's abstract form. Colli concocts a scheme to eliminate this excessively honest husband by fabricating criminal accusations against him. Baldovino is to be charged with embezzling a considerable sum from the funds he has been assigned to manage. In a Pirandellian twist of events, however, the intended victim has observed the strategy and outmaneuvered his foe. Baldovino forces Colli to consider stealing the money himself, thus running the risk of apprehension. If Colli will do the actual crime, Baldovino agrees to play the thief. His loss of honesty would release everyone from the pact of respectability, allowing Agata to resume her interrupted rapport with Colli. Baldovino sees this solution as the only opportunity to imprison his beast permanently. For him it amounts to the ironic exchange of one assumed role for another. Nevertheless Baldovino insists on the mere appearance of form; he will not be a thief in substance, just as he has not been a husband in fact but the mere abstraction of an honest man. About to incur total loss Baldovino discovers that love can conquer all. In one of Pirandello's rare happy endings, Agata blocks the game of masks and illusions—the farce of honesty become criminality—by asserting the substantiality of their marriage. She and the boy will follow her husband, as is expected of a dutiful wife. Once so needy of respectability and self-respect, Baldovino discovers that honesty was only "a grotesque mask I chose to wear" (166), not his innermost self, and revolts. But in Agata's eyes he is a profoundly honest man, not an abstraction. At play's end he comes to accept her perception and love.

Angelo Baldovino insulates himself from life's pain by opting for a form that will imprison his tormenting impulses. Like numerous Pirandellian protagonists he sees himself and the consequences of his actions all too well. While others live "blindly," he is a marginalized observer: "when you're alive, you live and you don't see. I can see, because I came into this house in order *not* to live" (160). Release from implosion can only come in the shape of explanations, elucidations, and rationalizations—a stream of words to fill the painful voids. Baldovino, like Laudisi, Gala, and numerous other Pirandellian protagonists, is a theoretician of life, a master of words and concepts. Yet, Baldovino only finds joy when he risks the blindness of loving Agata. The protagonist of *The Rules of the Game,* Leone Gala, also marginalizes himself, suffocating his emotions beneath a dispassionate, cerebral facade. He too hides behind a superimposed mask. His logic is intimidating and devastating to others, but it removes Gala from the need for painful self-revelation and destructive relationships by creating a protective barrier of thought.

Pirandello's suggestive Italian title for *The Rules of the Game* can also be translated as "the game of roles"; both interpretations apply to this drama of tricks, strategems, bluffs, masquerading, and role-playing. Leone Gala is separated from his adulterous wife, Silia, who is currently involved in a long-term affair with Guido Venanzi. Gala and Silia maintain the facade of an unorthodox marriage, however, to preserve her social acceptability. In their first years apart Leone would formally visit his wife for one half hour each evening to give some credence to their marital farce. At the time of the play's action, that visit has generally been limited to no more than a punctilious and unacknowledged knock on Silia's door. Yet neither spouse seems ready to separate totally. Silia is both drawn to, and repulsed by, her husband's cold logic; his apparent imperturability clashes with her sensuous, imperious emotionality. She wants the collapse of his self-control under the pressure of her repeated goads. The fact that Gala does not break down breeds rabid resentment in Silia, who views her spouse as an intruder on her freedom, a presence she cannot erase from her mind. Gala haunts her, she declares, by his very existence. Hers is a paranoid obsession. Like many female characters in the works of Pirandello, Silia is a creature of instinct. The antithesis of her cerebral spouse, she is caught between hysteria and neurosis. For his part Leone accepts the role of figurehead husband to a wife he once loved deeply and later learned to hate—a wife who repeatedly betrays and taunts him. His is a life of detachment and observation. Theirs is a fatal attraction, doomed to erupt in crisis. The explosive occasion presents itself when a group of inebriated gentlemen mistake Silia for her neighbor, a woman of easy virtue, and invade her apartment. The group leader is one Miglioriti, a feared duelist. Seeing her opportunity to eliminate Leone permanently, Silia creates a scene, publicly accuses the drunken intruders of assault, then rejects their apologies and demands restitution of her honor. In short she wants a duel to be fought by the man whose name has seemingly been sullied: Leone Gala.

The situation is patently absurd: the adulteress, with her lover hiding in the bedroom, insists on the restitution of a respectability to which she has no moral claim. Silia's honor is a veneer, not substance. Unexpectedly, however, Gala accedes to his wife's demand that he issue a challenge; he is apparently willing to do her bidding and play the role of outraged husband to its conclusion. It is a cunning move in Gala's own game of cat and mouse. His appointed "second" will be the somewhat reluctant Guido Venanzi, for the role suits him ideally as Leone wittily and sarcastically points out. But Gala possesses a clever mind and sharp analytical skills, as well as the temperament of an iconoclast. On the appointed day he refuses to meet Miglioriti in the scheduled duel to the death. Having understood Silia's desire for his elimination, he knows that the restitution of her reputation in an affair of honor is a bluff, part of her deadly game plan. Therefore he neatly and logically turns the tables on his wife and her lover. As the official husband he has completed the formalities required of him by issuing the challenge. The required proprieties have been met. He is a husband in name only, however, and it is now up to Guido, the husband in all but name, to meet Miglioriti and fight for Silia's honor. As the second the lover must accept. These are the rules of the game, after all. Inevitably, Guido Venanzi is killed as Leone Gala prepares to breakfast.

In *The Pleasure of Honesty* and *The Rules of the Game,* Pirandello presents marriage as a formalistic sham that affords little personal solace or joy for the unloved protagonists. In both plays the rapport with false wives is the impetus forcing the main character out of his intellectual shelter and assumed roles into the world of passion and instinct he fears. To preserve themselves, Angelo Baldovino and Leone Gala employ reason, which allows them to fabricate a front, a formal identity, that buffers them against the pain that accompanies living. The philosophical Baldovino exists as thought, transforming himself into the abstraction he has willed himself to be, sowing confusion in his wake. To establish an acceptable modus vivendi of his own, Gala, concentrating his entire passion into two things: thinking and eating, has buried his emotional side. As he explains to Silia, at the end of act 2, to avoid the necessity of killing her, first out of love, then out of rancor, he caged his emotions in the "self-imposed role of tamer of [his] feelings." According to Frank Laurence Lucas's insightful categorization, Gala is both stoic and epicurean, without hope and without fear. Yet, for both these characters, the assumed mask is only partially successful. Baldovino and Gala constantly struggle against the possibility of being stripped naked for the world to see. Baldovino fears his hidden beast. Gala prefers the role of beast tamer. But the beast of passion lies in wait, hidden beneath each man's controlled facade.

The cerebral Gala and his emotional wife actually have a great deal in common. Both are highly conscious of their state of hopelessness and uncomfortable with their physical and spiritual selves. Silia feels imprisoned by her beautiful woman's body, the object of male gaze and desire. Briefly glimpsing her ontological alienation, she encounters moments of estrangement from her face in the mirror. On an emotional level Silia feels the same pain of existence Leone perceives intellectually. However, Silia comprehends neither the existential origin of her anguish nor its connection to the human condition. She relates her lack of autonomy to her husband's omniscient presence and finds herself imagining his watching her, knowing her every move, foreseeing her behavior. In her mind's eye Leone possesses the power of a cruel and remote deity to destroy her. To rid herself of this phantom presence, she prepares her deadly little game. For his part Gala has consciously pursued the path of dissolution through self-effacement, doing his utmost "to exist as little as possible" for both himself and others by emptying himself.[9] Leone Gala has constructed a voyeur of life, especially of his own life, watching himself live "from outside." As he attempts to explain to Guido, who acts but does not observe, Gala's existential despair derives in part from his mastery of "every move in the game" of life (13). While Silia allows her impulses and feelings to sway her, rendering her moody and fickle, Leone seeks "the thrill of the intellectual game that clears away all the sentimental sediment from your mind" and replaces it with a "clear, calm vacuum" (15). Like so many of Pirandello's fictional spouses, they are doomed to mutual misunderstanding.

Leone Gala's refusal to fight in the game of life and death concocted by Silia's perfidy and seconded by Guido's inaction is his checkmate. Leone has altered the rules of their game and created one of his own, based not on the regulations of dueling or the codes of high society, which he categorically rejects, but on a ludic realization of their own triangular relationship. In his cerebral, distant way Leone warns Silia and Guido that the game being played is serious and that the roles are set: "But you must play your part, just as I am playing mine. It's all in the game. Even Silia has grasped that! Each of us must play his part through to the end" (40). Clearly Gala has not attained the long-sought "Nothing that lies inside yourself." It is in the role of husband betrayed by both wife and friend that he lashes out, ever so cleverly, yet ever so fatally, shedding the final role assigned to him in Silia's game: dead man. Far from being the apathetic, unfeeling, even comical figure that Silia and Guido imagine, Leone Gala settles the score; he is a passionate angry man who has outplayed the opponents and won his life. Endgame comes quickly in a deadly mix of murderous intent and revenge. The trickster removes his mask and the grim reaper appears. In the final scene with his wife, Gala allows his avenging beasts to emerge, however briefly:

> LEONE (in a low voice, gripping her arm): I have punished you both!
> SILIA (as though biting him): I see! But at the price of your own dishonour!
> LEONE: You are my dishonour. (58)

Responding to persistent accusations of excessive philosophizing in his plays and to repeated criticism of the verbosity of cerebral characters such as Laudisi, Baldovino, and Gala, Pirandello often sought to clarify the relationship between intellect and emotion in his dramatic works. In the following statement, excerpted from a press interview held in 1924, the playwright also speaks to the novelty of his dramatic solutions as his contribution to the new theater of consciousness: "People say that my drama is obscure and they call it cerebral drama. The new drama possesses a distinct character from the old: whereas the latter had as its basis passion, the former is the expression of the intellect. One of the novelties that I have given to modern drama consists in converting the intellect into passion."[10] By creating a panoply of reasoning, self-analyzing, and self-aware characters, Pirandello stretched the familiar limits of naturalist drama. His self-conscious protagonists seek to justify, explain, understand, and come to terms with themselves and their world, on both conscious and subconscious levels. *Raisonneurs* open up the metaphoric potential of thought, engaging their fellows and the audience in a challenging, complex dialectic that dares theater to be far more than a place of entertainment or amusement. These characters expose the nooks and crannies of their surprising minds, the illusions behind logic, the multiplicity of being, thus enriching the text. The objective "facts" of naturalist discourse are challenged by the subjective interpretations of ideas, events, and experiences doggedly pursued by Pirandello's masters of logic, who, seeking to make sense of it all, need to constantly delve beyond the surface into the morass of the human psyche. Briefly stated, Pirandello's bourgeois dramas offer a new interpretation of the individual's struggle, based on both feeling and reason, against the oppressive forces of existence and society.

Ever the humorist writer, Pirandello blends comedy and tragedy, pathos and parody, anguish and laughter in these early bourgeois dramas of his vast repertory. Operating in the realm of seriocomedy, as does *Right You Are, The Rules of the Game* is equal parts farce and fatalism, with elements of black humor. Like Lamberto Laudisi, Leone Gala is as much the sophisticated eccentric as the world-weary philosopher of absence. In act 1 the absurdity of his cat-and-mouse game of equivocation with Guido, as husband and lover cordially converse in Silia's living room, is concurrently droll and ludicrous. So is the disconcerting image of the intellectual Gala, wearing a chef's hat and apron, beating eggs while discussing Bergsonian philsophy at the opening of act 2, or the entrance, in pajamas and slippers, of a sleepy and totally placid Leone emerging from his bedroom on the morning of his scheduled duel to the death in act 3. Pirandello employs these visual images to project the grotesque duality of the face and the mask. The appearance of lightheartedness covers the painful human torments experienced by the protagonist. Gourmet cook, nonchalant man of the world, amiable logician: these are masks worn by Gala to tame the beasts tormenting the inner self. But, as theatrical devices, masks and farce provide comic relief and amused chuckles in a play filled with dark impulses. Gala knows full well that roles, either those assigned by society or those constructed by individuals in their games of life, are disguises. He wears the mask of apathy as well as one of amiability, but in the end the face of pain emerges. Soon Gala will permanently assume the mask of dishonored coward for his society, but he will have won his game.

The mixture of laughter and tears is the outward manifestation of the humorist's "feeling of the opposite," or understanding of reality. The bourgeois dramas of 1917–1918, composed in the final years of an international conflagration that submerged Pirandello, as well as millions of others, are as concerned with conflictual feeling as they are with paradoxical ideas. In these plays Pirandello blends the elements of intellectual comedy and passionate tragedy, thus striking a difficult balance. Since theater is envisaged as both imagery and words, the finales of these three dramas connote the depths of Pirandello's attachment to the innovations proposed by the Grottesco, thereby leaving powerful impressions on the audience. The climax of *Right You Are* is visual and verbal. The veiled woman is the physical embodiment of the crisis of reality: an enigma wrapped in black, to be punctuated by Lamberto Laudisi's laughing commentary on the voice of truth. Tears mark the conclusion of Angelo Baldovino's story: uncontrollable tears from a living abstraction who has finally released some of his beasts, finding joy and a man. But for Leone Gala, master of *The Rules of the Game,* the last image is stasis: deprived of either tears or laughter, he is an immovable statue in a tragic silence, as his breakfast sits on the dining-room table. Writing about the theatrical impact of the Grottesco in a scholarly review published in 1920, Pirandello defined not only their drama but his own. "The farce of the Grotesque," he wrote, "includes in its tragedy its parody and its caricature, not as extraneous superposed elements, but as its own shadow, the awkward shadow of every tragic gesture."[11]

CHAPTER FOUR

Moscarda's Nose, or the Disintegration of the Individual

One morning Vitangelo Moscarda is observing himself in the mirror when Dida, his wife, blithely remarks that his nose tilts to the right. Previously unaware of this fact, Moscarda is fascinated by its truth and his own ignorance. Demanding further examples of his physical peculiarities, Dida casually enlightens her husband: his eyebrows resemble circumflex accents; his ears are not attached properly; his pinky finger is a bit crooked, his right leg slightly curved. The mirror confirms it all. Vitangelo realizes that for his twenty-eight years, he has not known his own body. If not the body, what is knowable? Suddenly Moscarda is self-aware, drawn to his reflected image again and again. All mirrors begin to fascinate yet repel him. From a casual event, the exploration of his body in the looking glass, Vitangelo Moscarda has entered the murky waters of self-consciousness. Thus begins Luigi Pirandello's last completed novel, *Uno, nessuno e centomila* (1925–1926, *One, No One, and One Hundred Thousand).*[1]

Notwithstanding the comic tone of the novel's exordium, Vitangelo Moscarda's tilted nose is a terribly serious matter that will initiate his perilous quest for identity and authenticity. Continually drawn to the mirror of self-contemplation, Moscarda gradually distances himself from human fellowship to search for greater self-knowledge. He requires solitude for his narcissistic explorations so he can be "without himself" but with "the outsider inseparable from himself." Having broken out of the familiar patterns of his existence, Moscarda goes on to challenge the elements that compose his social identity and finds that they do not correspond to his own self-perception. Attempting to establish a public persona that projects this inner dimension, Vitangelo quickly discovers that there is no single persona, but many. Finding that others view him as inept, superficial, even ridiculous, Moscarda, hoping to redefine himself publicly and privately, rebels against these acquired images. Like Mattia Pascal, Vitangelo Moscarda, yearning for a reflection that is neither fixed nor false, but true and recognizable, takes to watching himself live, repeatedly confronting his image in mirrors, windows, eyes, and minds. Inevitably he is doomed to failure. The initial disruptive gaze into the mirror reflecting the physical self is transformed into an obsessive disquisition on the construction of identity and humanity. The mirror image has produced a stranger, made all the more foreign to Moscarda because others seem to recognize the stranger in the mirror as his actual self. Moscarda's narrative echoes a conclusion Pirandello himself once reached about his own identity: "There is somebody who is living my life and I know nothing about him."[2]

Vitangelo Moscarda has begun a voyage into the depths of self-knowledge, quickly progressing to the realization that he is even more unfamiliar with his inner self than with his outer self. Roaming the streets of his Sicilian town, the young man questions friends and neighbors about his nose, his body, his identity. Each respondent becomes a new mirror. In each he discovers another view, a new perception, a different but not necessarily complementary Vitangelo Moscarda. While none of the images matches his own, each is firmly upheld by the reflector. The protagonist's dilemma is clearly ontological, as an endless series of presumably false, inaccurate selves are projected onto him by others. To duplicate the perceptions of his human mirrors, Moscarda attempts to catch himself in the act of living, in motion, as they see him. Whereas his fictional ancestor Adriano Meis looked into a mirror and saw Mattia Pascal, Vitangelo Moscarda gazes upon a mysterious cipher. Like the Wicked Queen in the tale of Snow White, he endlessly consults and challenges the glass by asking, in effect: "who is the Vitangelo among them all?" No answer is given because no one clear identity exists, except in the individual's self-consciousness. Notwithstanding his initial unified sense of self, Moscarda, fascinated by the growing multiplicity of masks and images, discovers he is no more—or less—than their sum.

In *One, No One, and One Hundred Thousand,* the mirror is a signifier of dichotomies, of doublings and splittings, of divisions in the self, and of multiplied perceptions. I or other? madman or sane? Vitangelo or Gengè? They all appear in Moscarda's mirrors, whether they be the armoire looking glass or his wife's eyes. The mirror soon expropriates Moscarda's life. At first only duality concerns him: "he was that one who existed for the others and whom I couldn't know, whom the others saw living and I didn't."[3] Eventually other selves begin to haunt the protagonist. His wife's Moscarda, nicknamed Gengè, is sweet but slightly ridiculous, an ineptly kind man-child. In Dida's mind Vitangelo's body and being belong to *her* Gengè, the man she loves, married, suspects. Considering him a fabrication and a rival, Moscarda categorically rejects Gengè as his real self. Vitangelo soon comes to loathe his wife's image. He agonizes over the thought that Dida passionately embraces Gengè, not himself as he knows himself to be, in their lovemaking. Other "selves" begin to anguish him: the "dear Vitangelo" dismissed by his business associates, the shiftless ne'er-do-well perceived by the local well-to-do, the usurer detested by the community, his father imprinted in his own anatomy. Vitangelo Moscarda makes a supreme effort to see himself from the outside, as others see him, as he cannot see himself. Soon he intuits that the belief in a unified personality is a mirage, one of the comforting assumptions on which human certainty rests: "that reality, as it is for you, must be and is the same for everybody else" (25). The novel's title is exegetical: man believes in his unity (one-ness) but is actually many persons, a changeable chameleon reflected by endless mirrors. Being the object of an infinity of external perceptions, there are one hundred thousand "I's" and actually no one self.

Aware of being the daily construction of himself and others, Vitangelo is galvanized by this discovery, by feeling imprisoned in his body, his name, his house, his reputation, his town, his roles, and his historical situation. These are all imposed upon him, and, being fabricated by others, they are inherently falsifying. Analyzing his social roles, Moscarda quickly rebels against them; he is determined to decompose the masks by which others identify him. Desperate to be for others what he is for himself, Moscarda is propelled into rejecting "normal" behavior. For example, to prove he is not a heartless moneylender, he first evicts an indigent tenant, thus creating considerable ill will, and then proceeds to donate an attractive new home to the poor man. This effectively eliminates the image of Moscarda the usurer by replacing it with a new, equally charged identity for the community: Moscarda the madman. In a frenzy to take control of his life, Vitangelo challenges one and all to reassess his identity. His actions are out of the ordinary, "ab"normal according to established patterns of social behavior. His intimates react in disbelief for they do not recognize "their" Vitangelo Moscarda. In time Dida, having lost her Gengè, leaves him. His business managers banish him as a dangerous idiot. Having inherited his wealth, he plots to donate all his material possessions because they came from his wheeling and dealing father and are not really "his."

Nearing novel's end, Vitangelo has found narcissistic solitude but also its emptiness. Seeking some form of human communication after losing his wife, he attaches himself to Anna Rosa, Dida's confidante. A mature virgin embroiled in her own issues of identity and narcissism, the woman is both fascinated by Vitangelo's lengthy philosophical disquisitions and repelled by her developing sexual attraction. In a dichotomous act of her own, the bedridden Anna Rosa one day opens her arms to embrace Moscarda, then shoots him with a concealed revolver. It is during his lengthy recovery that the protagonist determines on a decisive existential step. Seen as lacking common (that is, collective) sense, seeking self-determination free of all encumbrances and all masks, and frightfully aware of the innate isolation experienced by all men—since no man can ever truly know another—Moscarda finds liberation in nature. Divested of everything material, separated from human intercourse, living in a shelter financed by his abandoned wealth, and deemed "mad" by his community, Vitangelo Moscarda is finally at peace. Pirandello's last novel concludes on the same paradoxical note of *The Late Mattia Pascal:* to be someone, the hero must resolve to live as no one.

As is generally the case in Pirandello, there is an underlying note of social criticism in *One, No One, and One Hundred Thousand.* To achieve some form of authenticity, Moscarda first calls into question the validity of the institutions that form the foundation of modern bourgeois capitalist society. Marriage, even its most intimate sexual aspects, is presented as a union based on false assumptions; it is depicted as the joining of two separate beings with differing, even antagonistic, images of themselves and each other, who never share genuine mutuality. Vitangelo comes to realize that Dida loves not him, but her own creation, Gengè. Equally important is his increasing awareness that she too possesses unknown selves; gradually Moscarda is forced to question his own fallacious constructions of Dida's identity. With no ontological stability possible, dissolution soon follows. Once Vitangelo begins his journey through the looking glass, not only is his marriage doomed but so is his entire relationship to family, work, and community. The surname Moscarda, imposed by social custom, offends his sense of self because of its fortuitous association with the word for fly, *mosca.* His reddish coloring denotes a foreign presence, his father, coursing through him because of heredity factors. Indeed, each analysis of the building blocks forming his constructed identity weakens Vitangelo's hold on a unified self. By demolishing all the architectural elements, Moscarda hopes to build again, according to his own blueprint.

Moscarda's repudiation of the family business, a bank, is an act of rebellion against the continuing power of money and ancestry to define his life. The protagonist knows full well that his deceased father's associates are not bankers but profiteers and capitalist exploiters. His own collusion is limited to an occasional signature and good profits, but the label of usurer, inherited like the business, is attached to him in the community's perception. Undeserving of the appellation "banker," only indirectly a "usurer," Vitangelo rejects both designations, thus putting his own income and that of all the shareholders at risk of financial collapse when he attempts to withdraw his monies. The willed obliteration of his participation in the bank is reflective of Moscarda's break with the structures that organize the workings of society. It is also a symbolic patricide: killing the bank allows him to kill off the one person he holds most responsible for shaping his multiple identities. Vitangelo Moscarda is a bourgeois who does not accept the capitalist world order, a man with no profession, no job, no financial preoccupations. Even before his leap into the mirror, Vitangelo personified the failure of the bourgeois order: a middle-class "banker" who does no work; a child of privilege who has no direction; a husband who has no authority; a paterfamilias who produces no heirs. It is no wonder the family and community turn on Moscarda and declare him mad. In their eyes his folly is not just psychic imbalance but social disruption as well.

Vitangelo is deemed mad because he rejects the world as he knows it, with all its limiting roles. However, the effacement of thousands upon thousands of Vitangelo Moscardas requires a leap into a new dimension of social alienation. Like Mattia Pascal he too stages a suicide of sorts. For Moscarda, to be is commensurate with not to be. One equals no one. Like a reclusive hermit opting for a Franciscanate contemplation of nature, Moscarda denies the world and embraces sister poverty. If the city is "a constructed world," nature offers infinite fluidity and mutability. Of course, Vitangelo's city is a representative microcosm, the macrocosm being human civilization, or "man" himself, who "takes as material even himself, and he constructs himself, yes, sir, like a house" (41). Only by voluntarily dissolving his individuality can the protagonist find a workable solution to the dilemma of his concurrently disintegrating and multiplying identity. Nature offers him timelessness and formlessness, a place outside of history. As Moscarda says, "You can't know yourself in a pose: a statue: not alive. When people are alive, they live; they don't see themselves. To know yourself is to die" (148). Anna Rosa is Vitangelo's antagonist in both love and self-awareness. While he thirsts for the disappearance of his multiple images, she is determined to preserve her every look, attitude, and gesture in a multitude of photographs kept in a drawer and regularly admired. Her choice is death, not life. In her pronounced virginity and narcissitic need to arrest her likeness on paper, Anna Rosa represents fixity in form, a hyperbolic surfeit of masks, rather than the liberating evanescence of life in nature.

Vitangelo Moscarda's solution, requiring the disintegration of his identity to the point of its elimination, is also a loss. If Being exists in nature, the individual self is diminished and fleeting. Garbed in institutional, thus unidentifiable, clothing as he roams the countryside, Vitangelo yearns for merger with nature, not in the Romantic sense of a subjective feeling of convergence, but in the abandonment of self-consciousness to an unthinking, unseeing, unreflecting, unconscious life-form. It is a return to Mother Earth, to the womb of preconsciousness. To achieve it, the individual must become like the objects found in nature, who are what they appear to be—unlike man. Fluid and thoughtless, Vitangelo can merge with every object encountered, in a continuous mystical union with Being, dying at every moment and being constantly reborn. Subsumed by Being, Vitangelo Moscarda is released from all falsifying constructions, thus attaining a blessed state of harmony:

> I am alive and I do not conclude. Life does not conclude. And life knows nothing of names. This tree, tremulous pulse of new leaves. I am this tree. Tree, cloud; tomorrow book or wind: the book I read, the wind I drink. All outside, wandering. . . .
> . . . I die at every instant, and I am reborn, new and without memories: live and whole, no longer inside myself, but in every thing outside. (159–160)

Some critics view Moscarda's existential solution as a new religious dimension in Pirandello's works. The protagonist's contemplative disposition, retreat into nature, renunciation of the world, and communion with all Being clearly evoke the hagiography surrounding St. Francis of Assisi, to whom Moscarda has often been compared. Indeed, Vitangelo's relinquishment is mystical, supporting comparisons with blessed Franciscan folly, a holy madness joining man, God, and nature. This relinquishment is, nevertheless, a dissolution. Having rejected social roles, names, and identities, as well as institutions, Moscarda cannot return to his past. As Douglas Radcliff-Umstead has pointed out, the protagonist's tale can be interpreted as a story chronicling either the development of self-awareness or the descent into insanity. Read the latter way, it is not pantheism but dementia that moves Moscarda into nature. Other scholars consider Vitangelo Moscarda the prototypical modernist antihero, in disharmony with his society, rebellious to its dictums, and incapable of establishing solid human connections because of his inability to communicate. Interpreted in this manner, the protagonist is abdicating, not fulfilling, life.

Pirandello conceived of *One, No One, and One Hundred Thousand* as a summation of his thoughts and as an original representation of the decomposition of the personality, a decomposition taken to its extreme consequences. Stefano Pirandello indicated that his father required more than fifteen years to complete the novel: an unusually long gestation period for an author known to write profusely and quickly. Excerpts were published as early as 1915, ten years before the entire work was serialized in the literary magazine *Fiera letteraria* over a six-month period in 1925–1926. Speculation and meditation form the core of *One, No One, and One Hundred Thousand*. The novel itself is stylistically complex, operating on two distinct narrative levels. One level recounts episodes from the protagonist's life in a sequentially chronological order; the other offers metaphysical conjecture and psychological self-analysis. Both narrative levels propose the first-person voice of Vitangelo Moscarda as the mediating glue holding the text together. Unfolding as a continuous interior monologue, Moscarda's narration nevertheless implicitly moves toward the creation of dialogue: dialogue between Vitangelo and his other selves; between Moscarda and other characters, including Dida's lapdog Bibí, whose expressive eyes shine with a Gengè of their own; primarily, however, the novel is a dialogue between the narrator and his readers. Moscarda's sense of personal evanescence, dissociation, irreality, and ambivalence is projected through a highly rhetorical narrative strategy in which the protagonist carries on this dialogue with a hypothetical addressee, whose own identity continuously shifts—a "you" to whom his thoughts and ruminations are directed in a calculated act of persuasion. Vitangelo's discourse analyzes the minievents of his existence to expose the movements of his developing consciousness, but it also suggests the universality of his singular experience. Even after the transcendent leap into nature, Moscarda maintains outreach, creating an audience to receive his communication and empathize with his choices.

While the contents of Pirandello's last novel depict dissolution and evanescence, its form is a careful construct that builds meaning by merging ideas (Moscarda's thoughts) and images (his multiplying identities) in a complex narrative discussion of identity. In fact, the book is a cleverly crafted literary object that connotes Moscarda's experience through its structure. Multiplicity is suggested by the novel's sixty-odd chapters of varying lengths and contents. The chapters are organized into two distinct sections composed of four parts each. The first four-part section traces the protagonist's gradual process of fragmentation—Moscarda strives to define his image for himself and for others, only to encounter a plethora of selves. The second grouping of four parts recounts the protagonist's attempts at reframing his identity according to his self-perception, an act which results in the leap into contemplative transcendence. Like Mattia Pascal, who attempts a redefinition of self by constructing Adriano Meis, Vitangelo Moscarda seeks to do away with numerous public personae to impose a single one of his own making. Employing a retrospective (then and now) first-person narration, as in *The Late Mattia Pascal,* this last Pirandellian novel functions as a statement on the impossibility of constructing a viable unified identity within the social sphere, which imposes multiple selves on the subject.

One, No One, and One Hundred Thousand is a compilation of some of

Pirandello's most familiar motifs and devices, from doubling mirrors to intro-spective narrators. Like numerous other Pirandellian protagonists, Vitangelo Moscarda is caught in the vise of feeling himself living. Extraordinarily medi-tative and painfully logical, Moscarda effectively elucidates a series of recurring Pirandellian themes through the narrative transmission of his case history. These include the multiplicity of personality, the relativity of truth, the impossibility of certainty, the hopeless search for a unified identity, the need for beneficial illusions, the inevitability of social alienation, and the conflict between form, in its stasis, and life, in its constant becoming. Unlike other Pirandellian works, this novel offers its protagonist an alternative to the inauthentic social order: nature. The plunge into nature is Moscarda's attempt to reestablish the Edenic world, which existed before sin (civilization) diminished the integrity of the individual. In the simplicity, fluidity, and organic quality of his new state, Vitangelo can erase himself to begin anew outside the anguished chaos of so-cial life. By refusing society's roles and masks, Moscarda is an exemplary Pirandellian character who dies "the symbolic death of insanity."[4] Vitangelo Moscarda's story is a tale of social constructions being destroyed to reconstruct a genuine self. Yet the protagonist's final self is also a social construct: the madman. As madman, Vitangelo is allowed the freedom to "be" in nature's fluidity but at the cost of exile from his own self-consciousness and flight into a peopleless world. While masks hamper the knowability of the inner self, mad-ness permits the individual to emerge, but only as an outcast, a wise fool, or a feared lunatic.

Pirandello's earlier novel *Si gira . . .* (1916, Shoot!), later retitled *I quaderni di Serafino Gubbio, operatore* (1925, *Shoot! The Notebooks of Serafino Gubbio, Cinematograph Operator*), introduces another self-conscious and watchful nar-rator, intent on setting forth his unique life story. Set in the frantic Roman world of silent moviemaking, *Shoot!*'s plot unfolds in the pages of diaries, or jour-nals, kept by Serafino Gubbio, cameraman by accident. Gubbio comments upon what he observes through his lens, his eyes, and his memory. "Seeing" is Gubbio's particular characteristic; his watching is actually study, an attempt to glimpse in others what he himself lacks, namely "the certainty that they under-stand what they're doing" in the midst of their frenetic lives. Seeing is also part of the protagonist's job: he is the mind's eye of his inanimate camera. Gubbio's life has been reduced to pure sight, a remote gaze. The immobile movie camera is a metaphor for Serafino's seeming imperturbability before the passionate and irrational behavior of his peers; it embodies the stasis of Gubbio himself, as immobile in his own way as the many-legged "black spider" he operates.[5]

Through his watchful gaze Serafino Gubbio views the foibles and dramas that surround him on the lot and in his quarters. The espied lives of the inhabitants of Kosmograph resemble nothing more than the adventurous, titillating, passionate, or pathetic films the studio produces for mass consumption. One of the objects of the cameraman's visual study is the actress Varia Nestoroff, a Russian femme fatale whose shady past had touched his former life before his retreat into imperturbability. Part of Gubbio's journals recapture the charm and pain of the past revisited in the mind. As a young man Serafino lived an idyllic intermezzo with the family of a gifted painter who loved the Russian beauty purely. Unable to bear the artist's devotion and idealization, the woman intentionally seduced his handsome friend, Aldo Nuti, then engaged to the painter's sister. The affair inevitably led to the tragic destruction of the young artist and his loved ones.[6] Having formed one of Gubbio's few bright memories, the devastated family was then irreparably destroyed by the foreign siren he now beholds daily in all her sensual allure. Nestoroff herself is racked by inner demons and the weight of her secret guilt. As the camera's human eye, Gubbio notes that the woman's histrionic acting is the externalization of her inner being: violent, dramatic, sensual, and overpowering. Gradually he feels compassion for the actress: he breaks his self-protective impassiveness.

For a brief period the protagonist allows himself to be sucked back into life with its messy passions and chaotic emotions. Nestoroff is only one of the objects of his compassionate gaze. He also befriends his pathetic landlord, a tiger caged on the set, a homeless violinist, and the tormented Aldo Nuti, who joins the film company as a leading man. Gubbio also falls hopelessly and silently in love with sweet little Luisetta who, in turn, is equally and hopelessly fond of the uninterested Nuti. The leading man, for his part, is struggling with the memory of his abandoned fiancée, his suicidal friend, and the exotic woman who seduced him into betraying them both. The past swarms unchecked into Serafino's memory as well, filling him with nostalgic regret for the tragic family he had loved. Emotional involvement ruptures Gubbio's isolation: "I am no longer a *thing,* and this silence of mine is no longer an *inanimate* silence."[7] But the return to human feeling inevitably leads to pain, the inescapable existential pain of participating in life. Nudged out of his impassiveness, Gubbio soon realizes the futility of his emotional expenditures. After reaching out to others, he quickly retreats. Finding his isolation more secure, he returns behind the glass eye of his "black spider": it is a desire for oblivion.

In front of Serafino Gubbio's eye the imitation of life with all its frantic manifestations—the movie scenes—plays on as he automatically turns the camera's handle. According to Gubbio, the mechanical spider, in its dual function of recording life while killing it off, saps the life force of the actors. The "*live* action of their *live* bodies" disappears on the screen, to be replaced by a fleeting and dispersive visual projection (106). As a medium of soundless imagery, film is Pirandello's symbol for untruths and insubstantiality. Critic Arcangelo Leone De Castris suggests that shooting pictures is a way or portraying one's own absence from life and it is to nonbeing that Serafino moves, distraught by his recent and anguished reconnection to human fellowship. The camera, transforming the operator into an extension of the machine, functions as a barrier between him and others. In the role of passive mechanical spectator, in the final pages of his notebooks Serafino Gubbio becomes imprisoned in a "thing's silence" and is returned to an inanimate, therefore unfeeling, state. Yet, while shooting the last scene of an important jungle film, the cameraman is inexorably and permanently caught up in the tragedy of Aldo Nuti, Varia Nestoroff, and the caged tiger. The film's absurdly melodramatic storyline finds an even more dramatic finale in the last moments of the actors' lives. Instead of killing the cat as required by the script, Nuti turns the gun on his former mistress, only to be torn to pieces by the enraged tiger. Ever the perfect machine, Gubbio obeys the call of the camera, automatically registering it all, hand glued to the handle. Shocked into traumatic muteness, Serafino is forever a willing thing in its/his silence. If not a stone or a tree like Vitangelo Moscarda, Gubbio metamorphoses into a thing among things, a cog in the machinery of modern life.

Gubbio's is the most current of Pirandello's alienations: a man in the service of machines. Seeking to become machinelike himself, the cameraman, having already determined he had no need of a soul, acquires an automaton's imperturbability. Serafino Gubbio allows himself to depersonalize as a protective measure against the pain of living—he hopes to become as desensitized to his surroundings as the camera he holds. If Mattia Pascal tried for an impossible authenticity and Vitangelo Moscarda for evanescence, Gubbio prefers to escape his humanity altogether by watching everything, including himself, from a distance. He wishes to separate from the "superfluity" that plagues people and pushes them to seek impossible certainties, rather than contenting themselves with a natural existence and animal satisfactions. It is a logical conclusion to Gubbio's marginal position, described in the poignant chapters of the novel dedicated to memory. An orphan, a wandering student, and a failed intellectual, Gubbio has lost all ties to people, places, and roles. All that is left him is to sever altogether ties with life by reverting to the observant gaze of his machine self: "Or rather I cease to exist. *It* walks, now, upon my legs. From head to foot, I belong to it: I form part of its equipment. My head is here, inside the machine, and I carry it in my hand" (86).

One of Italy's most astute Pirandello scholars, Carlo Salinari interprets the rapport of man and machine in this novel as a sign of disconcerting historical transformations. In preindustrial society people had used utensils to better life, but, in the new world order of industrial production, machines use individuals and condition human life. Humanity has come to serve the machinery of modern industrial society, like the cameraman cranking his spider's handle who is incapable of responding adequately to the pain, misery, love, and passion that appear before his mechanized eye. Even Gubbio's hand becomes part of the machinery, as he lives up to his nickname and identifier on the movie set: "Shoot!" Having lost the identity and integrity implied by a name, Gubbio has been reduced to a function. In Serafino Gubbio's journal Pirandello represents the disconnection of the individual from the social fabric. The protagonist's robot life of isolated solitude stands in opposition to the myth of nature's vitality and power, a contrast which concludes *One, No One, and One Hundred Thousand*. As Gubbio himself notes, "as I turn the handle, I am what I am supposed to be, that is to say perfectly *impassive*. I am unable either to hate or to love the Nestoroff, as I am unable either to hate or to love anyone. I am *a hand that turns the handle* " (57–58).

Pirandello is reaching beyond melodrama into the realm of metaphysical symbolism in the sensationalist conclusion of *Shoot!* Gubbio, stricken with horror and fear, loses his voice while his hand continues to turn and turn, fixing the tragedy of Nuti's hatred and Nestoroff's death on film for posterity and capturing a reality stranger than most fictions. Just as his new friend, the homeless violinist, cannot play his enchanting music for others because they misunderstand, the cameraman can no longer produce the sounds of human communication—language—because mutual understanding is impossible. The presence of the doomed tiger serves to emphasize the folly of people caught in the traps of their own emotions and subject to explosive, if bestial, responses. On the one hand, the tiger embodies the predatory nature of Varia Nestoroff, a woman of great beauty and voracious appetites, but it also symbolizes Nuti's bestial desire for her. In the end the unleashed tiger devours life, in the person of Aldo Nuti, but Gubbio too has fed that same life to his devouring machine. If the tiger is a natural predator, true to its animal self, Gubbio's black spider is an unnatural mechanical carnivore feeding on souls. Ironically, Gubbio's film becomes a box-office smash, insuring the cameraman some professional stability and rewarding him financially for his metamorphosis into the hand that turns the handle.

Serafino Gubbio does not achieve the transcendent epiphany or joyful madness of Vitangelo Moscarda. Nor is he a total automaton, a mere extension of his camera. His notebooks indicate the continued need to transmit experience and being in some form, if only to give utterance to the impossibility of relationship. Having rejected living, writing becomes Gubbio's alternative existential space, where representation is made possible without direct participation in the life depicted. In some ways the cameraman resembles the films he shoots: silent, he nevertheless inscribes a story in words that flash across the white screens of his notebooks. Yet Gubbio can only record what he sees, not attribute meaning or value to it. Nevertheless writing offers Pirandellian protagonists the possibility of somehow reconstructing the conscious self and expressing it concretely: Serafino Gubbio takes up the pen to voice his unspoken and unspeakable words; Mattia Pascal tells his story as a way to recuperate his lost lives and unstable personhood; Vitangelo Moscarda's text reunites his fragmented identity. But an inherent dilemma subsists between the living and the narrating of life: the one intrinsically excludes the other. As Pirandello himself wrote a friend in 1921: "Life, you either write it, or live it. . . . I've never lived it, if not by writing it."[8] For Luigi Pirandello and his self-conscious fictional narrators, writing is a means of combating life's continuous changeability and fluidity by channeling them into the ideal form of art.

Stylistically experimental, *Shoot!* is often considered an uneven, somewhat disjointed, literary work. One critic, Umberto Bosco, accuses it of being three novels in one: an exemplary tale of the destructive mechanization of modern life, a nostalgic idyll unfolding in Gubbio's retrospective memories, and a depiction of the early years of Italian cinema with its odd denizens. The novel is held together by virtue of the coexistence of all three narrative threads in the single consciousness of its protagonist-narrator, as presupposed by the book's categorization as a personal journal.[9] In *Shoot!*'s fictional universe the narrative "I" of romantic and naturalist narrative has been replaced by the inconsistent, dehumanized figure of the protagonist, while *One, No One, and One Hundred Thousand* proposes a self-absorbed "I" divorced from external reality and deterministic logic. Moscarda's self-conscious narrator is a far cry from the omnisicent author of romantic fiction or the dispassionate one of verismo, much less the objectively viewed "human document" of naturalist fiction. Similarly Pirandello's stylistic experimentation is formulated to mimic the disquieting contents of his novels. The fragmented style of *Shoot!* is a reflection of the fractured reality of human consciousness and life. As Radcliff-Umstead has aptly stated, the protagonist's writing and recording of events in fragmentary passages "form the novel's film clips."[10] In keeping with Pirandello's progressive decomposition of realist conventions, begun with *The Late Mattia Pascal* and continued in *One, No One, and One Hundred Thousand, Shoot!*'s collage technique places this novel in the literary avant-garde and foreshadows the development of the *nouveau roman* in the 1950s and 1960s. Like the new novel, *Shoot!* treats "things" as fictional subjects, suggesting that people too can be viewed as things. Pirandello's depiction of the fragmentation of individuals and consciousness in *Shoot!* was echoed contemporaneously in other artistic renderings, such as cubism, and in fields outside of the arts, such as Freudian psychoanalysis, with the concept of id, ego, and superego, and physics, with Einstein's theory of relativity, which rethinks spatial and temporal relationships with the understanding that human knowledge itself can only be relatively true. Like other modernist protagonists, Pirandello's fictional characters repeatedly express the futility of all human constructions, the elusiveness of personality, and the alienation resulting from their renunciation of "normal" life. Vitangelo Moscarda and Serafino Gubbio embody the impact of growing human fragmentation by taking it to its extreme consequences: the disintegration of the individual.

CHAPTER FIVE

Henry IV's Sane Madness

The imposing presence and tortuous lucidity of Luigi Pirandello's imperial protagonist, *Enrico IV* (1922, *Henry IV*), impel his companions, as well as the play's audience, to confront the power of madness to demolish certainties, producing dismay, even terror, in onlookers. "Do you know what it means," he challenges all, "to find yourselves face to face with a madman—with one who shakes the foundations of all you have built up in yourselves, your logic, the logic of all your constructions?"[1] In his conscious folly Henry penetrates the arbitrariness inherent in human institutions, social relationships, and value systems. Possibly Pirandello's most arresting dramatic characterization, Henry IV possesses great power, albeit limited to the boards of his personal theater, where he is concurrently producer, director, and star. While men are constantly at work constructing themselves and donning their masks, the "mad" Henry IV has abolished his original biographical reality by appropriating a fixed historical identity which permits him to deconstruct the fabrications of others. His story is one of the most complex, and possibly the most tragic, invented by Pirandello. Henry has substituted form for being by borrowing the life of a man long dead. By making it his own, he lives out the pages of history in the plays of his imagination. Truly masked in the trappings and events of the past, Henry dominates the present by rejecting it. He dresses in medieval clothing, dyes his greying hair blond, rouges his cheeks, and inhabits a medieval castle whose location—that is, whose identity—changes according to the ruler's whim. The castle is his extended stage, where he can re-create his living illusions. It is also his asylum, possessing that word's dual meaning of madhouse and shelter. Henry is surrounded by attendants, servants, valets, and occasional visitors who masquerade for his benefit. But he alone chooses the script for the day while the supporting cast improvises lines in keeping with his direction. The game, the play, has become a living reality, for Henry is "mad."

Henry's story takes shape in bits and pieces culled from the dialogue of other characters and, in the second half of the play, from his own admissions. Facts emerge piecemeal in a disorderly fashion that imitates the fluid character of the life Henry has abdicated. In a technique often employed by the playwright, critical background information is not presented chronologically or sequentially within the dramatic action; instead he requires audience participation in laboriously reconstructing events introduced throughout the drama in dialogue sequences. By untangling the assorted testimonies presented, the audience retrieves the key episodes in Henry's life story. From a wealthy family, the man now known as Henry was obsessively in love with Matilda Spina, a beautiful and equally coquettish aristocrat. To celebrate the upcoming Carnival season, their social set planned an elaborate masquerade: everyone would dress in historical costume and, together, form a lively cavalcade before partying into the night. Matilda opted to go as her celebrated namesake, the eleventh-century Matilda of Tuscany, a staunch political supporter of the papacy and an equally ardent rival of the Holy Roman Emperor, Henry IV. The enamored suitor immediately chose the monarch's role for himself, promising Matilda that he too would kneel at her feet: an overt reference to the historical episode during which the emperor supplicated Matilda of Tuscany for help in convincing the pope to lift his excommunication. The day of the long-planned masquerade arrived. During the cavalcade the young suitor fell off his mount, hit his head, and awoke as the emperor himself. Given the family's affluence, the young man's delusion was seconded. Henry was given a small, properly decorated castle, costumes, and servants. In this country haven he lives out his existence as the medieval German emperor.

A dozen years passed. One morning the amnesiac simply remembered. Initially he was eager to rejoin his interrupted life, only to realize that he had grown middle-aged as Henry IV. Society, he knew, would not welcome him back. Instead he would be subject to snickering, misgivings, and finger-pointing as the recovered "madman." Even before his fall he had been somewhat marginalized as an eccentric, suffering profoundly at his exclusion from fellowship and love. Therefore Henry elects to live out his days as a medieval monarch and a modern madman. His feigned madness allows him to exist within the fixed confines of history, an established and unchanging reality, in contrast to the fluid, contingent, and unknown quality of the average human life. While this biographical information is provided in the dialogue, the actual dramatic action takes place decades after that fatal Carnival when a talented, if odd, young man became permanently fixed in the role of a medieval German emperor.

After the death of Henry's beloved older sister, his nephew fulfills a death-bed promise to bring in another psychiatrist to examine his crazy uncle. This mission of mercy proves both enlightening and fatal. The nephew is accompanied by his fiancée, Frida, and her mother, Marchesa Matilda Spina herself,

Henry's great lost love. Matilda is no longer young, if still beautiful in an flashily sophisticated manner. The fifth visitor is Tito Belcredi, an old friend who is the marchesa's current lover. Unlike the others Matilda is fascinated by the idea of seeing the madman who had once loved her desperately. In the first act psychiatrist, lost love, and current lover put on medieval garb for a madman's masquerade and appear before the intimidating emperor in his throne room. The meeting is disturbing to all. Matilda is convinced she has been recognized; Tito Belcredi is visibly shaken by Henry's open hostility, for the erratic monarch clearly expresses loathing for him, accusing him of being a papal spy; only the psychiatrist is professionally unperturbed. Adopting the doctor's conviction that the presumed madman can be cured, a plot is hatched to shock the lunatic into sanity. Henry will be forced into the awareness of the passage of time, resulting in rejection of his delusionary state. The psychiatrist's stratagem is simple and, on the surface of things, quite logical.

The doctor's shock therapy hinges on two life-size portraits hung in the imperial throne room. Painted during the long-ago Carnival preparations as souvenirs, one depicts Henry as the youthful emperor, the other, Matilda Spina as his political enemy, Matilda of Tuscany. The psychiatrist plans to substitute Henry's nephew and the marchesa's daughter for the paintings, thus surprising the unwary madman. The living portraits will talk, the hidden electric lights will be switched on, the real Matilda will appear, and immediately Henry will be cured. The flaw in this stratagem is clear: Henry is no longer a delusional amnesiac. During the stage action at the end of act 2, he has revealed this astonishing fact to his attendants, who proceed to inform the marchesa, Belcredi, and the doctor. But at the beginning of act 3 the new masquerade is well underway. Henry is indeed shocked to see paintings move and speak; he is equally shocked to see the woman of his dreams reincarnated in the full splendor of youth. As all the principals gather, angry recriminations and emotional revelations follow, leading to the astonishing discovery that the distant accident had been provoked. Perhaps as a joke, perhaps to eliminate a dangerous rival for Matilda's affections, Belcredi had purposely pricked Henry's horse, thus causing the fall which brought about years of madness. But the middle-aged Matilda Spina does not interest Henry: her daughter does. She is a prodigy, a miracle, his dream become reality, a static image brought to vibrant life. Grabbing the young Frida and acting every inch the emperor, Henry declares she is his. Attempting to rescue the girl from the unmasked madman, Belcredi continues to incite his wrath, only to be mortally wounded by an unexpected sword thrust. In a matter of seconds Henry's assumed role has become his permanent reality. Behaving like a vengeful feudal lord, he has destroyed his enemy with a weapon only intended as a theatrical prop for a madman's masquerade. His actions are the proof of his lunacy.

Masks, masking, and masquerades dominate *Henry IV,* both as defining metaphors of the text and as integral elements of the dramatic action, including the Carnival cavalcade whose ludic quality is transformed into tragedy for one participant, the costumes and borrowed identities the visitors wear to study the madman, and the invisible masks all people wear within society to survive. Masks and, by extension, identities are constantly shifting, evincing one of Pirandello's defining concepts: the multiplicty and changeability of the human personality. Characters in the play possess at least two identities and names, a divisive doubling between their daily realities and the fictive selves adopted to enter Henry's medieval world. It is a doubling across time and perception, made all the more complex by the fictional reality of the play itself. As June Schlueter has stated: "every character, already fictive, plays the part of a fictive character in the fiction within the fictive world of the play."[2] Dubbed a metafictional character by Schlueter, Henry is the focus and epitome of these doublings, embodying a multiplicity of dualities and masks within himself. He is a "sane" man masquerading as a madman. Middle-aged, he declares he is twenty-six to his masked visitors: to corroborate this chronological duality, his hair is half blond, half gray. During his grand entrance his dress is equally emblematic and schizophrenic; in reference to his penitent abjection before the pope at Canossa, he wears sackcloth over imperial garments. He is also himself—whosoever that may be—masquerading as a medieval ruler. In the end the protagonist *is* the emperor for a moment, the same moment that he becomes the madman forever. Henry IV is the embodiment of Pirandellian paradox; he is the sane madman, the self-conscious mask, the imprisoned maverick. Henry has willingly chosen the mask of insanity, a state that liberates him from conventional constraints while permitting him to manipulate consciously his own masks and those of others. The playwright called this protagonist "il grande Mascherato," the great Masked One. Henry's final, seemingly irrational, attack on Belcredi confirms his insanity in society's eyes and justifies the permanent assumption of his chosen identity. But the attack is also directed at the mocker and spoiler of Henry's "play": Belcredi cannot abide the seriousness of Henry's existential masquerade, just as he cannot experience empathy for the sufferings of the man in the imperial mask.

Other characters are swept into layer upon layer of identifiers to second the "madman's" delusionary beliefs and the playwright's ideas on multiplicty. The attendants switch between their historical roles and contemporary selves; the doctor doubles as an abbott while Belcredi is a fictive monk and the abhorred medieval figure Pietro Damiani as conceived in the emperor's rich imagination; the nephew becomes the portrait image of his crazed uncle, and so on. The representations of the Matilda figure alone are bewildering. The Matilda Spina of the past, dressed as the medieval Matilda of Tuscany, is stopped in time in the life-size portrait. The present-day Matilda, no longer in her prime, is masquerading as a young woman with her bleached hair and excessive makeup. This Matilda assumes the role of the emperor's mother-in-law to appear before him, a clear prefiguration of later dramatic action when Henry seizes her child. Frida, Matilda's young daughter, is her mother's double: the physical reincarnation of the past and the embodiment of the portrait, the woman Henry has indeed loved. Frida masquerades in the costume worn by her mother twenty years before, literally replacing Matilda as the living portrait. The marchesa herself is the first to understand this substitution: "look again; it's you, not I, there" (150), she tells her daughter while observing the painting. Indeed, Matilda Spina is no longer herself, as she once was, but another person Henry barely recognizes and no longer desires. By wearing a gown identical to the one in the portrait, she does not represent the beloved image become older (as the doctor anticipated) but the embodiment of the ravages of time, which changes individuals, rendering them unrecognizable. In *Henry IV* roles accumulate without coherence or continuity, which points to the fragmentary and changeable nature of personality and identity.

Reiterating, as well as expanding, the motif of individual fragmentation and multiplicity, *Henry IV* also explores the related topic of the mutability and fragmentation of time itself, a theme already introduced within the first scene, set in the imperial throne room. A layer of times is suggested by objects, references, and gestures: the room and decor are medieval; the paintings are representational but modern; one of the attendants lights a cigarette. Soon a recently hired masker, "Bertoldo," arrives on the scene, visibly dismayed by his own temporal lapse: he has studied for the wrong part, the wrong monarch, the wrong century, the wrong country. Having "assumed" he would be serving Henri IV of Renaissance France, he is unprepared to face the medieval world of his new role and its temperamental ruler: Bertoldo is off by several hundred years. This secondary character's confusion is transmitted to the audience. Time, ordered diachronically in the play, repeatedly fluctuates in the dramatic action and dialogues: present, present perfect, remote past, now, eight, twenty, nine-hundred years ago. These temporal movements correlate to Henry's shifting moments of self-consciousness and identity. Centuries, decades, years, moments appear and disappear. Henry, the master impresario, purposely shifts the times of his own historical re-creation, which has no need to follow the constraints of sequentiality and/or chronology. Like a script history possesses the freedom of its predetermined outlines, so that the action can reprise at any point.

Henry's destiny is to live another man's life, speak another man's thoughts, see another man's reflection in his self-assumed mirror, the portrait. The image itself portrays a temporal split and a fictional mask, for it is the painting of himself as he was and will never be again, pretending to be a German emperor. But Henry is also the great Masked One, adept at tearing the masks off the hidden faces of others around him—he is both party to, and observer of, his directed masquerades. His visitors and all those surrounding him, in their assumed roles, are his puppets and he alone pulls the strings. It is a sense of power life seldom affords. The mad Henry, like Vitangelo Moscarda, challenges the basis of human thought: reason. People fear Henry and seek to accomodate his whims as a way of dismissing his vision, for all the mad cast doubt on the existence of certainties, deny the validity of logic, shake all human constructions. In the mad, people see mirrors of their own irrationality. To keep their constructed order whole and unharmed, the threatening outcast must be exiled.

In the public perception Henry is repeatedly defined by his delusions and illusions: he is mad for all. But for the man behind the mask, there is no such consistency of identity, no intact self to call genuinely "I." During his lengthy amnesia Henry knew himself as the absolute monarch of the Holy Roman Empire and behaved appropriately and unconsciously. Upon reawakening to his actual self, the protagonist chose illusion, or pretense, as his self-conscious identity. Caught between the historical past of the Holy Roman Emperor and the present of his social exclusion, for eight years he has lived a dual overlapping consciousness. At its most positive the situation allows him the freedom to choose between two existential dimensions. After killing Belcredi, however, the mask of madman is permanently imposed on Henry as his sole possible identity: he will be forced to forever reenact the life of the emperor but will be deprived of his prior autonomy and feeling of choice. In actuality, the identification of the self ("I") with Henry IV has come to dominate the face behind the mask. The protagonist has learned to be genuinely the medieval emperor even in the most elemental motions of his daily reality: eating, sleeping, scratching his back, "clothing yourself in the dream that would be no more a dream, because you would have lived it, felt it all alive in you" (195). In the end Henry, having lost any other identity, any name other than that of his assumed role, has become the prisoner of his own construction. Having hoped to conquer contingency, Henry has embraced the life of the dead.

In its willed construction Henry's world resembles a theatrical production. The emperor's life is transformed into a series of scenarios for an improvisational theater of the mind, complete with props, makeup, historical costumes, a permanent set, and a brilliant impresario-actor. Henry himself selects the script to be performed from the dramatic possibilities provided by the monarch's tragic life: the dialogue must be improvised, but the action is fixed by history. However, like many writers and directors, the protagonist also takes liberties, by inventing episodes and characters to suit his vision, most significantly in the creation of an historically inaccurate but personally true love story between the emperor and his enemy, Matilda of Tuscany. Equally significant is the realization that theater and life reflect each other. Makeup, role-playing, costuming, and masking is an integral part of both, covering reality behind illusions, as Henry continually suggests to his visitors and companions. They are all quick studies, if occasionally poor actors, and confirm his power by performing at his command. Henry's attendants tell the visitors, who are symbolically dressing for their "roles" in the new masquerade, that they only need follow the madman's lead. Henry himself gives shape to their parts, as he is the playwright of his own personal drama. It is a position he relishes for the control it provides over others. Revealing his long ruse to his companions, Henry glories in this power:

> Don't you understand? Don't you see, idiot, how I treat them, how I play the fool with them, make them appear before just as I wish? Miserable, frightened clowns that they are! And you . . . are amazed that I tear off their ridiculous masks now, just as if it wasn't I who had made them mask themselves to satisfy this taste of mine for playing the madman! (189)

Since role-playing is central to Pirandello's concept of self-construction, Henry's acting prowess is key to the play's development. Known as a brilliant amateur thespian before the accident, acting, that is, his ability to project fictions of self through his roles, is at the core of Henry's new existence. He embodies the human desire to create personae or public images to hide the incongruities, fragmentations, and fractures of an all-too-human personality. The protagonist's choice of madness can be justified as an appropriate response to the crisis of living. A fixed construction, the mask of Henry IV is more secure than the flimsy, unstable, unprotected, and socially imposed constructions of others who struggle ceaselessly against the daily disintegration of their identities and the eternal changeability of life. The mask of emperor may be less real but more true than the pretenses of daily life and the impossibility of fellowship or, in Henry's case, love. Moreover the world of popes and monarchs, wars and excommunication, enemies and ambition is heroic in its grandeur, in sharp contrast to the daily life of the visitors, who bicker, complain, criticize, and mock each other, lost in their trivialities. Theater exposes the fictional nature of such constructions as well as their extreme vulnerability.

Like many Pirandellian protagonists from Mattia Pascal to Leone Gala, Henry is articulate, cerebral, and painfully self-reflective. Like them he is a social outcast, unable to conform to the demands of his society or the boundaries imposed by his social roles. Madness affords one type of liberation: an expansion, even a rupture, of the social limits that is accompanied by the possibility of openly challenging people and events and declaring the truth without fear. Having been literally insane, Henry has come to recognize the ever-present figurative madness in life itself: "I am cured, gentlemen: because I can act the madman to perfection, here; and I do it very quietly, I'm only sorry for you that have to live your madness so agitatedly, without knowing it or seeing it" (205–206). Unable to live with preexisting images, Henry constructs a new identity outside all traditional models. He alters himself by escaping into the personality of a dead man whose life supplies great emotions, reactions, and power. Having found his own life wanting, Henry chooses the pleasure of history over the extreme difficulty of social integration. His role as a historical personage grants him a fixed identity an average man cannot have and a control over his surroundings impossible in everyday existence. But the role also robs him of his original identity and of human fellowship. His life is fixed, etched in historical stone. Nevertheless Henry, attempting to impose meaning and order where they do not normally exist, consciously plays it with complete seriousness. The world that comes alive in his personal theater is derived from history books, and its immutability is attractively comforting: in a universe where little is knowable, every outcome is known. No surprises will shake the foundations of his psyche or require the constant construction of personal masks. Part of Henry's individual tragedy, however, is that he cannot move beyond the limits of his chosen material but must continually employ it to hide the inner man. Unlike Mattia Pascal, Henry understands that he cannot fake the suicide of his alter ego: nothing would be left but the weight of the word *mad*.

Time is Henry's greatest enemy. During the years of his amnesiac delusional state, the real self had been submerged in the fictive creation, which was equivalent to life, not to masquerading. Having lost the "real" quality of his illusions, the protagonist nevertheless maintains madness through lucid choice. Awakening from his trauma, Henry discovers the painful fact of time's passing: his hair has gone gray, his body grown older; he has "lost" his youth in a mad haze. Life, like time, moves irretrievably forwards, and he has not: the continuity of time has been shattered for Henry by madness. The past cannot be recovered, as he understands all too well: he will come to the banquet of life like a famished wolf, only to find that the table has been cleared. As a man Henry is the victim of life's temporal limits. History, on the other hand, is fixed; outside the flow and mobility of life, it transcends time. By immersing himself in the biography of a Holy Roman Emperor, Henry hopes to defy time. Past, present, and future can be mastered, stopped, and relived. Amid the fluidity of life Henry fights to capture the permanent. At age fifty he can be twenty-six in his assumed role of the penitent Henry at Canossa, as he appears to the visitors. He can replay life, the emperor's life if not his own, as an actor can resume a treasured role. If the script is unsatisfactory, another can be substituted, for he is immune from time's forward motion. There are no temporal uncertainties in historical time, no befores, no afters. By embracing history, Henry has conquered chance and mystery: all is ever-present and known. Age can seemingly be overcome with a bit of hair dye, a little rouge, and the right temporal reference. By imitating the semblance of youth, Henry reasserts his freedom of self-determination. Fashioning himself, he experiences some control over his being—no matter how ephemeral. One of the protagonist's tragic realities, however, is the fact that he can never totally eliminate his awareness of the fiction, or pretense, of his choice. Life as Emperor Henry IV is essentially a fiction, an existential absurdity.

Pirandello perceived life in Bergsonian terms as continuous flux, that is, a flow of constant change, movement, and uncertainty. One can neither stop the flow nor control its chaotic disorder, so he counters its perilous motion with fixed forms. Human roles, illusions, belief systems, and institutions are all attempts at stabilizing the flow, controlling it, fixing it in knowable and determinate forms, so that it does not overpower the individual or society. Beyond these measures to arrest life lies darkness: the mysterious, unknowable, and terrifying void. For Henry history is one such form, chosen to stem the flow, at least temporarily, until the moment his closed world, his madman's stage, is invaded by the movement of time and the memories of the past: his own past, not the emperor's. Skipping a generation, obliterating twenty years, life ironically draws Henry back to the emotional turmoil of his youth by offering him the portrait of his lost love in flesh and blood rather than in canvas and oils. Frida's presence breaks the forward continuum of time, for time repeats itself in her. Like Matilda twenty years before, Frida too is the illusion of love, but this time he grabs for it, defends it, embraces it. Henry is attempting to hold on to the image of youth in himself, the same youth that was lost to madness.

Building himself on the life of another, Henry's chosen identity is rooted in two differing realities and times, so that the divisions between imaginative reconstruction and personal actuality are inevitably blurred. The contours of the man and his historical mask are indistinguishable. More tragic still, Henry's dual identity is inexorably fixed in time, a state symbolized by the portrait's hanging in his throne room—the portrait is paradoxically a true representation and a false reality. As he poignantly declares to the assembled group, he cannot free himself from the "magic" contained in the painting in order to "live wholly and freely [the] miserable life" from which he has been excluded: "A man can't always be twenty-six" (172). In many ways the life of Henry did stop near age twenty-six, during the Carnival masquerade, just as the emperor's most critical moment occurred in the snows of Canossa, while he was begging papal forgiveness and the intervention of Matilda of Tuscany when he was aged twenty-six. In this play the life-size portraits function as Pirandello's omnipresent mirrors, casting back living images into a created world which comes to life under Henry's able direction. The paintings are Henry's instruments of self-knowing and the material manifestations of time's import.

Having regained his sanity, Henry gazes upon his portrait as the fixed symbol of his lost youth, as an irretrievable moment in time. But the portraits are also self-conscious reminders of the passage of time, the movement from youth to middle age, and the reality of loss. Nor do the portraits actually depict the characters "as they really were," but as Alan Roland and Gino Rizzo note, "an unknown individual is frozen, first by tragic accident and then by psychological necessity, into an old self, or more precisely, into an idealized, grandiose image of that past self; at the same time he is unable to fulfill the yearnings and needs of his real self."[3] In his portrait Henry stands frozen in his past, eternally and frustratingly twenty-six, but the beautiful young woman displayed in Matilda's portrait has moved from frozen form to vital life in Frida. Henry's unlived life, the life of the twentieth-century man, is reborn in its obsessive passion. Merging the longing for his unlived past—the yearning to return to the lost self and begin anew—and the arrogance of the historical emperor, Henry strikes: the costume sword of his theatrical production has metamorphosed into the destructive weapon of a medieval warrior bent upon vindication.

One thematic link joining past and present in Pirandello's tale of lucid madness is the denunciation of the moral, social, religious, and political conditions oppressing man throughout history, whether that be the medieval Holy Roman Empire or contemporary Italy. All times, the author implies, destroy ideals and corrupt life. Incidentally, *Henry IV* is Pirandello's only "costume" drama, the only play that camouflages characters behind the trappings of a historical time and place different from their own. Yet, the pain emerging from the text does not belong to the historical emperor but to the man hidden beneath the imperial garments who is invisible to others because they only perceive a lunatic. Without the consolation of human sentiments, however illusory, such as love, fellowship, or community, Henry is painfully conscious of every man's destiny of loss, decay, age, and, inevitably, death. Seeking a space in which to exist, Henry is caught in the conflict between his inner truths, external realities, and the demands of his masquerade. While the protagonist may praise the possibilities open to him by madness, he is nevertheless trapped in himself, in his lucid ability to analyze and dissect. His strongest prison bars are fabricated by his own mind. Once the motivations for Henry's sane madness are sympathetically exposed to public view by Pirandello the humorist, the audience is invited to experience the ensuing feeling, or sense, of the opposite. Touched by the individual's existential crisis, the spectators respond. But as John L. Styan has pointed out in *The Dark Comedy,* the audience also empathizes with the visitors plunged into Henry's world. As representatives of social "sanity," they find their sympathy challenged by their "sense of the cowardice of a sick man trying to stop the movement of time" and make the transitory permanent.[4]

More than a historical drama, *Henry IV* is the drama of history for a self-conscious protagonist who—unable to exist in the present, denied the opportunity of recovering the past, and blocked from any satisfying future—lives in permanent isolation. History is the protagonist's defense against external reality; it is his beneficial illusion.[5] Luigi Pirandello defined *Henry IV* as "a tragedy in three acts." There is much of the tragic in this story of a passionately brilliant man who is completely alone, cut off from all authentic human community, enclosed in the castle of his imaginary life, unable to communicate his inner self or thoughts, and inhabiting an endless masquerade. Pirandello's title also explicitly connects *Henry IV* to the long Western tradition of tragedies and tragic figures, which reaches back to the ancient Greeks through Shakespeare and the neoclassicists. The audience anticipates viewing larger-than-life characters and events in an atmosphere of sacrifice, tragic flaws, divine retribution, and grandeur that leads to a final catharsis, or purge, arousing pity and fear. Like conventional tragedies this play's atmosphere is charged with a current of inevitability and hopelessness. But *Henry IV* is a modern tragedy, divorced from the shared religious or moral experience of simpler historical eras. Henry is not purified by his crisis nor is any traditional catharsis offered either the character or the spectators of his drama. The only catharsis afforded the audience is its participation in the frustration of Henry's existential checkmate, where no final solution is forthcoming to resolve the dramatic action. Indeed, classical tragedy is avoided by Henry's persistent role-playing and by his own self-conscious ambivalence toward his role. If anything, Henry's modern tragedy lies in his acknowledgement of the need for masks at the cost of personal self-fulfillment.

Anthony Caputi declares that *Henry IV* celebrates the protagonist as a twentieth-century tragic figure, a scapegoat who embodies the self-conscious choosing of a life based on lies, a life that is a fictional expression of the ontological identity he can find nowhere else.[6]

Henry is marked by difference: he embodies alterity both before and after his tragic fall. "Henry IV is the drama of modern existential man. The tragic situation has become grotesque. The hero's ultimate choices are arbitrary, irrelevant, or meaningless, no longer conditioned by conflicts between universal and temporal values. But there are choices, and a certain dignity in decision."[7] However, many critics see no tragic intent in Pirandello's drama. For Eric Bentley, Henry is an orphan whose position has been worsened by accidental insanity and virtual incarceration. In Bentley's eyes the "tragedy" *Henry IV* is only a Sicilian melodrama, or opera libretto, of love, jealousy, and revenge, that is enclosed in a Gothic quasi-history or a Germanic quasi-philosophical treatise. "[Henry]'s aim in life is nothing less than to attain to tragic seriousness.... The protagonist insists on tragedy; the author does not. The protagonist is a character in search of the tragic poet: such is Pirandello's subject, which therefore comes out absurd, grotesque, tragicomic."[8] Pirandello's own staging of the play supports its humoristic origin as a tragicomedy rather than as a conventional tragedy.

As A. Richard Sogliuzzo has shown, Pirandello's production of *Henry IV* for the Teatro d'Arte, starring Lamberto Picasso,[9] evinces the author's highly theatricalized conceptualization of the play. The cast photograph shows actors dressed in historically inaccurate costumes, better suited to a carnival party than a historical recreation. The principals are heavily masked by powder, rouge, and eye shadow. The false-nosed, pointy-bearded, balding psychiatrist is deliberated made-up to resemble one of the Commedia dell'Arte's stock figures, *Il dottore* (the doctor), a charlatan who occasionally pretends to be a physician. Belcredi and Henry present exaggerated, clown-white faces with deeply shaded eyes that recall death masks. The physical appearance of the characters underscores their grotesque participation in a madman's charade and suggests farce rather than tragedy.

In recent decades *Henry IV* and *Six Characters in Search of an Author* have been the subject of serious psychoanalytical and medical analyses in an attempt to get at their deeper, subconscious levels of meaning. The characterization of Henry, for one, invites examination as a case study in madness. Tellingly, Luigi Pirandello himself had several personal encounters with mental illness, a condition he often depicts in stories, novels, and dramas such as *Henry IV*. During the writer's early years it appears that a younger sister suffered from a brief case of adolescent frenzy, while his cousin and fiancée, Lina, had a mental breakdown during their engagement: her growing hysteria demolished Luigi's uncertain feelings for her. Most important, however, the author came face to face with the power of madness during his long cohabitation with the paranoid Antonietta Portulano. His wife's psychological decline particularly colored Pirandello's views on the relativity of identity after he experienced Antonietta's power to define him according to her own disturbed perceptions. Seeing an alternative self forming in his wife's delusions, the author found it necessary to accept this imagined but seemingly real second identity. All three episodes taught Pirandello to respect the validity of subjective perceptions, which can make illusion truth and give form to the chaotic imaginings of the mind. These insights found their way into numerous representations of madness and psychic aberrations throughout Pirandello's creative production.

Given the biographical and literary facts, some critics in the post-Freudian era were unavoidably prompted into exploring the nature and origins of Henry's mental state. Thomas Bishop states that Henry's story reads like a case history of amnesia compounded with schizophrenia. Less categorically, Eric Bentley sees the protagonist's confused behavior as a clear sign of psychopathology, which suggests the presence of a madman or, at the very least, a deeply disturbed individual. For Rudolph Binion, Henry is an example of emotional arrest, which dates from his traumatic fall. Alan Roland and Gino Rizzo seek clues in the play's structural aspects to define the protagonist's drama in terms of wounded narcissism (low self-esteem), masochism, and deprivation.[10] To compensate for his narcissism, Henry defends himself by creating an idealized role-identity as emperor; masquerading allows him to achieve self-worth. Literarily speaking, however, Henry's story was intended not as a clinical study but as an artistic rendering. Readers and spectators must interpret the function of mental illness in *Henry IV* metaphorically, as well as realistically, as part of the author's complex imaginative creativity.

Henry IV is about masks and masquerading, living and performing, profusions and confusions of identity, and the alternately conflicting and merging dialectical qualities of the antithetical pairings madness/sanity, reality/illusion, past/present, art/life. Henry's doubling is a symbol for the uncertainty of identity; his manipulation of retainers and visitors alike demonstrates the importance of assigned roles, as well as the power of external pressures to imprison people in these fixed forms. Other characters behave like puppets flexing under the knowing fingers of a master puppeteer, himself the great Masked One. Therefore it is not surprising that drama critic Adriano Tilgher would turn to *Henry IV* as the first exemplar of his theoretical formula defining Pirandellian theater as the contrast between life and form.[11]

The dichotomy of life and form had already been suggested by Pirandello himself in *On Humor,* in which he declares life to be a continual flux one tries to stop and fix in stable forms that are "the concepts, the ideals with which we would like consistently to comply, all the fictions we create for ourselves, the conditions, the state in which we tend to stabilize ourselves." But internally the flux continues as the life within, which individuals seek to arrest by fashioning consciousness and personality—fictitious forms that can collapse under the thrust of flux, that "in certain moments of floodtide, overflows and upsets everything."[12] Although Tilgher had been reviewing Pirandellian works with great acumen for a half-dozen years, the 1922 piece on *Henry IV* was the first to articulate the life/form formula that would be applied to Pirandellian drama for decades to come. Using his formula, the critic quickly expanded his initial analysis of one play to include an extensive retrospective examination of all Pirandellian output to date. Tilgher's conclusions appear in a lengthy essay in his *Studi del teatro contemporaneo* (1923, Studies on Contemporary Theater).[13] Seeking to define the underlying theoretical system operating in Pirandello's writing, Tilgher proposes the antithetical coupling of life/form as the writer's working metaphor, thus demonstrating how life is forced to enter a determined form, even becoming imprisoned in it as takes place in *Henry IV,* in which life is suffocated by the imposed fixed identity. While the tragedy of the sane madman demonstrates the working formula as a clear-cut dichotomy, other Pirandellian texts are less sharply outlined, such as in *One, No One, and One Hundred Thousand,* whose main character struggles with infinite numbers of transitory forms without discovering the essence of his selfhood.

According to Tilgher, it is an artist's categorical imperative to give current aesthetic form to the life of his own time. In Luigi Pirandello's works the critic found an artist capable of rendering the irrational, anti-intellectual movements of the day and a writer out to renew the aging conventions of realism. In Adriano Tilgher, Pirandello found an ideal advocate for the organic nature of his literary production. For several years Pirandellian plays would look to the Tilgherian formula as an organizational device and thematic framework, signaling exceptional codependency between a writer and his critic. Eventually Pirandello would restate the formula in terms of a conflictual dichotomy between movement and form within life: form gives substance to life, while movement repeatedly demolishes forms. As Tilgher notes, the opposition between form and life is intrinsically theatrical, defining the core of dramatic action.

Tilgher's theoretical formulation had considerable influence on the construction of several late Pirandellian plays, notably *Diana e la Tuda* (1926,

Diana and Tuda), *Quando si è qualcuno* (1933, *When Somebody Is Somebody*), and *Trovarsi* (1932, *To Find Oneself*). Whereas *Henry IV* offers history as the prevailing form, these plays propose art or fabricated images as alternative means of "fixing" life's fluidity. The three dramas deal with the contrast between life, or movement, and art, or form, as this struggle is enacted in the heart and mind of a several artists, including sculptors, writers, and actors. Originally conceived as a dramatization of the life/form formula, *Diana and Tuda* has been criticized for its excessive adherence to theory, to the detriment of the dramatic action and the credibility of the characterizations. The play has even been declared the mere "mechanical dramatization of Tilgher's dialectical analysis."[14] The two women of the title are the embodiments of the antithesis: as life, Tuda is a vivacious model whose lovely body inspires a statue of the goddess Diana, or form. The sculptor is Sirio Dossi, a young man obsessed with his need to achieve perfection in stone, thus eternally fixing the beauty of a living woman into a lifeless artistic representation. Tuda loves Dossi selflessly. She voluntarily submits to his will and molds herself into the image sought. Jealous of her physical perfection, Dossi marries his model to prevent any other artist from capturing her beauty on canvas or in marble. Eventually the statue consumes both the sculptor and his inspiration; the figure sucks the vitality from Tuda, who cannot shift the artist's attention away from the emerging statue. Dossi loves his perfect creation, not the woman whose image he sculpts. As the living Tuda wastes away, the stone Diana comes into splendid artistic being: form consuming life.

Consumption is the guiding trope of *Diana and Tuda*. The three principals waste away physically or psychologically because of their obsessions. The model is consumed by her marmoreal image; its beauty grows—feeding Dossi's all-consuming craving to produce an eternal monument to his talent—as hers diminishes. Tuda, the woman, is eventually saved by another artist, Giuncano, an older man who values the warmth, beauty, and vivacity of a living being over the frigidity of stone. Consumed by his age, his impossible love for Tuda, and his yearning to possess life, Giuncano has destroyed his art because it is intrinsically dead; his statues were only cadaverous monuments to lifelessness. When Dossi violently pursues Tuda to prevent her from embracing, possibly destroying, her nemesis, Diana, in her impossible desire to merge with the being he actually loves (life impossibly seeking to be form), Giuncano comes to her defense and kills the younger sculptor with his powerful hands in an act of "blindness." Clearly the two sculptors represent conflicting interpretations of the function of art. One sees permanence in form, the other the death of life. If art is immortal but inanimate, life is animated but mortal. In the play, as Robert Brustein has rightly pointed out, the Tilgherian antithesis is transformed into a conflict between life and death: "Pirandello's demand for form is literally a death wish, since, as he tells us, whatever is fixed in form is really dead."[15] As has often been noted, the contrived plot of *Diana and Tuda* also contains a paradoxical reversal of the Pygmalion myth in the account of Sirio Dossi's love for his statue. Rather than bringing an ideal image to life through love, the modern sculptor transforms his loving model into lifeless perfection.[16]

In the concluding scene of *When Somebody Is Somebody,* the Pygmalion myth is revisited with a singular metamorphosis. Sitting on a great stone seat in a moonlit garden, the unnamed protagonist *** (somebody) slowly levitates above the stage. Immobile, rigid, drained of life, he is transformed into a statue of himself. "All this in a silence which seems to belong to the centuries."[17] *** is a famous writer, a celebrity, and a great man. Forced to adhere to the masks of his legendary past, he is also the prisoner of his fame. ***'s forms suffocate his spontaneity and creativity, for he is continuously forced to reproduce himself artistically, unable to break out of the categories assigned him by critics, publishers, academicians, and literary historians—similar to the fate that befell Luigi Pirandello late in life. Like so many celebrities *** is trapped in his public image; he is impotent to disengage his vital self from the petrified statue he has become.

***'s impasse is twofold, yet both aspects relate to his desire to break out of the fixity of his deadening form into the fluidity of life. As an artist *** desires to give voice to a revolutionary lyric vein, long denied. Thanks to his ageless spirit, as a man he finds love in a young woman who inspires his creativity by fostering his rebellion. As a result the old poet composes passionate, joyous verse and publishes it under the pseudonym Délago. But both his love and his new lyric voice are sacrificed at the altar of Somebody. The poet cannot abandon his long-standing public image, which he constructed painfully over the years. Its advantages provide the solace of knowability and surety. Because he is not *Nobody,* but *Somebody,* he can be nothing else to the public. Therefore he must deny the Délago in himself. To do otherwise would totally destroy the youthful self and the beautiful poetry produced in his name: "If I reveal myself to be Délago, if I shout it to the whole world, then good-by! Délago is done for! He's just a mask, don't you see? A mask of youth that I've put on for a joke . . . (with passionate anger) I can't have any flesh and blood; I can't have any life of my own; I can't have even what belongs to me" (223). As a famous man *** is the object of a collective mythology which has fashioned his personality, life story, and creativity into inalterable shapes. As an artist, in the guise of the invented Délago, *** had hoped to recreate himself, only to find that option rescinded. Délago becomes his literary rival, the poet of youth, in whom he cannot be recognized: he is permanently crystallized as Somebody for the world at large and, by play's end, for himself.

***'s dilemma expresses in dramatic terms the theories suggested by Adriano Tilgher's dualist formula. Man is caught between two antithetical drives. The first is dynamic and fluid, withstanding form; the second, seeking out stasis and immobility, is opposed to change. In the story of Donata Genzi, the protagonist of *To Find Oneself,* the quest for a vital personal identity encounters not one, but multiple forms. Donata is a celebrated actress known for her exceptional craft. As she explains in act 1, she "lives" her stage roles by losing her sense of selfhood, much like Henry "is" the emperor. Once the performance is completed for the night, Genzi finds it difficult to "find herself" outside the role. Aware that her characters are fictions she assumes, the actress is anguished by her self-annulment and abnegation in the protagonists she represents. Suffering constant dislocation, Donata finds she possesses no life of her own outside of the characters she becomes onstage. She lives as the multiplicity of identities she plays but not as herself. Like Henry, Genzi inhabits her role completely. Once she embodies her characters, they are real, not fictions, for she experiences artistic transfiguration.

Donata Genzi's crisis arises from the realization that she does not know who she truly is. She has lost her sense of individuality in her repeated embodiments of other lives. The actress is forced to confront this situation when she falls in love with Elj Nielsen, an impulsive seafaring painter whose maritime odysseys symbolize the open invitation to life in all its flow. Even in this temporary emotional fulfillment, Donata finds that she is ever the actress creating her roles. Desperately trying to "live" as herself, she discovers that, to give expression to her own feelings, she invariably reverts to the words and gestures of her characters, not finding any of her own. This awareness mortifies her and hinders any spontaneity. She repeatedly catches herself in a familiar gesture, a known tone of voice, a banal movement, or a dramatic situation redolent of her theatrical incarnations. Not wanting "to see herself" in the act of living, Genzi covers all the mirrors in Elj's house to block out her reflection, the symbol of her self-consciousness. Submitting to Elj's impulsive zest for living, however, Donata finds that she is losing her identity as an actress without finding an alternative self. When asked to abandon the theater for "life," Genzi cannot. Nor can her lover accept her transformation from the woman he knows into the actress who transmits life to a series of "ragdolls" by lending them her body, voice, and gestures.

Seeing Donata on stage, Elj rejects her. Because she is an actress, her most intimate self belongs to everyone, not to him alone. Correspondingly, with her lover in the audience, Genzi intitially "loses" herself, unable to merge with the role for the first time in her career. But, with a supreme act of will, this negative experience is overcome, liberating her. Through her art the actress experiences an epiphany, "re-finding" herself.[18] A self-conscious artist who controls every response, movement, and tone to obtain a perfectly harmonious union of actress and character on stage, Donata Genzi finally realizes that the theater is the space where life is created with freedom. She is absolutely authentic only when she portrays a character, when she lives provisionally in her role. Genzi's identity is dependent on her masks: her pretense is more real than her life. Like Henry IV, Donata finds her vital space in a theatrical rendition of life, in the knowing acceptance of role-playing as an identity. She is her masks. Like him she chooses isolation with her phantoms—she is aware that nothing is true except that finding oneself depends on an act of self-creation. Like the sane madman the actress has constructed a false identity to mask her ontological insecurities and unsatisfactory existence; she prefers the forms she can control to the emotional risks of Elj's impulsive plunge into the sea of life.

Rejecting the imputation of *Pirandellismo* that surfaced with increasing vigor after the publication of Tilgher's essay, the playwright repeatedly emphasized his creative freedom, rejecting any theoretical categorizations, including the Tilgherian formula, as the sole yardstick for judging his writing.

My works are born of living images, the perennial source of art, but these images pass through the screen of concepts which have taken form in my mind. My works of art are never concepts trying to express themselves through images. Quite the contrary, they are images, often very vivid images of life, which through the operation of my mind assume universal significance by themselves, through the formal unity of art.[19]

Although Pirandello was influenced by Tilgher's formula, he did not imagine his dramatic characters as theoretical personifications, but as thinking, passionate beings whose stories reflect the universal human condition. By finding forms to channel the frightful uncertainty of living, Pirandello's characters achieve compromises that permit them to exist, albeit in paradoxical, isolated, and painful ways. Devoid of an authentic life of their own, Pirandellian protagonists such as Henry IV, Donata Genzi, or *** seek certainty within immutable forms. By impersonating identities or acting out assigned roles, they find some stability and gratification in the process. In the drama *Vestire gli ignudi* (1922, *To Clothe the Naked*), however, the protagonist Ersilia Drei can neither achieve authenticity nor find a suitable form in which to mold herself.

Seeking a respectable self-definition, Ersilia finds a series of uncomprehending males ready to demolish her inventions. She is alone, vulnerable, naked to the world, and overcome by life's unstoppable floodtide.

Prior to the stage action of *To Clothe the Naked,* a seduced, abandoned, and guilt-ridden Ersilia Drei has attempted suicide in a Roman park by taking poison. On her deathbed she weaves a romantic tale for a trusting reporter, dressing up the squalid motivations of her act. The renditions of her life story that emerge during the stage action are far less sympathetic than Ersilia's subjective reworking. Employed as a nanny in Smyrna, Ersilia was seduced by an attractive naval officer who abandoned her after promising marriage. Sexually awakened, she reluctantly became the mistress of her employer, the Italian consul. Caught in flagrante delicto by the diplomat's wife, an altercation ensued. Meanwhile Ersilia's small charge, left untended by either her parents or the babysitter, fell to her death. Disgraced and racked with guilt, Ersilia returned to Rome only to find her naval officer about to wed. Destitute, the young woman turned briefly and disastrously to prostitution, from there to suicide. Seeing an opportunity to change the ugly facts in order to die with dignity, Ersilia Drei paints a positive self-portrait for the journalist by depicting herself as a defenseless young woman, wrongfully accused and without prospects. Distraught to discover her first love had abandoned her, this construction of Ersilia Drei is willing to die for love. This pathetic version of the facts allows Ersilia to construct a self-affirming identity as the wronged heroine of a sentimental potboiler. Unfortunately the deathbed confession proves premature and harmful to all parties concerned. Ersilia does not die, but, accepting her self-justifying lies as truth, the press directs its unwanted attentions to the consul in Smyrna and the naval officer.

The stage action begins after the recuperating Ersilia Drei is released from the hospital. Homeless, she is taken in by a middle-aged writer, Ludovico Nota. Wishing to build a novel around her fabricated story, the author needs to examine his intriguing new heroine at close range. Soon, however, Ersilia's sordid past enters this shelter, shattering any hopes of rehabilitating herself or her biography. This intrusion of life is captured acoustically on stage through a series of street noises entering the open window of Nota's apartment: traffic, horns, bells, hawking vendors, shouting newsboys, the swarming din of voices. The protagonist cannot escape the tumult of life anymore than she can escape her own past. Ersilia is caught in her inventions as her story is repeatedly challenged and recast by others. The journalist enters, demanding the facts behind his published and possibly libelous account. The naval officer arrives, proposing a compensatory marriage. The consul follows, accusing Drei of mendacity and wantonness but also suggesting they resume their relationship. Stripping away layer upon layer of her construction until only the naked self is left, each meeting is devastating to Ersilia's fragile new identity. What remains to identify her are memories of guilt, sordidness, and lust. It is an identity Ersilia Drei cannot accept as her own because of its unworthiness. Unable to face life with no masks of decency and respectability to sustain her, Ersilia has only death as a remedy. She poisons herself a second, fatal time.

There is no heroism or grandeur in Ersilia Drei's story, but there is much humanity in her unrelieved frustrated need for self-justification that is repelled by the unmasked, naked self's being repeatedly and mercilessly exposed to the world. While the newspaper account and then Nota's promised novel allow her to project to the world a positive image, "a decent little dress" in which to die and be reborn in the orderly and fixed universe of writing, these too prove illusory as her uncensored past emerges. Ersilia's attempt to construct a new self is doomed from the start. Unable to create a suitable form for herself, however fictive, she is personalityless, like clay to be molded by chance, a nothing. Within the play this lack of coherence and individuality make Ersilia Drei the easy object of a series of inaccurate external perceptions: male gazes that deform and misrepresent her. The naval officer wishes to confine her to his image of a victimized, abandoned woman whom it is his duty to redeem. The consul recalls scenes of mutual desire that are the sexual urges of a middle-aged man taken with a young woman. Even Ludovico Nota, the writer, has his version of Ersilia Drei. He does not perceive a hopelessly suffering woman, but the object of his desire, who offers an evermore intriguing series of selves to his creative gaze. "She has been an enthralling necessity, a ceaselessly changing source of new configurations. Thus is is not her actuality that interests him, only the possibility she carries within herself. And possibility suffers irreversible damage at the hands of actuality."[20] Confronting Ersilia, the men distort even the sordid truths of her tale, each attempting to protect his own image, each projecting another variation of the facts, another dimension to the story, and each demanding that Ersilia conform to them all. They are like dogs tearing away at her dress, her masks. Unable to live in fortuitous fluidity, Ersilia dies formless, denied her dream of a bride's dress in which to be buried, if not married. The dream of wedded respectability, of innocence and self-respect, of conforming to established patterns of female normalcy, is embodied in this imaginary dress that is only an illusion she has been stripped of, like all the others. Alone in her nakedness Ersilia Drei dies with dignity. But the protagonist's choice of death over life proves the inadequacy of that decent little dress—her last illusion—to sustain the wearer. It is meant to clothe a corpse, not a woman.

Pirandello's world of masks, illusions, and masquerades is fundamentally agonizing and pitiable in its depiction of the need for some measure of certainty. Henry IV, Donata Genzi, Ersilia Drei, ***, all dream of an absolute self freed from the uncertainties of life's flux. Sirio Dossi attempts to realize such absoluteness in a work of art, the statue of Diana, at the cost of Tuda's spirit and vitality. Each dream requires a death, a denial, a diminishment of the individual creating his or her necessary form. Henry fades into the identity of a long-dead medieval emperor to find fixity in the secure knowledge of historical fact. Donata Genzi lives only in her roles, thereby effectively abolishing her personal needs and emotions. To be *Somebody,* *** must be metamorphosed into a living statue: a petrified man. For Ersilia Drei only the final dissolution of death is possible in an existence where all illusions, masks, and decent little dresses have been stripped off.

CHAPTER SIX

The Theater Plays

Luigi Pirandello's major biographers, Federico Vittore Nardelli and Gaspare Giudice, offer a revealing anecdote about the author's creative process in action. As they tell it, several masons working in a neighboring building observed the noted but reserved writer at his desk "talking to himself, fidgetting, gesticulating with wild and staring eyes, and making the oddest faces in the world."[1] The masons had caught a rare glimpse of Pirandello busily occupied at constructing his fictional universe and dramatizing its inhabitants in the privacy of his study. In her own memories of life with Pirandello, daughter Lietta recalls family dinner conversations when the author would talk at length about his characters, their foibles and happenings, as though they were actual acquaintances. After a long conversation with Pirandello in 1924, when he was at the pinnacle of international success, French critic Alfred Mortier found himself reassessing the playwright's creative personality. Casting aside the prevalent image of a cerebral intellectualizing writer, Mortier saw a different Pirandello, an *onirique,* or visionary dreamer, "a man haunted by his own creations. They obsess him without respite until he has put them down in writing."[2] In several reminiscences actors and members of the Teatro d'Arte describe the playwright-director's vividly dramatizing his scripts during rehearsal readings for the company and recall his standing in the wings during actual performances while spiritedly mimicking the dramatic action onstage. In these "enactments" Pirandello would give resonance and personality to each of the characters, animating them through the intonations and modulations of his extraordinarily expressive voice and gestures. Besides such anecdotal proof of the author's obsession with "bringing to life" his characters, a few Pirandellian tales fictionally depict the rapport between writer and protagonists in metaphorical terms, notably "La tragedia di un personaggio" ("The Tragedy of a Character"), first published in 1911, and "Colloqui coi personaggi I & II" (Dialogues with Characters I & II) of 1915.[3]

These stories portray the assertiveness of characters seeking artistic life and the consummation of their identities as created beings. In "The Tragedy of a Character" Pirandello's writer-protagonist humorously depicts his weekly open-house interviews for aspiring characters that are held Sundays from 8 till 1. They are attended by a vast assortment of "the most discontented people in the world" (94), who are seeking admission to a suitable story or novel. Among these malcontents is Dr. Fileno, a worthy character whose (artistic) life was "miserably unfulfilled" in a bad novel by an undiscerning author. Fileno, demanding the fulfillment of his potential, proceeds to invade the writer's weekly audience, thus anticipating the invasion of the empty stage by the Six Characters. Like the Six, Fileno is in search of a better author to give depth to his existence as a character in an appropriate venue. As he explains to the writer-narrator, in words that reappear in the dialogue of *Six Characters in Search of an Author:* "No one can know better than you that we are living beings—more alive than those who breathe and wear clothes. Less real, perhaps, but more alive" (99). The life of the character, Fileno continues, is immortal. The being born a living character will never die, unlike the human artist who is the instrument of creation but fated to mortality. The insistent Fileno is nevertheless rejected as a candidate for the writer's literary attentions; the same fate will befall the Six Characters some ten years later.

According to Pirandellian invention, characters are the incarnations of a conceptual truth generated in the authorial imagination. This idea is developed extensively in the 1925 introduction to his greatest and most influential play, *Six Characters in Search of an Author.* Once conceived, Pirandello writes, characters live on: "Creatures of my mind, those six were already living a life which was their own and mine no longer, a life I was no longer in a position to refuse them."[4] Using the biological analogy of reproduction, Pirandello compares the "vital germ" of life developing in the imagination to human conception, "though on a higher plane of life" (xiii). But the author can deny the life conceived, because it does not have the value or meaning sought by him as a "philosophical" writer. As prefigured in the tale of Dr. Fileno and his rejecting author, the homeless Six Characters, with no text to call their own, torment Pirandello ceaselessly, "magically transported outside the pages of a book" never written (xiv). Unable to lightly abort his characters, deeply implanted in the imagination, the writer resorts to modifying their sad, sordid story into a humoristic situation involving realism, fanatasy, comedy, farce, tragedy, and pathos. It is no longer just "their" story, it has become the new story of unrealized characters searching for another author to set down their drama, their sole permanent means of existence. Eventually "their" story will be told, but in fragments, as the Six justify their being and significance to the uncomprehending theatrical company they find rehearsing in an otherwise empty theater.

By concentrating the dramatic action on "characters as characters" rather than on "characters as people," the playwright immediately plunges his audience into confronting the essence of theater itself, touching issues of creativity, invention, and the fabrication of illusory realities. By viewing characters interacting on a bare stage stripped of the props of theatrical deception, the spectators necessarily question the nature of their experience, situated as they are in a space built to give life to fantasies and to materialize fictions. The first of three Pirandellian plays about theater, *Six Characters* directly explores the multiple constructions of illusion in a place where illusions are repeatedly manufactured. But theater is also the space where reality is re-created, where art imitates life. Entering the auditorium and viewing its undecorated boards, Pirandello's audience is made immediately aware of the stage as a formal space to be transformed and controlled by directors, actors, technicians and, last but not least, by themselves as spectators. Pirandello's theater trilogy is intended to explore the numerous constitutent elements making up the total theatrical experience, ranging from the presentation of a scene using costumes, make-up, lighting, and sets to the role of the audience in formulating meaning, from the function of actors and directors to the importance of the written text. *Six Characters in Search of an Author* and its companion pieces, *Each in His Own Way* and *Tonight We Improvise,* deconstruct the elements, conventions, and artifacts of stage reality to establish, or at least suggest, new relationships between art and life by dissolving the traditional separation between the two. The trilogy plays assert that the reality of theater is illusion, while explicitly and effectively constructing and collapsing that illusion before our eyes as well as revealing the element of pretense while concurrently creating it. These three plays invite the onlooker to suspend any and all disbelief. Inevitably these works also examine the rapport uniting life on the stage to life in the world, as the two intersect, copenetrating. In these plays theatrical and existential illusions and realities join in a self-consciously provocative manner.

By dismantling the component parts of theater and exposing them to view, Pirandello is involved in the demolition of the invisible "fourth wall," which traditionally separates the public from the dramatic action taking place onstage. Realist theater had invited the audience into the lives of characters by removing this wall and letting theatergoers view the action as passive voyeurs. In the spirit of modernism Pirandello's trilogy shakes all four walls: it both builds them up and tears them down, thus revealing theater as process and showing stagecraft at work materializing fictions. Blurring divisions between art and life, the theater trilogy manages to break down the partitions between characters and audience members, or between dramatic action and passive reception. No longer protected by the invisible barrier separating the auditorium from the stage, the spectators are assaulted, forceably involved in the theatrical events encircling them in the lobby, in their seats, even in the street, so that they become temporarily uncertain of what is reality and what is play. In doing so, the dramatist also exposes the paradox of naturalist make-believe that presumes to present itself as actual life. Notwithstanding the awareness of theater's artifice, which is clearly revealed, Pirandello's audience becomes involved in the action, caught up in the magic of the illusion, even on the bare stage of *Six Characters,* where Pirandello's naked masks go about their business.

All three theater plays contain two levels of action: the framing action is concerned with the theatrical elements of the drama; the other level is a melodrama within the framing play. In all three works the inner story is violent, passionate, and antagonistical. As Robert Brustein has rightly noted about Pirandellian melodramatics, "hyperbolic expressions of grief, rage, and jealousy alternate with murders, suicides, and mortal accidents; wronged wives, maddened hubands, and bestial lovers foment adultery, incest, illegitimacy, plots, and duels. At times his monologues turn into arias, and would be more appropriate set to Verdi's music."[5] Because of their unsuitability and excesses, these plays within the plays have often been labeled potential dramatic failures the author quite properly never composed for the stage—stories like the one explicitly rejected by Pirandello in his rendering of the Six Characters' odyssey in search of completion. However, the outer framing action allows for novel interpretations of the enclosed story by providing for greater complexity in characterization, multiple viewpoints of the action, and a theoretical structure. Likewise, the inner story represents the concepts outlined in the framing play in human, rather than philosophical or theoretical, terms. This mutual exchange shifts audience attention from the details of the plot to the tensions created between the two levels and enriches both with new meanings and possibilities. The spurned dramatic action is transformed by its placement within Pirandello's philosophical investigation of the nature of theater and of the construction of illusions onstage and in life. In this context the inner plays vividly dramatize the creative ideas discussed in the framing action.

In *Six Characters* the inner story concerns a dysfunctional family with a history of objectionable social behavior, including abandonment, illegitimacy, prostitution, and suicide. The original nuclear family—Father, Mother, Son— was dissolved at the husband's instigation after he realized no communication existed between himself, an intellectual with pretensions of solid moral health, and his simple wife. After being sent away, the Mother starts a new family with her husband's male secretary, a far more congenial partner. The illicit couple have three children: the Stepdaughter, Boy, and Child. Over the years the Father loses sight of this second family he helped form, once they move away to avoid his persistent attentions. Following the death of the Secretary, the Stepdaughter quietly turns to prostitution to provide for the Mother and siblings. In this position she meets a new client (the Father), is discovered, and soon shepherds the entire family into his home. Trying to win her abandoned son's love, the Mother's neglect of her second family leads to a tragic conclusion of their drama. The untended Child drowns in a pond, the depressed Boy shoots himself, and the Stepdaughter takes to the streets.

Less harrowing but somewhat sordid, the inner story of *Each in His Own Way* is presented as a drama being performed onstage for both the real audience and a fictive one. Drawn from the novel *Shoot!* this play within the play concerns the public scandal following the suicide of a promising young artist who had just discovered his fiancée in the arms of his closest friend. After the suicide Delia Morello, an actress, and her lover Michele Rocca separate, but their past continues to give rise to gossip, extensive criticism, and social pressures. Branded quasi-murderers, they are expected to pay for the artist's untimely death. To reinforce the impact of public opinion on the principals, the dramatic action is not set in *Shoot!*'s bohemian cinematic world but in Turin's conservative high society. In the third entry of the trilogy the actors of *Tonight We Improvise* are putting on a Sicilian melodrama of jealousy, honor, and patriarchal oppression. The female protagonist is Mommina, a young woman raised in a family of daughters whose Neopolitan matriarch rejects the restrictive proprieties generally inflicted on Sicilian girls. Her daughters are relatively free, musically inclined, and given to flirtation with officers from the local military base. After the violent death of her father, Mommina marries one of the officers, Rico Verri, only to find herself imprisoned in their tower home by a pathologically possessive spouse. The young woman quickly ages, sickens, and grows melancholy, trapped with her small daughters in her jail/house. When one of her sisters comes to town with an opera troupe, she is forbidden to see the performance. To console herself and her babies and to somehow reproduce the lost experience of theater, Mommina reenacts the melodramatic opera, Verdi's *Trovatore,* for the girls, her only audience. Singing a powerful aria in her beautiful but useless voice, Mommina dies in the effort.

The sensationalism of the trilogy's inner stories serves as an efficaciously straightforward illustration of the devices, methodologies, and emotional impact theater employs to convey meaning. Many of the playwright's basic techniques are already masterfully developed in the earliest and best known of the three works: *Six Characters in Search of an Author.* The familiar Pirandellian dialectic pitting the fluidity of existence against the stability of form (in this case, art) is literally embodied in the two sets of protagonists. On the one hand, there are the Six Characters who enter a theater—the symbolic spatial microcosm for *The* Theater—proposing to "be" the subject of a drama. They are unfulfilled characters, conceived but never written down, seeking the eternal life of art. On the other hand, the actors, directors, and technicians who encounter them embody the flux and mutability of life. The two groups inevitably clash. The Actors mimic the words and gestures of the Characters only to deform them, to the pained realization of the Six that they can never be resurrected onstage, but only approximated at best. Art and life remain separate. Within this principal framing action the "melodrama" of the Characters' story reiterates familiar Pirandellian motifs: the inevitability of human misunderstanding and isolation, the lack of love, the impossibility of communication, the multiplicity of personality, the imposition of social and private roles, the tragedy of the disintegration of ties, and the passionate expression of suffering through reason and logic. It is the Characters' dilemma that they can neither change their past, for it is Form and has been fixed, nor can they find absolute realization at the hands of a new writer or within the imitation of themselves offered by the thespians.

If *Six Characters* defies traditional notions about a play's content and naturalist ideas about verisimilitude, it also challenges expectations about theatrical form.[6] Technically this innovative play marks the end of the traditional stage. The dramatic action overflows onto the main floor and behind the scenes. Formal acts are abolished in favor of "accidental" divisions, such as the gradual, uncontrived departure of protagonists from the stage to continue a conversation or the sudden, unintentional drop of a curtain. There are no sets or backdrops, so that the bare stage is exposed to the full view of the audience. Characters come and go utilizing the entire theater: aisles, doors, orchestra seats, proscenium, and wings. The empty stage is symbolically so: ready to receive the undefined material, examine it, rework it, adjust it, until it moves toward completion. Even today the effect is astonishing; it was more so in 1921. The audience is coaxed into assuming that the play, ostensibly begun as a rehearsal in progress, is part of the same reality found outside the playhouse walls. In similar fashion the Actors casually enter the theater by utilizing the doors and aisles just employed by the spectators, further welding the worlds of fiction and daily life. The dramatic action seeks to maintain this realistic feel of spontaneity throughout. The first scenes concentrate on the residents of the theatrical world—actors, directors, managers, prompters, and stagehands—as they gradually come together for the rehearsal.[7] Once the Characters arrive, they contrast sharply from the troupe in physical appearance and tone, but they too react "spontaneously" to the theatrical environment for which they were conceived. When called upon, the Six recite their parts with natural ease, for they are not acting but reliving or reexperiencing. When an additional Character is needed for plot development, a few referential items are gathered on stage and the procuress Madama Pace is conjured up from nowhere, like a bottled genie, ready to assume her part. Pirandello regarded the mysterious and otherwise inexplicable arrival of Madama Pace, summoned by dramatic necessity to participate in the action, as the supreme example of the artistic imagination at work. Her sudden appearance is a dramatization of the *process* of creation rather than its results. With the apparition of Madama Pace before the terrified company, Pirandello has captured art in the making. As stated in the introduction of the 1925 edition, "the birth of a creature of the human imagination is the step across the threshold separating nothingness from eternity" (xxii). In such scenes the demarcations between art and life disappear. In other scenes the Characters relive their story for an audience, while the Actors, becoming characters in turn, re-create the Six. In short the creation of illusion is made concrete for the audience, thereby causing considerable intellectual and psychological discomfort.

Six Characters is about a play in the making that involves all the protagonists, as well as the audience, in the process of literary creation and its elaboration onto the theatrical stage, where the material is received and reworked by actors, managers, directors, set designers, and so on. The Characters are the core of the drama because they are manifestations of the imaginative process, not because of their sensational story. As "created realities," they are distinguished from the "human" participants in the play by a series of theatrical devices ranging from simple contrivances, such as the use of distinctive colors and differences in clothing styles and fabrics, to the complex manipulation of lighting. In the stage directions Pirandello asks the Actors to dress cheerfully and move naturally to contrast immediately with the somber blacks, whites, and purples of the solemn Characters. The playwright even recommends the use of masks for the Six to emphasize their identities as "immutable constructs of the imagination" with fixed motivations, such as revenge for the Stepdaughter or sorrow for the Mother, who is visualized as the religious icon of the Mater Dolorosa. Even ignoring such suggestions,[8] the staging of Six Characters requires a clear manifestation of difference in gesture, movement, tone, and appearance between the two groups. Every special effect or distinguishing feature is used to separate the Characters from the day-to-day humanity of the theater people. This is done to highlight the fundamental Pirandellian concept of the multifaceted nature of human personality, with its kaleidoscopic shifts and changes, which conflicts with the fixity of the Six artistic artifacts. The celebrated Pitoëff production in

Paris, which marked the beginning of Pirandello's international reputation as a revolutionary dramatist, masterfully used props to separate the two groupings, with stunning results. The entrance of the Characters was conceived with care and originality: lowered to the stage in an old scenery elevator, the Six, sheathed in green light, appeared to descend from the ether (Pirandello's "higher plane of life"). By pure (Pirandellian) happenstance the Pitoëff elevator jammed before reaching the boards, forcing the Six to clamber down one by one onto the stage, adding to the overall effect. Pitoëff had created memorable visual images to represent the author's metaphysical concepts.

As characters, the Six personify different stages of the creative process by demonstrating different degrees of characterization, in keeping with the author's original conceptualization. In his self-analytical introduction Pirandello states that the Father and Stepdaughter are fully realized as Mind or Spirit, the Mother less so as Nature, whereas the Boy and Child are merely underrealized presence. The Son remains peripheral, refusing to participate in the dramatic action in any way. "They had to appear at the exact stage of development each had reached in the author's imagination at the moment when he decided to be rid of them" (xvi-xvii). Inert and silent, the Boy and Child are ambiguous beings, caught between dissolution and form. Having supposedly died in the inner story, they nevertheless play out their small but pivotal roles, wordlessly reliving their own deaths onstage: appearing only to disappear. The Mother, as Nature, does not comprehend her reality as a character, but she experiences it as emotion, an anguish that never ceases. "I am living my agony constantly, every moment," she declares to the assembled company, "I'm alive and it's alive and it keeps coming back again and again, as fresh as the first time" (52). Fixed forever in timelessness, the artistic creation repeats its life. In every reading of a book, in every performance of a play, the action and characters are once again present, unaltered by time or repetition. Thus the Characters are indissolubly tied to the reality of their imagined lives, no matter how desperate they are to change the plot and alter their roles.

Notwithstanding the predestined results, the Characters repeatedly attempt to redefine the nature of the inner story according to their subjective vision, each inevitably clashing with the others. The Father insistently endeavors to justify himself using reason to cover up the bad faith and meanness of his acts, from his dubious marriage, to his abandonment of familial responsibilities, to near fornication with the Stepdaughter. He articulates his views in order to remove the mask of guilt forced upon him by one act of sexual need, a single event in a lifetime of events. Yet his condemnation to the fixity of that act reinforces his identity as a Character, an immortal being tied to an eternal moment, to be forever relived. The Stepdaughter, equally Mind, passionately struggles to further her agenda, forcing the Father into ever expanding guilt and blame, beyond what is justified by his role in the storyline. The Mother also wishes to rewrite the script in her own maternal way by adding a nonexisting conversation with the Son. While the Father uses reason to cajole the Actors and Producer into scripting their drama, the Stepdaughter employs her sexual charms to seduce them. Both Mind Characters share a desperate need to to act the roles for which they were born, but they also seek to alter the construction of events, to slant it toward their self-justifying interpretations. Like Dr. Fileno the Characters are in revolt against an unacceptable collocation in a fixed world that does not fulfill their individual needs. As Malcolm Bradbury has shown, each Character is also a perspective, and these perspectives constantly clash. This fact places *Six Characters* squarely in the midst of Pirandello's lifelong exploration of relativity and truth. Yet, it is the Son's rejection of the action that most clearly demonstrates the Characters' attachment to their original story. Wanting no part of the search for an author, the Son attempts to leave the stage altogether, yet he cannot move beyond it. Held back by some mysterious force, he is "tied and chained by a bond that's quite indissoluble" (62). Like the others he is cemented in the fixed form of art; he is unable to abandon his created reality any more than he is able to alter the situation or refuse his participation.

The story of the Six Characters, which is extrapolated from the action, finds its meaning in the dialectic with the "human" Actors who attempt to re-create it theatrically. Primarily the Characters desire to be heard, understood, and transcribed; their need clashes with the practical considerations of the Actors, led by their spokesman, the Producer.[9] In opposition to the passion of the articulate Characters, who are fighting for their existence, the Actors, preoccupied with issues of staging, balance, and propriety, view the story in functional terms. Whereas the Characters demand life through art, the Actors speak of illusions and the artful imitation of life within a tightly structured organism. As the Producer explains, in theater no one character can dominate the stage, conventions are to be upheld, and morality is to be considered. Characters, he declares, figure in scripts while actors appear onstage. What the Producer terms "literature," the Father considers passion and life. Since the Characters' drama lives immutably within them, they are dismayed by the ease with which their story, their sole medium for existence, is transformed. A green divan substitutes for a flowered lounger; the Stepdaughter must remain clothed during the sexual-encounter scene; events taking place in multiple locations must be collapsed into a single set. The Characters feel betrayed, even mutilated, by a process they cannot control. This disillusionment reaches a dramatic zenith in the crucial scene between the Father and Stepdaughter that is enacted at the play's midpoint, a scene repeated by the leading Actors.

In this key scene of *Six Characters,* the two levels of existence in the play encounter each other and coalesce, as the created reality of the higher plane yields to the artifice constructed by the Actors. Faithful to the truth of their being, the Father and Stepdaughter reexperience their first encounter in the backroom of Madama Pace's disreputable dress shop for their audience of professional theater people. This is the defining moment of their life story, which is immediately re-created by the Leading Actors, using the same words and actions. In the Actors' hands the scene is accomplished with practiced skill, but it is "completely different." As Martin Esslin remarks, "the actors only translate the truth of the imagination of an author back into stage stereotypes."[10] Such a rendering, no matter how well performed, is inevitably a clichéd distortion of the Characters' "truth." Having already been rejected by the Author, the Six find themselves unrecognizable in the Actors' rendering. Yet such interpretations are essential to the production of any drama. The Pirandellian text implies that any interpretation is inherently a deformation of the original work or, in this case, of its character(s). Protesting such falsification, the Six are told by the Producer, "Truth's all right, but only up to a point!" (49). The comment is clearly a double-edged judgment on the potential and limitations of theater. From the authentic audience's point of view, however, the Six persistently emerge more real, vital, and substantial than the acting company. In the conflict between created and living realities, moving from the plane of the imagination to the level of performance represents a loss, a diminution. Conceptually the infidelity and imperfection of the mirrored scene underscores the ontological difference between Characters and people, thus exemplifying the dialectical rapport of form and life, as form (the Six) encounters life (the Actors) through art. Understood in this light, the bewildering conclusion of the Characters' melodramatic story is of secondary importance. It is not essential to Pirandello's vision that the dramatic situation find logical resolution. Are the children actually dead? Was the dramatic action real or fictive? Was it all a mere illusion of the sort represented daily on the world's stages? Such questions are left to either the Actors or the audience to answer for themselves. Pirandello is far less concerned with the factuality of the inner drama than he is with the fate of any creative work after it falls into the hands of the cast, directors, and writers who control its passage from conception in the imagination to final expression as theater.

Within the trilogy plays Pirandello exploits the familiar metaphors of life as a stage and the individual as a player to convey his philosophical insights into the human condition in the modern world. Through the exploration of the dichotomy between the real and the fictive, the playwright dramatizes several recurring themes found throughout his literary production: the fluid mutability of identity, the interaction of reality and illusion, and the relationship of life and art. As Richard Gilman has perceptively remarked, the tension between the two sets of "characters" in the drama, with the fate of the story at stake, "corresponds to the [tension] we feel in our own lives between 'truth' and fiction"[11]—or, to use different terms, between imagination and reality. The relation of the Characters to the Actors has been seen as an analogy for the relationship of inner person to social self: the individual is persistently acting, taking up roles, when living among others, while continuing to affirm the personal vision of selfhood. Yet, in *Six Characters* the fictions within a fiction suggest a deeper reality, once again bringing into question the authenticity of human identity and foregrounding familiar Pirandellian musings into areas such as the subversion of the philosophical categories of seeming and being. Within the play the Characters provide six multiplying clashes of reality and appearance as they interrelate, each attempting to project his or her perceptions while demonstrating the isolation of the individual in community. Similarly the doubling of the actor into the character is a symbol of dissociation indicating the tragic impossibility of communicating one's innermost self to others, just as the Actors cannot "be" the Father or Stepdaughter but appear as inferior copies or counterfeits. This is the typical Pirandellian universe of subjectivity, where reality is reflected in the mind as life continually changes, creating instability and havoc.[12]

Like *Six Characters in Search of an Author,* the second entry in the theater trilogy, *Each in His Own Way,* is a complex dramatic disquisition on the interactions between various theatrical elements composing a play. Both works portray the separation between fictional representation and human reality while attempting to demolish this very difference. In *Each in His Own Way* Pirandello has constructed an intricate structure housing various levels of characters, role-playing, and audience participation. In so doing, he multiplies the opportunities to tear down the walls dividing the constructors of the drama from their audience. By setting the early dramatic action in the lobby and, if possible, on the street itself—outside the playhouse proper, the playwright is seeking to erase the spatial boundaries between spectators and stage even before the "play" officially begins. As Pirandello explains in the foreword, a special edition handbill should be distributed by newsboys in the foyer or in front of the theater. This flyer announces that the play about to be premiered is based on actual events. Naming names and giving scandalous details, the handbill warns the incoming spectators to be prepared for the unexpected, it being likely that "tonight's performance will result in some unpleasant repercussions."[13] This material intrusion into the daily lives of the entering audience is aggravated by the arrival of the notorious woman mentioned in the flyer: the actress A.M., known to all. Her entrance into the lobby justifies the handbill's promise of "repercussions." A similar scene is occurring in another part of the foyer with the arrival of Baron Nuti, the man named in the scandal. Both A.M. and Nuti are accompanied by supportive friends. The separate groups, pacing, emoting, and nervously conversing, create some disturbance. Naturally these individuals are actors playing roles, although the theatergoer is not necessarily aware of this fact. It is the playwright's intent to surround the real audience with the living fictions of the drama, thus involving them continuously with the dramatic action. Pirandello's elaborate superstructure assaults the spectators further once they enter the auditorium.

Each in His Own Way contains two acts of a naturalist drama that are actually performed for the audience. This play within the play is a fictional representation of invented situations based on the personalities of A.M. (Amelia Moreno), and Baron Nuti, whose identities are barely concealed under the character names Delia Morello and Michele Rocca. Each of these two traditional acts, when finished, is followed immediately by a staged "choral interlude." In these sections parts of the external theater corridors are re-created on stage while talking "plants" are placed in the actual auditorium aisles and seats to lend further credibility. Moreno and Nuti are also located somewhere in the audience. In the interludes Pirandello depicts reasonable spectator reaction to the unfolding drama. His purpose is to question the differences between art and life, illusion and reality. The numerous protagonists of the intermezzos are actors pretending to be spectators emerging from their seats to comment on the performance or on the irritating nature of Pirandellian drama in general. Like the lively scenes representing the acting troupe in *Six Characters,* these interludes are to be spontaneous, unrehearsed, casual encounters between theatergoers or drama critics discussing the merits or failures of the play in question. These miniscenes, played out both on stage and elsewhere in the auditorium, are amusing in their self-parody. The planted audience-actors and actor-critics replay all the familiar tropes on Pirandellian mirrors, distortions, illusions, cerebralism, and multiplied realities. Inevitably the interested voices of Baron Nuti and Amelia Moreno join in, expressing their anger and dismay.

The second act of the play within the play concludes with the characters Delia Morello and Michele Rocca's falling frantically into each other's arms, unheeding of the scandal, public censure, and private guilt sure to follow and overcome by their own shared love-hate. The second choral interlude reprises the audience-reaction scene of the first, only to have Amelia Moreno rise from her seat and invade the stage as some of the "audience" grows wilder, shouting and clapping. The actual invasion is not seen but commented upon by the fictive spectators. Moreno has rebelled against the fictionalization of her life as propagated by the play. As an actress she well knows the power of art to make illusions appear reality. Through this scene Pirandello also dramatizes the frame and merges it with the inner play, thereby doubling the impact of the dramatic action. The play within a play never concludes, however. After Moreno strikes the leading lady who is playing her fictional double, the actors depart in protest against the management for producing such a risky enterprise and against the author, Pirandello, for having created such a dangerous work. At the end of the second interlude, Baron Nuti challenges the Theater Manager for making him say words he had never spoken and do things he would never have dreamed of doing. Nuti's anguish is echoed by Amelia Moreno, who sees not falsification but imitation: "But she said what I said! She did what I did! Exactly what I did! It was me! I was watching myself!" (131). Nuti and Moreno inevitably meet in the fictional corridor onstage. The audience—both real and illusory—sees the fiction just experienced reenacted before their unbelieving eyes as life. Swept away by their passion, Nuti and Moreno leave together, as did their fictional doubles, while the administrators cancel the unfinished show. Without actors drama cannot exist.

In *Each in His Own Way,* Pirandellian dialectics are taken to their logical (or illogical) extremes. The play's dual structure (two acts and two interludes) sharply focuses on the doubling of reality and illusion, life and art, through the representation of "real" versus "fictional" characters and "real" versus "fictional" responses to the dramatic action. Illusion regularly intrudes upon reality and reality upon illusion since the action of the play within the play is immediately reflected and answered in the interludes. As Oscar Büdel has eloquently noted, "this is the limit of theatricalization. The actors' space has been made to coincide with, is the same as, the actual space of the audience. The play element has been carried into the reality of life to the point where both seem inextricably intermingled, thus suggesting, making, proclaiming theatricality as a form of life."[14] Pirandello described *Each in His Own Way* as the dramatization of the conflict between spectators, the author, and actors. The two parts of the drama, onstage and in "life," form a whole that is being transmitted to a real audience. But several critics have indicated a possible flaw in the successful transmission of this play's message. The choral interludes are also fictions, clearly staged pieces, made all the more "theatrical" by being placed onstage. Pirandello, obviously cognizant of this flaw, did plant what he terms "fluid characters," most particularly Nuti and Moreno, within the larger framework of the lobby, orchestra seats, and actual aisles of the physical space composing the total theater. However, as Robert J. Nelson notes, it becomes a doubly unreal business for the authentic spectators, who are perfectly aware of the frankly asserted artificiality of theater. Thus, while outer and inner plays reflect each other, suggesting reality and its illusory re-creation in art, the element of dissociation given by the double fictionality of the drama stretches the audience's suspension of disbelief on two levels.

For those spectators who approach theater as a naturalist experience, that is, as an imitation of reality, the suspension of the dramatic action, the lack of resolution, and the unended plot of *Each in His Own Way* are particularly frustrating given the realistic tone of the inner play. As the choral interludes make clear, however, the disruption of naturalist expectations is undertaken purposefully. In these interludes Pirandello the writer becomes the subject of Pirandello the playwright, thus making him an invisible, multifaceted character of his own drama. By offering divergent appraisals of himself through a variety of "spectators" and "critics," the dramatist is pointing to the contents of his unfolding play, to the relativity of human interpretations and opinions, and to his function as theatrical demolitionist. The emphatic self-referentiality of these snippets of dialogue brings the audience repeatedly back to the notion of authorship, to the pros and cons of dramatic conventions, and to the play as a constructed fiction. Pirandello emerges from the series of miniconversations as a controversial figure possessed of an assortment of antithetical interpretive keys to his own works. To understand the meaning of theater, the author seems to be saying, the conventions of drama must be dissolved and evaluated, only to be revived in new, strikingly revolutionary forms. Another function of the choral interludes is to give dramatic voice to what is audience participation. Like a hall of mirrors the real audience reacts to the responses of the stage audience, which is responding to the play both groups are watching and interpreting. In the play itself characters are reacting to each other's differing viewpoints with viewpoints of their own, thereby producing viewpoints in the audience: both real and fictive. In this play, where reality and pretense cannot easily be distinguished from each other, Pirandello is concerned with "human" illusion as well as theatrical illusion.

The inner play of *Each in His Own Way* centers on the "true" nature of the Delia Morello–Michele Rocca affair, bringing to mind the truth seekers of *Right You Are (If You Think So)*. As in that earlier bourgeois drama, the dramatic action takes place in private spaces that are opened to public use: the grand drawing room of an aristocratic house in act 1; the sunrooom and garden of another wealthy home in act 2. Both acts have assorted secondary characters who discuss the "facts" of the affair and interpret its potential meanings. A *raisonneur* figure focuses and analyzes the group conversations. In the play within the play of *Each in His Own Way,* several irreconcilable versions of the notorious alliance are suggested in a series of conversations, thus forming another mirroring image that unites the inner play's discussions of the scandal to the outer frame's discussions of the play. In one version of the events, the actress seduced Rocca as an act of pure altruism to prevent her fiancé from contracting a disastrous union with her. In another Morello is portrayed as a vindictive femme fatale who enticed Rocca because he opposed her marriage to his future brother-in-law. In a third rendition the woman capitulated to Rocca the seducer, who wanted to save his friend from a horrible mistake. These interpretations of, or variations on, a single event are discussed heatedly by two adamant young friends, Doro Palegari and Francesco Savio. Both have definite—if temporary—views about the exact nature of the truth and about the moral character of the woman involved. Diego Cinci, the *raisonneur* figure, incites them and others by revealing the contradictory and prejudicial nature of their arguments; this obviously confuses his listeners as to what constitutes "truth." Like Lamberto Laudisi, Cinci, coming from a relativistic worldview, can defend all positions. The young friends, however, hold to their strong if fickle views; eventually they lose patience with each other, resulting in a challenge to duel. The arrival of Delia Morello on the scene in act 1 is no more enlightening than the appearance of Mrs. Ponza in *Right You Are.* Although she is neither veiled nor unresponsive to the questions posed her, Delia can give no answer to which of the versions provided is the "true" one, or which woman described is her real unadulterated self. Even while justifying her behavior, Delia's predicament is that all versions presented are somewhat plausible. Each offers some measure of truth in which she seems to recognize herself. The many opinions surrounding her, both partisan and antagonistic, confuse Delia Morello further. She is unable to decipher her own contradictory perceptions amid the swirling viewpoints. Teeter-tottering between champions and foes, Delia Morello simply does not know herself or her motives.

The second act of *Each in His Own Way* offers no resolution to the issue of relative truth and identity proposed in act 1. Upon discovering they have switched opinions about the affair, the adamant young men nevertheless prepare to duel. Each has been convinced by his opponent's arguments, yet both remain unalterably antagonistic. At this point Michele Rocca arrives to offer "his" version of the events leading to the artist's suicide. Altercations ensue, unresolved, over Rocca's points; these altercations reverberate in the reactions of the "audience" and real principals (Moreno and Nuti) in the second choral interlude minutes later. Onlookers and spectators, needing to reassess the data received and readjust their perceptions of the "truth," are once again thrown into confusion. The fundamental unknowability of this or any truth is made patently clear at the end of this act, however. Morello and Rocca fall into each other's arms and confess that none of the proposed versions was actually valid, the only truth being their immediate intense desire. Rocca says, "Our stories are both lies, yours and mine. . . . You wanted me, as I wanted you, right from the first moment" (124–125). This scene is melodramatic, exaggeratedly so, charged with repressed sexuality and emotional upheaval. All the uncertainly but adamantly held truths prove to be pretense, which demonstrates Pirandello's concept of the changeable nature of human reality. The scene underscores the individual's innate tendency toward self-delusion, as he or she attempts to fix fluid experience into set certainties. Like many Pirandellian works *Each in His Own Way* is concerned with fragmenting realities, whether it be the state of Delia Morello's personality or the contours of the theatrical space, the multiple possibilities inherent in any human situation or the frustrating dramatic text. Theatrical technique serves Pirandello as an instrument for rendering his ideas on the relativity of truth and the consequent unknowability of reality in concrete dramatic forms.

Whereas *Each in His Own Way* is a play about doublings, reflections, echoes, and dualities that join the world of theater to the world at large, *Tonight We Improvise* is an exposition of Pirandello's opinions on the roles of actors, directors, authors, and the audience in the construction of the play itself. A daring, experimental work which is seldom performed, *Tonight We Improvise* goes beyond Pirandello's previous attempts at defining the component elements of theater. Like its companion pieces in the trilogy, *Tonight We Improvise* opens up theatrical space beyond the stage to create the dramatic illusions of the play. At the start of the action audience plants loudly bemoan curtain delays while Hinkfuss, the "director," argues with the protesters. Hinkfuss lectures them on the nature of theater, which, he declares, is not founded on the fixed work of the author but on the realization of the text on the boards with the collaboration of numerous parties: this makes it fluid and different each time. To prove this point, Hinkfuss adds, he has made the decision to improvise a theatrical performance loosely based on a Pirandellian short story. The dialogue between Hinkfuss and the audience, actors and characters, dramatic action and spectator reaction, has begun. The inner play of *Tonight We Improvise,* a Sicilian tragedy, is somewhat blurred, confused, stopped and started, being regularly interrupted by the cast, director, and "audience." Initially this fragmented rendition of a tale of obsessive jealousy is often set aside to introduce elaborate effects or to explore the nature of varied theatrical expressions other than drama. The text integrates opera, dance, acrobatics, song, film, recorded music, even a light and sound show employing miniature sets. These "fantastic" scenes do not, however, necessarily enhance or further the dramatic action of the inner play. These scenes are introduced to demonstrate the quality of theatrical artifice that brings all manner of fantasy to life by creating pleasing illusions to amuse or captivate audiences, which is the declared intention of Hinkfuss, the play's director and master of ceremonies.

As a play about its own creation, it follows that *Tonight We Improvise* should concentrate on issues of stagecraft and illusion. In the first spectacular scene a religious procession moves from the back of the auditorium through the central aisle onto the stage and through church doorways. It is complete with regional costumes, altar boys, canopies, candles, figures dressed as the Sacred Family, music, chants, bells, and distant organ music. As the religious image dissolves, another section of the stage is lit as the white walls of a neighboring building become transparent: the scene has been instantaneously transformed into a decadent 1920s cabaret with a performing jazz singer and sinuous blond dancers. The prime function of these two set pieces is to represent the multifaceted nature of theater itself (that is, the procession, complete with the faithful masquerading as Mary and Joseph, costumed altar boys, and little girls in white), which pervades daily life even when it does not have an explicit performance value, as it does in the cabaret. In the following scenes, emerging from the make-believe street on stage, the La Croce women "arrive" at a fictional opera performance which is, however, being staged on the very boards where *Tonight We Improvise* is performed. The new set is not artificial, but real, as the characters noisily take their seats in one of the actual boxes, illuminated by a mysterious, preternatural light. The characters are now part of both the real and the fictive audiences at the theater. But, instead of viewing a Verdi melodrama onstage, a silent movie accompanied by a phonograph recording is shown to all the spectators. At the equivalent of an intermission, a miniature airfield complete with flying toy planes, buildings, and lights against the artificial night sky is assembled by Hinkfuss, who then proceeds to dismantle it. While diverting, these effects are pure artifice, unrelated to significant meaning production except as a commentary on the multifaceted nature of theater itself. In the meantime the actors playing the characters have joined the real audience in the lobby, where a series of distinct short scenes are enacted, allowing audience members to watch, observe, and eavesdrop on the play's "characters," as the spectators do in *Each in His Own Way.*

The coordinating voice uniting all the performances belongs to Doctor

Hinkfuss, himself a creature of dialectical qualities. Hinkfuss is a character constructed of opposites; he is possessed of conflicting physical and psychological attributes, concurrently grotesque and brilliant, rational yet impulsive, positive but also destructive. His appearance is innately theatrical rather than typically human: he is imagined as a tuxedoed dwarf with an enormous head of hair and little hands with tiny, pale, hairy fingers resembling caterpillars. Nevertheless this grotesque little figure of the imagination dominates the dramatic action in his varying roles as the master of ceremonies, the director of an unwritten play, the manipulator of situations, and a distorted Pirandellian *raisonneur.* As Bettina L. Knapp has noted, Hinkfuss is a magus, the archetype of the Spiritual Father emerging from the depths of the unconscious, who is acting as the agent of transformation. Returning to the recurring Pirandellian formula of the fluidity of life conflicting with the fixity of form, Hinkfuss offers controlled improvisation as an obvious resolution to this conflict. The fixity of art, embodied in the story, finds fluidity in improvisation, under an imaginative director like himself.[15]

As director, Hinkfuss is at loggerheads with his repertory company. The cast rebels against his insistence they perform an improvisational work while he continues to exert control over its disposition and their craft. Hinkfuss is not only the director of the scenario (or story) proposed to his actors, but he also tries his hand at authorship by revising the selected Pirandellian text in order to accomodate it to his own vision. He interrupts frequently, demands clarifications, manipulates his actors. In so doing he subverts the concept of improvisation. Again and again the thespians complain about his impositions, viewed as interference rather than authority. Craving the liberating aspect of improvisation, the actors banish Hinkfuss from the stage. In so doing, they banish the division between script and enactment by literally taking over the personalities of their characters or, possibly, imbuing the characters with their own traits. Throughout the dramatic action these performers will be playing simultaneous dual roles: as characters in the improvised play and as members of a theatrical troupe.

The success of the fusion of actor and role in *Tonight We Improvise* contrasts with the failure of the Actors of *Six Characters* to "become" the Characters. Several scenes capture the emotional depths such fusion engenders as it destroys the divisions between art and life or, as Hinkfuss suggests, makes art life. The astonishing element in these representative scenes lies in the playwright's ability to translate the actor's identification with his role from the thespian's point of view. In all cases the actor is as present as the character. For example, in a brief early scene the La Croce Matriarch/Character Actress soundly slaps her "husband," the Old Comic Actor and justifies this gesture on the grounds that improvisation requires real participation on the part of the artist—not imitation blows. All action rises genuinely from the actor's innermost being, she suggests, and stays with the artist throughout the performance. In another scene the Old Comic Actor steps onto the stage, seemingly soaked in blood and fatally wounded. Rather than playing a death scene, as expected, he complains that his entrance has been ruined and proceeds to exit and enter again. His second entrance is equally unsuccessful. Unhappy that he is not adequately prepared for a "proper" death scene, the Old Comic Actor once again interrupts the flow of the improvised action. Instead of "playing" his role, he treats his fellow performers to a moving narrative account of "how" he would have died that transforms his fellow players into his private audience and successfully moves them to tears. The action of the play within the play, however, is structured to build toward the climactic death of the main protagonist, Mommina. The leading actress, who is "living" Mommina's moving death scene, quite literally collapses, physically overpowered by her empathetic feelings. In these scenes Pirandello attempts to involve the audience in directly viewing the fusion between character and actor. As Olga Ragusa notes, this experience "is destabilizing because it is forced on [the spectator's] consciousness."[16] The element of theatrical artifice required to realize such identification with the role is also dramatized onstage, notably in the scene "creating" the deformed and sickly Mommina. The Leading Actress is aged before the audience's eyes by her "sisters" and "mother" through makeup and costume additions—she is metamorphosed from a beautiful young woman into "inert flesh." While the spectators remain perfectly aware of the construction of this illusion, it is nonetheless powerful, almost magical, in its impact. Yet, not all critics respond positively to either the inner play or the entire structure of *Tonight We Improvise*. Büdel maintains that this last entry in the theater trilogy makes no attempt at taking the play within the play seriously. George E. Wellwarth considers the drama's conclusion the "extremity of spuriousness," given the incapacitation of the Leading Lady. Others may challenge the dramatic validity of the internal melodrama, with its operatic overtones and nineteenth-century sentimentalism.

While improvisation can be defined as an act of life realized from one moment to the next, it can also lead to the shattering of the performance as it disintegrates into general anarchy. Art can be lost in the flux. Although the play cannot perform itself, the actors discover that unscripted performance is chancy at best, occasionally even dangerous. In their state of confusion they request a written text that can be securely followed and accept the return of Hinkfuss, needed for his direction. It appears that, in the dialectic between form and life, form has its place. In the trilogy improvisation also functions as a conceit for Pirandello's approach to theater. Demolishing conventional attitudes toward the stage, the playwright proposes a universe of the unforeseen, the sudden, the inconclusive, and the unknowable where imagination and illusion rule. But the theater plays themselves are far from spontaneous "happenings," where action is left to chance. Pirandello offers a highly structured set of works in which details are carefully pondered and stage directions abound. Indeed, *Tonight We Improvise* becomes a statement against haphazard improvisational art in favor of a rigorously constructed text by an author who is not a director but a playwright.

The theater plays also demonstrate the intricate interpretive layers that develop between the original creative work and its performance. Authorial intention is easily lost, for the dramatic text is open ended, subject to a multiplicity of readings, none of which necessarily coincides with the writer's initial vision, just as with the affair of Delia Morello and Michele Rocca. This fact gives poignancy to the consternation of the Six Characters when they see themselves falsified by the actors: a metaphor for the experience of the writer once his creation has entered the world beyond his imagination. For an author like Pirandello, seduced by the substantiality of a work of art, the issue of textual integrity is primary. It is not surprising, therefore, that the playwright would be fascinated by the practical elements composing theatrical performance, thereby becoming an ardent student of stagecraft. As a director Pirandello demanded that his actors identify as closely as possible with the characters portrayed so as to convey their essential nature. His own direction, emphasizing a natural acting style and avoiding the histrionic bombast then in vogue, has been described as fast paced, even comic in timing. This rendition of the text recalls Hinkfuss's comments on the function of the theater as a reflection of life with all its mutability and mobility. But, as Robert Brustein states, the conflict between life and art can only be resolved through the disappearance of the writer. Pirandello, however, was not an author capable of relinquishing tight control over his work.[17]

In the trilogy the dramatic form is repeatedly dissolved in the exchange of reality and illusion, inner and outer plays, dramatic action and critical reflection. Levels of meaning shift and move about, accompanied by continuous analysis and discussion. In this atmosphere the inner plays are not meant to stand alone as naturalist artifacts with a beginning, middle, and end. Rather they operate as dramatizations of ideas or expanded conceits for the creation and construction of the theatrical experience, which is the focus of the framing action. Thus *Six Characters in Search of an Author* concerns a play in the making which is never finished. *Each in His Own Way* provides a partial but incomplete text, a work purposely left unended. In *Tonight We Improvise* the play reaches resolution but not according to the original intent of the director-playwright: the text literally becomes the actors. All the theater plays, however, dramatize a dialectic of conflict. In *Six Characters* this dialectic is played out between the characters and the actors, between art and life. In *Each in His Own Way* spectators and actors collide as "real" and "fictional" characters encounter each other, representing fluidity and fixity, reality and illusion. In *Tonight We Improvise* the struggle for control of the dramatic material is played out between the director, his actors, and the "truth" contained in the story and its characters. In all three plays theatrical form is subjected to Pirandellian concepts of relativity and multiplicity, for the plays tear down conventions, spatial barriers, and the walls separating action and audience, characters and people.

Although the presentation of the dysfunctional family of the Six Characters is dramatically intriguing, the play's principal concern remains the opposition of art and form resulting in the struggle between illusion and reality. In the theater plays the standard Pirandellian themes of illusions, masks, and role-playing achieve metaphysical proportions because of their collocation into the larger discussion of the absolute nature of art. In this trilogy, as in most of his works, Pirandello is translating his views on the human condition into dramatic terms. The plays within the plays of the theater trilogy are teeming with anguished characters that enrich Pirandello's vision of the stage as the representation of life, as well as art. The protagonists emerging from the stage action are not mere personified abstractions or talking concepts but conflicted and passionate personalities that project messages about humanity's painful existential state through their fictions. Thus the tangled web of the melodramatic stories of the Six and the La Croce family engage the audience at the level of emotional, as well as artistic, reality. As embodiments of human experience these characters dramatize aspects of man's interior life and place in the world.

A representative figure, the Father of *Six Characters* is quintessentially Pirandellian in his struggle to control passion through reason. The Father is equally a cerebral and an emotive creation who expresses a gamut of feelings including self-confidence, torment, wit, anger, and condescension. He also personifies the mask of remorse imposed upon him by the playwright as his defining passion. Criticized, like many of the dramatist's *raisonneurs,* for excessive philosophizing, the Father reacts by declaring the "reasons of [his] suffering." His emphasis on the rational places him squarely in a Pirandellian universe but outside the traditions of melodrama, where emotions are not given an intellectual structure. As commonly occurs in Pirandellian drama, thought

117

and emotion are fused, not divided, in the character. The act of passionate re-flection is a fundamental quality of the dramatist's protagonists. Propelling the action of *Six Characters,* the Father is the story's prime mover, mouthpiece, advocate, and challenger. In recent years, however, literary criticism of this play has focused more and more on the subterranean, unconscious motivations underlying the dramatic action. Proceeding in such a psychoanalytical line, Eric Bentley remarks that the Father is the source of the Characters' catastrophes and the "base of that Oedipal triangle on which the family story rests."[18] The family story, the critic notes, begins and ends with the Oedipal image of father, mother, and son, the second family having literally or figuratively been killed off. Bentley sees the inner melodrama as a "great play of dead or agonized fatherhood," including the absence of the greatest father of all, God. In this vein the search for a welcoming author can be interpreted as a metaphor for humanity's need for the Author of our being, for the safety and protection of absolute fa-therhood. Moreover some critics employ psychoanalytic instruments not only to explore issues of character development and plot, but also to understand the creative genesis of Pirandello's works in his own psychological makeup. For example, in his article "The Play as Replay," Rudolph Binion attributes the tragic situations of *Six Characters* and *Henry IV* to the mechanism of "trau-matic reliving" of life-shattering dramas, in an existence termed "a chronicle of psychic gashes" (149). Binion states that a personal Pirandellian trauma is at the core of *Six Characters:* Antonietta Portulano's accusations of incest against her husband and daughter. These, Binion offers, are transformed into dramatic action in the scenes depicting the maternally interrupted sexual encounter of the Father and Stepdaughter.[19]

In his depiction of the Father, Pirandello is also expressing the failure of the individual's chosen masks, which is concealed beneath his self-justifying rational discourse. For all his aspirations toward "a certain moral sanity," the Father is stripped of his masks and exposed as a bad husband, a bad parent, an egotist, and a sensualist. Having been incapable of sustaining a satisfactory marriage, the Father becomes his wife's procurer when he sends her off with the Secretary. By this action he foreshadows the seventh Character, Madama Pace, who procures the Stepdaughter for him, with intimations of an incestuous bond. It is not coincidental that the play being rehearsed at the opening of *Six Characters* is Pirandello's own *The Rules of the Game.* Besides forming a comic self-referential aside, the mention and brief discussion of this earlier piece presage themes of the new text. Like *The Rules of the Game, Six Characters* is also about roles. On stage, these roles often clash: father versus child; actor versus character; husband versus wife. The Father is urgent about his personal tragedy; he has been caught in the compromising role of the middle-aged client of the disreputable Madama Pace and fixed in it. Madama Pace's own "nature" is visualized in her grotesque appearance. The corruption of her character is rendered by the monstrousness of her physique: a hideous old harridan wearing an orange wig, red silk gown, and a rose behind her ear, she is enormously fat.[20]

While *Each in His Own Way* focuses on the topics of relativity and consciousness, the inner play of *Tonight We Improvise* returns to some of Pirandello's earliest themes, derived from his naturalist roots in Sicilian verismo. In the account of Mommina and her morbidly jealous husband, Rico Verri, Pirandello once again explores the world of patriarchal culture, with its rigid codes, male chauvinism, oppression, and veneration of honor. Looking at this dehumanizing marriage and reaching far beyond the naturalist facade of objective facts into the subterranean darkness of the unconscious, the author delves deeply into the psyches of his characters. Unlike the spectacle presented by Hinkfuss in the first section of the play, no extraordinary special effects shield the audience from the tensions and psychopathology depicted through the craft of the actors and the innate "magic" of performance. For example, Mommina's cloistered existence is materialized in a brief scene in which the actress merely touches her forehead against the three walls of her jail/house that were previously invisible to the audience. As her forehead touches each wall in turn, it is illuminated briefly, only to disappear. At each touch Mommina cries, "This is a wall!" With limited use of lighting and a paucity of words and gestures, Mommina's fate is indelibly conveyed to the spectators.

Powerful mythic topoi are at work in the play within the play of *Tonight We Improvise,* which will be developed further in Pirandello's myth trilogy. These topoi emphasize the force of the feminine principle in both negative and life-affirming ways. For example, the La Croce matriarch is both the fertile mother of daughters and a collective Great Mother who threatens the patriarchy by fostering artistic expression as an instrument of self-expression in her female children. Once married, Mommina is denied this outlet until her final "performance," when the music of a passionate Verdi aria becomes the sound of her anguished psyche. Her husband, Rico Verri, is haunted by his own unconsciously imbedded archetype: the pure and sacred wife-mother, the Madonna figure he cannot and will not perceive in Mommina, with her liberated upbringing and disreputable family. Caught up in his society's primeval sense of honor, he cannot escape its tentacles. No longer content merely to jail his wife to keep her pure, he is tormented by the need to control her thoughts and memories as well. In the end the fictional world of Verri's imagination comes to dominate his reality. In his subjective judgment Mommina's imagined infidelities annihilate her actual fidelity. Verri becomes as jealous of his wife's thoughts as he is of her person. Like so many Pirandellian characters his illusion is more real to him than the knowable facts. Mommina herself is the sacrificial lamb, a martyr to patriarchal marriage and a victim of psychological sadomasochism. Verri has delusions about his wife's faithfulness: he fantasizes the existence of impure thoughts which would make her spiritually, if not physically, unchaste. Mommina employs repression to survive, suffocating herself under her husband's relentless scrutiny. Eventually her traumatized psyche experiences apparitions; psychoanalytically oriented critics would classify these hallucinations as aberrations due to schizophrenia, but on metaphorical and theatrical planes they function as the scattered fragments of Mommina's broken mind.

Theoretically, dramatically, and emotionally Pirandello's theater plays reflect the playwright's vital imagination and creativity. Their innovative use of the total theater, their exploration of the creative process in action, and their invention of novel ways to express human experience make them unique in Pirandello's dramatic output and revolutionary within the framework of the European theater of his day. By exposing the illusion of theater and opening it to public view, Pirandello, fulfilling his goal of capturing the instability of life and fixing it in dramatic form, redefined the nature of the dramatic work and broke the conventions of naturalism. In so doing, he made the audience an active, as well as reactive, participant in the construction of drama. As the playwright declares in the introduction to *Six Characters in Search of an Author,* "I have set before them [the audience], not the stage now, but my own imagination in the guise of that stage, caught in the act of creation" (xxiii).

CHAPTER SEVEN

The Myths

Utopia, religion, art—these are the subjects of Pirandello's myths, a series of three plays encompassing some of the playwright's mature meditations on the individual's relationship to the shared values of humanity. Written in his later years, these works suggest a new dimension in Pirandellian drama through the exploration of some of the certainties affirmed by humanity throughout time. *La nuova colonia* (1928, *The New Colony*) proposes the myth of a new social contract based on fellowship and the commonweal. A group of desperate members of the underclass bands together on an uninhabited island to begin again by building their own utopian community, only to have their former hostile environment reassert itself, exploding into violence and destruction. *Lazzaro* (1929, *Lazarus*) contrasts the inadequacy of a repressively dogmatic religious belief to the instinctive faith of the natural woman, Sara, and her simple and sage mate. The third play of the trilogy is Pirandello's last, unfinished drama. *I giganti della montagna* (1937, *The Mountain Giants*) celebrates the magical mystery of the imagination. Fantasies come to life, dreams materialize, and reality is suspended in this myth of art. But it is a delicate balance, easily shattered. *The Mountain Giants* is both an affirmation of the mysterious power of art and a declaration of its fragility.

Pirandello designated these plays "modern myths," a term reflecting his long-standing desire to develop a theater that was closer to the imaginative capacity of the people while concurrently reflecting contemporary realities. The myths treat current events such as the growing conflict between science and religion and the oppression of capitalist industrialized society. It is generally accepted that traditional myths act as primitive explanations of the natural order and cosmic forces. Statements issued by the dramatist during this period confirm his understanding of just such a mythic function within his creative works. Pirandello declared his desire to capture the "primitive and natural forces of the spirit" and communicate them to all humanity. The myths, he stated, are also meant to convey the "elemental unbreakable events of earth's cycles, sunrises, sunsets, births, deaths" through a "fable of life."[1] As a "fable," or fiction, myth nevertheless conveys psychological truths and functions as a vehicle for beliefs by employing archetypal images, characters, and situations that are to be experienced at levels beyond the logical. These elements, as well as the involvement of a suprahuman being or event, are all present to varying degrees in these three Pirandellian plays, which add a new metaphysical dimension to his dramaturgy. In this trilogy the author is attempting a return of sorts to theater as a natural expression of life, a quasi-religious experience, as it existed long before becoming a traditional literary form.

The movement toward mythic theater signals a new phase in Pirandellian drama during the final decade of the playwright's life, if not a total break with the themes of his prior production. The myth trilogy is Pirandello's attempt at producing a less cerebral and less pessimistic, more life-affirming art by exploring the enduring, archetypal realm of myth. Although—or possibly because—his personal life was fraught with isolation and restless dissatisfaction, the playwright was seeking artistic renewal and a measure of permanence. Taken as a whole, however, the three Pirandellian myths are profoundly pessimistic about the human condition as it is manifested in the social fabric, organized religion, and art. The collective plan of evasion into the unsullied world of nature in *The New Colony* proves calamitous for all concerned. God and infinity are declared to exist within individuals, while mystery and illusions dominate other aspects of religious belief in *Lazarus*. Art as free creativity triumphs at the margins of life in *The Mountain Giants* but is misunderstood, manhandled, and soiled when in contact with the people. The masks and patterns imposed on the individual by society are destructive and powerful, the myths declare, yet they also announce hope for redemption in each of the three works, signaling a departure from the insistent relativism and fragmentation found throughout Pirandello's literary production. The subject of myth is, after all, creation: the explanation of how things come to exist. In its own way each play of the trilogy is concerned with seeking answers and developing strategies for creating—whether it be societies, morality, peace of mind, a belief system, spiritual contentment, fantasies, or a play.

The New Colony describes the hopeful construction and cataclysmic destruction of a modern Utopian ideal. Set on a deserted island subject to seismic activity, the colony is composed of the socially dispossessed: impoverished fishermen, smugglers, petty criminals, and a lone woman, a prostitute. They are a band of outcasts, one of Pirandello's familiar archetypes, who could not conform to the restraints of their unwelcoming world. Set somewhere in economically depressed southern Italy, the play's prologue opens in a seedy tavern with talk of the island, a former penal colony: "the paradise of wicked men." La Spera convinces her lover, Currao, and several others to escape the degradation that surrounds them by sailing to the island to create a better society for themselves. Initially the colonists are held together by the woman's selfless dedication and altruistic values. Emerging as the group's leader, Currao undertakes the formation of a social structure guided by a code of democratically approved laws. He conceives an egalitarian social contract: each will be accountable, contributing to the common good to the best of his or her ability. The imminent threat of extinction fosters self-sacrifice and cooperation among the colonists in the face of threatening nature. Yet, the first act of the myth already projects a pessimistic view of the men's ability to construct their brave new world.

In the desolation of its natural setting and crumbling houses, the island is a metaphor for the men's discontented spirit: lonely, outside familiar codes of behavior, and sexually frustrated, some of the colonists find it difficult to adjust. They are tempted by the presence of La Spera, who had been available to them all in her former life. Their unsated desires quickly find expression in quarrels and a growing resentment of Currao, leader and possessor of the attractive woman they all lust after. Crocco, the most agressive of the malcontents and the most profoundly corrupted by his past life, sets out to alter the colony to his liking. After leaving the island, he returns with a boatload of new settlers, including "respectable" women. They are the arm of the society the colonists had abandoned that is reaching out into their new world, ready to grasp it. The newcomers are led by Crocco and an ambitious entrepreneur, Nocio, a symbol for the unscrupulous greed of unrestricted capitalism; both men see commercial possibilities in the undeveloped island and intend to exploit it to their sole advantage. Rapidly the plague of modern society, with all its rapacity, prejudices, and claims, invades the community. The new order gives way to the old within an institutional vacuum devoid of all protections. However, the colonists cannot escape themselves, for they carry the germs of corruption and evil within.

La Spera seeks to reverse the effects of this shift in values, but Currao is seduced by the newcomers. He abandons the former prostitute for the well-to-do and untainted Mita, Nocio's daughter, whom he plans to marry. Having been the queen, saint, and guardian angel of the new colony, La Spera is once again a pariah because of her past immorality. Traditional patriarchy judges the value of women on the basis of sexual virtue. Therefore the new woman La Spera has become is irrelevant as the old order reestablishes itself. Finding social legitimacy in his new opportunities, the reformed smuggler Currao wishes to raise "his" son properly with his respectable bride, not with La Spera. Warning the community that the earth will quake if the boy is wrenched from her, La

Spera flees. "As if it participated in the mother's desperate embrace, the earth does tremble," the stage directions note.[2] Taking refuge on a rocky promontory, La Spera and her baby are saved, surrounded by the sea. The earthquake and tidal wave that sink the rest of the island are allegorical manifestations of the greed and corruption which have drowned the community's fellowship. The biblical allusions are clear. The destruction of the island recalls the tale of Noah and the Flood, with which God punished humanity's evil by sending forty days of rain and preserving only a chosen few to repopulate the earth. It also evokes the destruction of Sodom and Gomorrah, the cities of vice, where the lust for pleasure and wealth led to unforgiveable transgression and unforgiving justice. La Spera is the only colonist true to the newfound ideals of love and faith. Spared from the holocaust visited by the sea, the former prostitute and ber innocent son emerge from the waves like a beacon of hope for the future. But as Susan Bassnett-McGuire has shown, the conclusion of the play offers little hope for humankind's ability to construct a new social order. Reinforcing Pirandello's bleak vision of humanity's helpless condition, La Spera's salvation, a miracle of sorts, is due to forces outside human control. Either an act of divine intervention or irrational chance—a deus ex machina that destroys her enemies—preserves La Spera. This fortuitous cataclysm may be intended as the manifestation of the suprahuman event found in traditional myth.[3]

As a statement on humanity's utopian dreams, *The New Colony* signals a clear failure. The impoverished idealists, who so hopefully set forth to create an egalitarian community outside the bourgeois ideology of property and possession, are condemned to return to the oppressive inequities of the society they had abandoned. Their utopian attempt is defeated by their greed, cravings, and desire for supremacy. Petty quarrels over ownership, serious disagreements over sexual possession, and rebellion against any rule of law tarnish the dream from the start. Seeking freedom, the malcontents actually want license. The failure of the New Colony is Pirandello's implicit social statement on the need for institutions and conventions, no matter how stifling to the individuals involved. Without the general acceptance of law and order, anarchy reigns. But the play also rejects the degradation of people in a dehumanizing and judgmental social environment. The altruistic interventions of La Spera on behalf of all the settlers are nullified by social prejudice: the moral woman is invisible behind the prostitute's mask. In the end even the idealistic leader Currao is corrupted by subtle promises of money and position as befits the son-in-law and heir of the exploitative Nocio. Currao, seeing his position altered from oppressed "have-not" to oppressing "have," agrees to serve Mammon. Together Nocio and Currao can establish a degraded imitation of the world left behind and rule it, to the detriment of the commonweal.

A role written for Marta Abba's talents, the central protagonist of *The New Colony* is the former prostitute La Spera. Throughout the dramatic action this character brings to mind a series of archetypal Christian figures with strong religious connotations. In some ways La Spera is a Mary Magdalene, the harlot redeemed by pure love. In this role she embodies the Pirandellian message of human solidarity struggling against the imposition of societal labels which deform the authentic self. Having cast aside the debasing identity she held in the old society, La Spera seeks to create herself, becoming the symbol of evangelical *caritas,* love as charity, by serving the community with devoted altruism. On her archetypal quest for redemption and meaning, La Spera achieves a personal truth: freeing herself by offering herself to others. As she tells a group of men lusting after her, wanting to return her to her discarded identity: "I can belong to you all, the way I do now, just because I belong to one man, the man of my own choice. Whereas the way I used to belong to you all, I really belonged to nobody, not even to myself!" (145). Moreover La Spera embodies the maternal archetype, represented in Christian iconography as Madonna and Child. She generates life and love, directed not only to her own son but to all the men for whom she cares, who become her spiritual children. She is the mother of them all, the intermediary of a better existence, the promise of their redemption. This spiritual identity is revealed physically in the first "miracle" of the play. At the end of the prologue, about to embark on the journey to the new land, La Spera discovers that her breast milk has returned after months of having her baby wet-nursed. The breast milk is a sign of her full spiritual and physical motherhood: she has given life, and now she can sustain it from within herself. The theme of the regenerative powers of maternity is developed symbolically and physically in the person of the transfigured prostitute, but it appears frequently in Pirandello, from his earliest works. The Christian image of motherhood is transformed into the mythic image of the great earth mother, or the pagan fertility goddess of ancient civilizations, in the concluding scene of the play. Earth and sea become La Spera's champions just as her maternity, the original foundation of the New Colony, is threatened. Like sea and earth La Spera assumes the power of life and death. Earth and water are the symbols for fertility and regeneration, which hopefully suggests that "the new vital energy of modern life will rise from a sea of anarchy and destruction. The annihilation of the new colony by Spera's will to save her son is creative destruction; from it perhaps a new historical cycle is meant to begin."[4] Suggestively, La Spera's name means hope.

Although well received at its Rome premiere by the official Fascist press, which saw a different, morally positive, and auspicious Pirandello in the work,

The New Colony has seldom been produced because of its length, large cast, elaborate staging, and concluding special effects. The play also contains stylistic problems that effect production values because of its inherently dichotomous nature. A. Richard Sogliuzzo rightly remarks that the work consists of two conflicting dramatic forms. The first is a drama in the naturalist vein about members of the desperate underclass attempting to rebuild their sordid lives. The second operates like a "quasi-religious allegory of Western humanism and socialism— more suitable for a libretto than a play."[5] In fact, because of its realistic aspects and tone, *The New Colony* has been compared to Giovanni Verga's *The House by the Medlar Tree,* whose poor fishermen are the downtrodden of history and the vanquished of life. Unlike most of Pirandello's dramas this play explores the raw language and crude brutality of an environment peopled by criminals, police spies, and streetwalkers. On the other hand, the religious imagery, excess of sentimentality, and mythic qualities of La Spera's conversion from sinner to saint pull the play in a symbolic direction, far from the documentary style of verismo. Without a Pirandellian influx of humor or irony to balance the tones, *The New Colony* suffers from its stylistic duality.

Lazarus, the second of the myth plays, continues the religious investigation touched upon symbolically in *The New Colony.* As the title suggests, the drama concerns death and resurrection through the mediation of belief by alluding to the New Testament account of Jesus' calling the dead Lazarus forth from his grave, in deference to the faith of his disciples. In actuality the medium for resuscitation in the play is not faith but science, thereby originating the crisis of belief that is the focus of the dramatic action. The drama centers on the isolated Spina family, which the playwright immediately associates with a series of deaths and losses illustrated by the setting described in the opening lines of the stage directions. The Spina residence is surrounded by a wall topped off with broken glass; at its center stands a huge black crucifix with a depressing image of the dying Christ—the suffering lifeless emblem of Diego Spina's rigid Catholicism. In the first act a series of past and present losses for the family is enumerated: the loss of the mother Sara who could not abide Spina's joyless faith and abandoned her husband; Sara's loss of her children; theirs of her; the loss of health in daughter Lia, crippled from neglect; and the loss of faith in son Lucio, a seminarian. These "little deaths" of the psyche become actual physical deaths when first a rabbit, Lia's pet, then the father, Diego Spina, die. Both animal and man are "resurrected" by science through the miracle of a shot of adrenalin. Seeing the rabbit resuscitated, Diego Spina is shaken by medicine's power to play God with life and death. Later he finds himself completely unprepared to accept his own after-death experience. Revived forty-five minutes after being declared dead, Diego remembers nothing: neither his demise nor its aftermath. Having assumed that he would have experienced an afterlife, the cornerstone of his rigid faith, Spina is traumatized. His nescience is proof that heaven and hell—therefore, God—do not exist. It is a ravaging blow for a zealot devoted to ritual, fundamental pieties, and unbending standards of personal behavior. The experience erases a life led according to the most puritanical of rules, thus unleashing Diego's suppressed passions and resentments without the controlling mechanism of his unbending sense of good and evil.

From the first act to the last, *Lazarus* offers a series of metaphysical inquiries, exploring the mysteries of existence, love, and the universe, and inquiring into humanity's role in a godless world. From the perspective of an individual of unquestioned, albeit dogmatic, beliefs the issue of resurrection through science rather than faith is more damning than miraculous. Having lost the secure harbor of his zealotry, Diego Spina is left empty. Without his old certainties he is another victim of the Pirandellian void. As is made clear in the drama, Diego's reawakening from death is also a reawakening to the life he has stifled in himself and in others. Painfully self-aware without his protective pieties, Diego reopens the wounds of the past. Deprived of the promise of a heavenly reckoning, he rebels against the shape his life has taken. Convinced that the absence of eternal reward or punishment in the next life renders good and evil irrelevant in this one, Diego sets out to destroy his wife and her lover. More Frankenstein's creature than Lazarus, Spina rises from the dead in monstrous form, ready to kill the symbolic source of his losses: Sara's new mate, the peasant Arcadipane.

In keeping with his vision of God, before his "death" Diego Spina had accepted misfortune with Christian fortitude, tinged with a zealot's humble arrogance. His repressive views were transmitted to his children: the son he directed into the priesthood and the younger daughter he sent to a strict sectarian boarding school, where she fell ill. The three Spinas are repressed individuals, locked in their formalistic piety, isolated from the world beyond their wall, and living in the dark shadows of their cross. Yet their devotion brings them no joy: all three are mutilated in spirit, deprived of love. In contrast to this isolated, failed family, Pirandello creates a positive mirror image: the peasant Arcadipane with his two healthy children and their loving mother, Sara, who legally remains the wife of Diego Spina. Whereas cohabitation had been stifling with her spouse, Sara has found contentment in the simple joys of family and labor shared with a good man of integrity. Arcadipane is the salt of the earth, genuinely whole, unlike the inhibited, narrow-minded Diego. To indicate the paradigmatic qualities of the three characters, Pirandello chose their names with care. Sara recalls the biblical wife of Abraham, the "mother of many nations," a woman of great beauty devoted to her spousal and maternal roles. Arcadipane translates as "ark, or chest, of bread," alluding to biblical stories depicting the close bond between human and God (Noah's ark, the Ark of the Covenant) but also to humanity's basic staple, the bread of life. Spina means thorn, intimating Diego's character but also the crown of thorns worn by the crucified Christ, who towers over his house and his existence.

Like La Spera, Sara is a maternal archetype, a lifegiver in spirit as well as body. She left Diego Spina because he fosters death and deforms love; due to his rigid creed he is incapable of understanding the depths of her own profound faith. As Sara explains to her estranged husband at the end of act 1, in the crucified Christ she sees life, while he can only perceive death. Sara's community is the earth, the vital flow of living. Mating with a peasant, bearing children, tilling the soil, and nurturing plants are integral parts of Sara's (and nature's) cycles. Like the earth she too bears fruit; her fecundity is the fertility of nature, with which she is in communion and synchrony. And, like nature, she is eternally young: "She still looks like a girl of twenty! . . . It's just as if the sun were passing by! She's a **miracle!**"[6] To accentuate this supranatural quality of Sara, she first appears on stage dressed in red, with a black cloak, set against a blazing sunset: "she radiates freshness, health, and power" (174). Sara's power comes from her reciprocity with nature, with the earth and its fruits, from her femaleness. She is indeed an earth mother; as such, her sundered children inevitably return to her. First Lucio seeks her out, having come to "recognize" her, "to be born again" of her (178). Allusively, he finds her tending the natural fruits of her labor in her vegetable garden. At the end of the play Lia is called to Sara, hands outstretched to embrace her unknown daughter. Echoing one of the wondrous cures of Jesus, the paralytic girl rises from her chair and runs to her mother. The final word of Pirandello's second myth is *miracle*—the miracle of maternal love.

It is through reunion with Sara that Lucio rediscovers his shattered faith; thus he renews his vocation. The return to the mother is also a return to Mother Earth, as Lucio comes to recognize the value of the fusion of love, nature, goodness, and God found in Sara. It is *caritas* she transmits to her son, the love born of charity, to be expressed throughout God's house on earth. This practice of altruistic love defines both Sara and La Spera, the maternal archetypes of the myths. In both plays the mother figures save their sons through the moral wholeness of their beings, although both women are judged socially reprehensible—a prostitute and an adulteress. Recognizing that his mother's Franciscan peace of mind also derives from a loving union with the material world, the doubting seminarian develops a new source of faith based on immanentism, the belief that God exists within the world, in all things and all beings.[7] By accepting Sara and forgiving the past, Lucio forges a new vision of divine providence which declares that all things, all events, have purpose and meaning, no matter how hidden or mysterious. Like the father the son too has been resurrected. As his name implies, Lucio has found the light (*lux* in Latin, *luce* in Italian) to illuminate the darkness of his spiritual death to God. The miracles of science in *Lazarus* are followed by the miracles of a living faith expressed not in doctrine, which Pirandello, a lifelong anticlericalist, disdained, but through life itself. Convincing his father of his new certainties and liberating faith, Lucio averts a tragedy and helps the nihilistic Diego "see" the value of *this* life: "Which is His life. . . In order that you may live it . . . Toiling and suffering and rejoicing like everyone else" (222). Ordering his father to live, Lucio echoes the command of Jesus to Lazarus: "Arise and walk . . . Walk in the ways of life" (222).

As Anne Paolucci has eloquently stated, Pirandello's trilogy of myths "is grounded in the miracle of belief."[8] The final myth concerns one of Pirandello's most personally cherished beliefs: his belief in art. At the conceptual stage for years, *The Mountian Giants* was unfinished at the time of the playwright's sudden death, a fact making it all the more intriguing to critics and readers. Having composed the draft of two acts, the ailing author dictated a plan for the third, climactic act to his son Stefano the day before he died. Years before Pirandello had written Marta Abba about the projected play: "The mountain giants are the triumph of fantasy, the triumph of poetry, but at the same time also the tragedy of poetry in this brutal, modern world."[9] While *The New Colony* is about the idealistic construction of an egalitarian social order and *Lazarus* concerns the creation of a life-affirming faith, Pirandello's last work, his myth of art, is the drama of a failed communication: the transmission of poetry, the art of literature, to an unprepared, uncomprehending audience.

Ilse—a brilliant actress—her devoted husband, and the remnants of their impoverished theatrical troupe are on an impossible mission. Ilse is obsessed by her desire to bring a dead playwright's masterpiece to the people: she tours endlessly in her fanatical determination to honor the work of the young poet who died for love of her. Their wanderings bring the company to the enchanted and isolated villa of the magician Cotrone and his Scalognati, or unfortunates. It is a magical place where reason is banished and illusion reigns. There the imagination takes wing, as fantasies come into being immediately as the mind contemplates them. But these visions can exist only within the limited confines of the villa. Ilse rejects the magician's offer of producing her play in the villa, where the mediation of actors and the presence of an audience are unnecessary because the performance emanates directly from the imagination, bringing puppets to life and transforming the written word directly into dramatic action. The actress cannot surrender her role in the production of art, for she longs to identify with the work written for her, to be its interpreter. Cotrone, the master of the realm of fantasy, warns Ilse that the unfettered creative imagination can only prosper in his small space, that it is doomed in the outside world. But Ilse will not listen. In the opinion of one of Italy's greatest contemporary stage directors, Giorgio Strehler, Cotrone's world is pure theater, the immediate expression of the creative spirit, whereas Ilse and her band are performance theater, the movement from the text to the actors who represent it: both are necessary components of the total theatrical experience. Offered the opportunity to appear at the wedding feast of the powerful Giants, the actress accepts but finds herself performing for their uncouth servants. The company's presentation is a misunderstood fiasco. The Giants' brutish henchmen seek entertainment, not art, from the players. Angered, Ilse lashes out at their ignorant lack of appreciation, only to be killed by the furious mob. This violent death of the protagonist is generally interpreted as an allegory of the impossibility of art's survival in a materialistic world—the land of the Giants.

The Mountain Giants is a plunge into the subconscious, irrational side of myth. The play teems with an extraordinary mix of grotesque and symbolic characters including deformed dwarfs, militant angels, and promiscuous madwomen, who contrast with the realistically drawn Ilse and her ragged company. Viewed in allegorical terms, the Giants, who never appear onstage, represent modern industrialized society, given to the production of technological feats, the logic of science, and the easy pleasures of mass culture but bereft of sensistivity toward the world of the imagination. It is a society that dehumanizes the spiritual side of humankind, as revealed by the descriptors the playwright uses to denote the Giants' workforce, which is the audience for Ilse's play and the embodiment of the masses: "raving Beasts," "ignorance," "illiterates," "vulgarity," "buffooneries," "bellowings," and "ever menacing storm." In such a setting art, like Ilse, risks destruction at the hands of a brutish public interested only in mindless entertainment.[10] To avoid these "cannibalizing" spectators, Pirandello removes theater, understood in its mythic dimensions, to the realm of the mysterious and the irrational, where it was housed by archaic peoples. The antithesis of the land of the Giants, Cotrone's arsenal of apparitions is the space of pure imagination, which empowers and evokes the phantoms of the mind. The arsenal is pure mental spectacle: fantasy, not logic. Cut off from human society, the villa of the Scalognati is a place of living dreams, ephemeral fantasies, animated ghosts, and magical marvels. To borrow Renate

Matthaei's description, it represents the mind "freed from all social and meta-physical ties that here toys with itself."[11]

The games enacted in Cotrone's arsenal are those of the imagination or the dreamworld, unfettered by the restraints of reason. Act 2 takes place in the arsenal, a vast room full of discarded playthings and useless objects. At first glance it appears to be a warehouse of dusty games, strange appliances, and life-size toys. As Ilse's companions enter this mysterious space, they find themselves taking part in a collective dream—they interact with animated objects such as dancing dolls, leaping ninepins, moving walls, and self-propelled musical instruments. Counter to any logic, the actors are in the arsenal while their bodies lie sleeping in distant beds: they have unleashed their unconscious and entered a dreamscape where anything can happen. A young actor, for example, is seen hanging himself out of unrequited love for Ilse, thereby imitating the death of the mourned suicidal playwright whose memorial the actress has become. A moment later the same young man is talking with the others about his nightmare, in which they shared. It is an irrational world of apparitions and magic tricks, a spectacle without script or structure that creates itself. As in the theater trilogy, a play within the play, an integral part of this Pirandellian text, is a dramatic instrument for denoting the creative process at work. When Ilse enters the arsenal and recites her role in the dead artist's lyric fable, the surrounding objects come to life and participate in the play by filling in for missing characters and props. The dead playwright's masterpiece is fully realized in this place dedicated to pure theater. The arsenal of apparitions is the dramatic representation of art reflecting on itself and creating itself, but it is also a misanthropic closed space excluding the uninvited, for the Scalognati use every trick in their magic book to block entrance into their special world. The Scalognati themselves, as their name states, are unfortunate marginalized members of society; rejected by others, they in turn reject external intrusions into their isolated dream house.

As actors Ilse's band of players must perform not only for themselves but for others as well so that their drama can endure, immortalized in the world of art and in the hearts of the people. For them, as expressed in Stefano Pirandello's play notes, "the poet's words are not merely the highest expression of life, but actually the only certain reality in which and on which one can live."[12] Rejected by audience after audience, the ideal nevertheless lives on, pure and integral, in the actress, the keeper of the flame. In her own way Ilse is as much the zealot as is Diego Spina. Her belief is in the poetry of the text and in herself as its ideal interpreter. Ilse, unlike Cotrone, does not accept the fact that "her" work of art can live outside of her on its own merits. Termed the "fanatical slaves of art" in the notes for the play's unwritten third act, Ilse and the actors cannot survive when confronted with the crass materialism of the masses, the "fanatical slaves of life" possessing no appreciation of spiritual matters such as poetry. Yet the troupe persists in their attempt to communicate their craft and the beauty of their text to the uninitiated, no matter the personal cost. Caught in her obsession, Ilse becomes the victim of art as she envisions it, a god to whom she sacrifices others and, finally, immolates herself. Her insistence on a single, specific text for performance, to be repeated again and again, contrasts sharply with the loose freedom of Cotrone's world, where art, ever fluid and vital, assumes shapes and forms without restrictions. Yet Cotrone's villa of unfettered imagination requires an immolation as well: the exclusion of the outside world—that is, an audience, other people—and the abdication from life itself to inhabit the realm of illusion. Ilse fails because of her insistence upon imposing her dream of poetry on a public incapable of receiving it. Cotrone's arsenal of apparitions also fails because of its evanescence and solipsism. To succeed as theater, Ilse's craft and Cotrone's illusion must come together with the poetry of the text and reach out to the people in a fusion of necessary components.

The violent conclusion of Ilse's tale suggests a Pirandellian reworking of the myth of Orpheus, the ancient archetype of artist-seer. Through their adventures in the arsenal of apparitions Ilse and her companions have made their descent into the underworld—the realm of the unconscious and the irrational, the kingdom of death, and the acknowledged source of poetry. The dead playwright is their Eurydice, whose body/text they futilely wish to recover. Finally, the actors' unwillingness to acquiesce to the demands of their brutal, orgiastic audience echoes the fatal encounter of Orpheus with the Bacchants—the frenzied revelers of the god Dionysus—whose rites include dismemberment and the mutilation of their victims. Indeed, two of the actors are torn to pieces by the enraged mob, while Ilse's body is "broken like that of a puppet" (100). In death, like Orpheus, Ilse becomes "dead Poetry." But the actress is not the poet, the creator, but his interpreter. In her own view, she is a life giver, the mother, or inspirational source, of the poetic text she ardently strives to deliver into the world. Actually the masterpiece Ilse imposes on an unresponsive public is one of Pirandello's own plays, a verse libretto set to music in 1934 by Gian Francesco Malipiero: *La favola del figlio cambiato* (The Changeling). Based on ethnologic folk legends of Sicily, this is a mythic story of maternity and the supernatural. A healthy child is stolen by fairies for a king. In the boy's place the sickly prince is left. Understanding the function of this exchange, the distraught mother sets forth on a quest for her real son. Meanwhile the peasant boy is brought up royally while the changeling grows deformed in mind and body.

Once the exchange is revealed, the substitute prince easily surrenders the unfulfilling benefits of the material world for a peasant's simple life and an adoring mother's love. In the performance of this fable Ilse is the mother in search of her lost child, an analogy for the dedication of the actress to her lost lover (the stolen son) and her quest to reclaim him by giving life to his art.

The maternal archetype, embodied in La Spera, Sara, and Ilse, is central to all three plays of the myth trilogy. But maternity was a persistent theme throughout Pirandello's long writing career, from his earliest short stories and novels to his final plays. In numerous works motherhood functions as woman's supreme value, her identifier. In the introduction to *Six Characters in Search of an Author,* the playwright defines the basic traits of the traditional maternal persona as embodied by the Character of the Mother. Unlike the Father/Mind, she is realized as Nature, consistent with the long-standing patriarchal division of male as intellect and female as instinct, intuition, or emotion. It is a cliché Pirandello appears to have embraced as a valid sexual distinction. In the figure of the Mother this gender duality is taken to extremes. Devoid of intellect, she has no consciousness of her being as a character with a part to play. "Her unawareness," the author states, "is a natural part of her," so natural that "it does not demand any mental exertion" but exists in "a perpetual state of unresolved emotion" (ixx). Unmind, Pirandello's Mother suggests stereotypical feminine traits, from passivity to mental obtuseness. She is, Pirandello concludes, "Nature fixed and perceived as Mother" (xx). As Mary Ann Frese Witt has noted, the writer tends to view the female sex as a series of categories, or dramatic roles, assigned to it by others, mostly men, which can be loosely defined as mother, wife, daughter, or (sexual) woman—the primary ones being mother and woman.[13] Leonardo Sciascia attributes Pirandello's views on gender differences to his Sicilianism, with its dialectical perspective of women. Females are either degraded objects of sexual pleasure to be exclusively possessed, an attitude derived from primitive pagan cultures, or figures of pathological veneration, denoting a Christian origin. In either case Sciascia concludes, Sicilians allow women only an instinctive form of life, thus denying their personhood. Inevitably these Christian and pagan perceptions operate dialectically, alternating between the exaltation and the denigration of the female sex.[14]

In most Pirandellian plays containing a strong focus on maternity, motherhood lifts women to a higher moral plane, as in *The New Colony,* where La Spera is transformed by the presence of her son. In the myth plays and elsewhere the meaning of motherhood is scrutinized with a particular sensitivity that entails broader emotional, social, and ideological issues. In the naturalist *La ragione degli altri* (1915, Other People's Reasons), a small child is contested in a struggle—reminiscent of that judged by Solomon—between two potential mothers: the loving but poor biological parent and the father's wealthy but sterile spouse. The wife's reasons predominate; after the repentent husband's return, she convinces his mistress to surrender the child so that a "legitimate" family can be formed. The biological mother altruistically agrees in the best interest of her offspring, thus garnering the sympathy of the audience. In *L'innesto* (1919, *Grafted*) a happily married but childless woman is brutally raped. Her husband is torn by the situation; repulsed, he cannot, however, bear to part from her. Finding she is pregnant, the wife tries to convince her spouse that the child is theirs spiritually if not physically. The infant will be the sign of her total love for him, a child grafted onto her body through the union of their souls. The delicate topic is handled seriously in the play, and the husband's gradual acceptance of his wife's viewpoint is another example of Pirandello's philosophy that reality is what we make of it. Moreover, the play privileges the spiritual bond of mother and child, a union that surpasses the biological considerations surrounding paternity. In *Come prima, meglio di prima* (1920, As Before, Better Than Before), Fulvia Gelli has abandoned her family for a life of freedom and sexual corruption. Thirteen years later she attempts suicide only to be saved by her surgeon-husband, who convinces the former prostitute to return home to care for their daughter while pretending to be his second wife. Now age sixteen, the girl rejects the new mother presented to her. Devoted to the sanctified memory of a parent she believes dead, the adolescent cannot develop any attachment to her supposed stepmother. Fulvia Gelli finds herself trapped within a series of identities: her young untarnished self, the prostitute, the respectable stepmother. Rejected by her child and unable to reprise her old identity or create a new authentic persona, Fulvia once again escapes, repeating the past. This time, however, things will be better. The protagonist has discovered her authentic nature by experiencing a death and resurrection of sorts; having confronted the past, she has been reborn to herself and maternity. Taking her newborn daughter with her, Fulvia Gelli, like La Spera, is ready to begin again.

As paradigms of the abstract idea of motherhood, Pirandello's maternal characters all reflect the atavistic universe of myth, as they find spiritual renewal through their life-giving love. Like Sara in *Lazarus,* these archetypal women participate in the ongoing cycles of nature, with its unending births and deaths. Other universalizing fictions comprise the three plays of the myth trilogy: they are stories about invented characters, but like all mythic tales they project general psychological truths about the human condition by representing individuals caught in moments of crisis. In his mythopoeia Luigi Pirandello seeks to develop modern fictions to explain ageless issues, which is in line with myth's intended goal: to interpret the natural order and the forces shaping life. How can people live together harmoniously? What is the relationship of humanity to death? What is the meaning of art? These eternal questions demand definitive answers. But Pirandello's answers, as always, are elusive, as he fashions his ambiguous fables of utopia, faith, and poetry.

CHAPTER EIGHT

Other Works

Poetry and Fiction

Luigi Pirandello was an exceptionally prolific writer. In addition to seven novels, he published numerous volumes of short stories, later collected in *Novelle per un anno* (1922, Stories for a Year), thus named because of the author's unachieved goal of writing a tale for each day of the year. There are also several volumes of lyric and narrative poetry; more than forty plays, gathered together as *Maschere Nude* (Naked Masks); a handful of screenplays; and a considerable number of scholarly essays, reviews, and journalistic articles. Much, but hardly all, of this vast production has been translated. Some works, however, exist only in older, somewhat inaccurate or abridged English-language versions. Only one novel, *Suo marito* (1911, Her Husband), has not been translated. The more popular short stories and plays have appeared in several versions. By Frederick May's 1965 count, ninety-odd short stories had received English dress;[1] new translations of Pirandello's short fiction have appeared since that date, including two anthologies. Unpublished English-language renditions of several plays have been performed on stage and can be located, with some difficulty, in archives. Pirandello left the copyright of his later plays to the actress Marta Abba, who translated most of them herself in somewhat stilted English. Finally, a few of the author's major theoretical works, notably *On Humor,* as well as some personal correspondence, have appeared in translation in recent decades.

Whereas Pirandello the playwright or Pirandello the novelist continues to attract a substantial audience, Pirandello the poet is seldom remembered. Yet the author penned six lyric volumes as well as a major translation of Goethe's *Roman Elegies* between 1883 and 1912, the early years of his creative life. Generally speaking, Pirandello's verse is conventional and uninspired in form, although its contents express the poet's inner restlessness. Some recurring Pirandellian themes, later developed in his fiction and drama, emerge: a feeling of existential futility, the desire for escape, occasional splashes of his unique humor. The first compositions recall the strong moral fiber and polemical tones typical of Giosuè Carducci (1835–1907), the most influential voice in late-nine-teenth-century Italian poetry, as well as the darkly pessimistic lyrics of then-popular Arturo Graf (1848–1913). Pirandello's later compositions are some-what influenced by the melancholia of the so-called Crepuscular poets. Stylistically Pirandello's poetry is closer to nineteenth-century prosody than to twentieth-century lyric innovation, in keeping with the "schooled" and deriva-tive nature of Pirandello's versifying. The poet closely imitated canonical models without achieving a particularly autonomous or distinctive voice of his own. Nevertheless these lyric exercises contain the seeds that will grow into the Pirandellian worldview. It is probably for this reason, and this reason alone, that the author's poetry has some resonance today.

The lyrics of *Mal giocondo* (1889, Joyful Ill) composed during the writer's adolescence and school years in Palermo, display late romantic traits but also hit a polemical note derived from Carducci. Like his literary mentor the young Pirandello displays dissatisfaction, even anger, with social mores, hypocrisy both private and public, and the degeneration of the ruling class: themes that connect the fledgling poet to the mature writer he would become. These motifs are reiterated in later poetry as well. The title character of the narrative poem *Pier Gudrò* (1894), for example, is a hero of the Risorgimento who is sub-merged in the decline of moral values, thus anticipating the vast tableau of the historical novel, *The Old and the Young,* in which Pirandello's Carduccian rail-ings and invective against the established political order find a more congenial narrative outlet. The oxymoronic title of Pirandello's first lyric collection, joy-ful ill, anticipates the concepts of the awareness and feeling of opposites at the core of the humorist's experience of life and art. The ambivalence of the term *giocondo* (joyful, or joyous), linked to the word *male,* which can signify ill-ness, difficulty, or even evil, suggests the dialectical conflict at the heart of Pirandellian discourse.

Pirandello's university years in Germany saw some shift in the contents of his verse, inspired in part by his romantic attachment to the lively Jenny Schulz-Lander. Composed while at the university, *Pasqua di Gea* (1891, The Easter of Gea, or Earth) and the later *Elegie renane* (1895, Rhenish Elegies) display Carduccian influence on their tone and form (the employment of the elegiac distich and "barbarian" rhymes made popular by Carducci) but also acknowl-edge foreign voices discovered in Bonn, such as the German Romantics. Springlike in theme and imagery, *Pasqua di Gea* emphasizes a pagan view of the "resurrection" of nature in its endless cycles through the motif of Mother Earth's acceptance, or rejection, of the Sun's fertilizing rays. The volume pro-poses a mythic allegory for the reawakening of earth and love which Pirandello will later employ to dramatic effect in his development of maternal archetypes. But the poems also suggest that nature deceives humanity with her beauty, concealing bitter realities. Moving from birth to death, the *Elegie renane* contrast the wintry landscape of northern Europe's Rhein valley to the poet's sunny Mediterranean roots. These lyric confessions of isolation and disorientation in a foreign land subtly hint at the motif of Sicilianism that permeates Pirandello's writing. *Fuori di chiave* (1912, Off Key) is the most Pirandellian of the writer's poetry volumes as well as being his last. Its title captures the contents: a lyric exploration of the individual's inability to harmonize either with himself or with others, within the fragmentation of reality and personality. Briefly stated, the motifs of Pirandello the poet are essentially those of Pirandello the storyteller and dramatist.

As a writer of short stories, or *novelle,* Pirandello was heir to a time-honored Italian literary tradition dating back to the Middle Ages. The author's fascination with the genre was life-long, beginning in adolescence and continuing throughout his maturation as a novelist and playwright. The short story immediately proved a congenial medium for expressing the stirrings of his rich imagination. Pirandello returned to the genre regularly throughout his creative life; he first published his compact narratives singly in numerous periodicals, then collected them in volume after volume, totaling fifteen and more by the time he died. Pirandello's first book of stories was issued in the 1880s, the last in the 1920s. In fact, the author's last published tale appeared in print the day before his death, although the majority of his stories were penned at the same time as the longer fiction. After signing with the prestigious Mondadori publishing house, Pirandello conceived the ambitious plan for *Novelle per un anno.* This final collection was to have included twenty-four volumes with fifteen stories contained in each. Fifteen volumes had been prepared and more than two hundred and thirty tales written by the time of the author's death. *Novelle* consists of previously published and revised stories, as well as new ones expressly written for the project. All of the writer's ample production is found in a two-volume edition of *Novelle per un anno,* edited by Corrado Alvaro for Mondadori in 1956/1957. Mondadori continues to issue the collection and has added stories left in manuscript form by the writer, variants, and single tales not included in any specific volume. In recent years the publishing house has prepared a new multivolumed critical edition of this work.

Novelle per un anno is a vast fresco of life colored in Pirandellian hues. The tone of the tales varies between comic, tragic, and grotesque, but, taken as a whole, the stories encompass the vast array of human experiences, thus leading critics to define the book as a variation of the *comédie humaine* (human comedy). Pirandello's characters range from the poorest of peasants to the aristocratic upper crust, with everything in between. They are often depicted during a single critical episode, an event that defines them by marking their existence permanently. Like his first novels Pirandello's earlier *novelle* were influenced by his involvement in verismo, Italian naturalism. Following in the footsteps of his literary mentors, Luigi Capuana and Giovanni Verga, the younger Sicilian storyteller also draws a pessimistic portrait of insular human life, stifled by social conventions and threatened by a tragic fatalism. Unlike his fellow Sicilians, however, Pirandello often adds the ingredients of his own fictional mix: irony and paradox—his well-known humor. The irrational pervades these narratives; characters fall prey to chance as the unexpected intrudes upon them, all attempts at controlling life being futile. As in Pirandello's novels the injection of the incongruous undermines the authorial objectivity and distance theorized by naturalism.

The world of the *novelle* is marked by the suffusion of pain, an absurd cruelty that touches every individual, thereby lightly echoing Verga's motif of the vanquished. Death and defeat emerge as major motifs in Pirandello's short stories. Numerous characters display resignation, bitterness, isolation, and surrender to a fate they cannot alter. A poignant rendering of this theme is found in the story "Prima notte" (1900, "The First Night"), the account of a melancholy wedding day. Death and loss are the reigning metaphors throughout the unfolding plot. The groom is a gentle older man, the local cemetery custodian and gravedigger; the submissive young bride weeps not with joy, but with dejection, at the thought of leaving her widowed mother's poor home; the trousseau chest resembles a coffin; the wedding procession leaves the couple at the gates of the burial grounds, where Marastella will make her new home. With the arrival of darkness the newlyweds spend the first hours of their life together alone; they are communing with the dead: the groom talking to his first wife at her grave, the bride weeping at the tomb of a beloved fiancé who perished in a fishing mishap. It is a marriage of pathos and heartbreak, a wedding transmuted into a funeral. The "two black shadows" residing in the house of the dead are drawn to their ghosts and sad memories. While the structure of "The First Night" follows the naturalist pattern of documenting social customs, regional types, and lifestyles, the story eschews the concept of impersonality by involving the reader in its sentimental tone and allusive imagery. Another vanquished man initially conceived in the naturalist vein, the clerk Belluca of "Il treno ha fischiato" (1914, "The Train Whistled") finds himself physically and psychologically overwrought by the unending struggle to support a dozen dependents. The monotony of Belluca's gray existence is shattered, however, by a

Pirandellian moment, a turning point, that liberates the clerk from his drudgery. The distant whistle of a train, heard in a state of semiconsciousness, opens new vistas of the imagination. Belluca discovers an exciting universe of travel and beauty in the voyages of his mind, only to be institutionalized as a madman. Back in society the clerk can nevertheless reach out to the world beyond his bleak walls whenever a train whistle invites him on the journey to jungles or mountains, forests or remote countries. Belluca has found a defense against the oppression of everyday life: the free flow of the imagination can invent realities of its own. Like many Pirandellian solutions it is a fragile victory. Belluca must guard against society's intrusions into his private sphere, for society is all too ready to define his joy as madness.

The precariousness of the Pirandellian universe, fraught with death, loss, chance, and fragmentation, does not necessarily lead to defeatism. The writer's characters often exhibit a strong instinct for survival and rebellion, for wanting to live and be free, like the late Mattia Pascal or the clerk Belluca. At other times death, or possibly suicide, is the avenue of escape rather than of destruction, as in "La veste lunga" (1913, "The Long Dress"). Sixteen-year-old Didì is being forced to abandon her adolescent dreams. Coerced into a marriage of convenience by her father, the girl analyzes her past and future during a symbolic train journey, a voyage of self-discovery. She realizes the trusting love she placed in her father has been reciprocated with self-interest. He has sold her like a valuable commodity to the highest bidder, thus condemning her to unhappiness while providing for his own economic security. Her revulsion is so keen that the girl reacts violently. Wearing her first long dress, the emblem of entry into the adult world of disappointment, sexuality, and hopelessness, Didì chooses rebellion against a fate she cannot envision. She makes her final journey into death ironically by swallowing her heartless father's heart medication. Like many Pirandellian works "The Long Dress" also adumbrates the failure of family as an institution meant to shield its members from external dangers through love and solidarity. Didì, attacked by those meant to protect and cherish her, like other Pirandellian children, siblings, spouses, and parents, is at the mercy of her own.

Not all representations of death in Pirandello's tales are tragic or melancholy. A comic vein, nurtured by the author's developing concept of humor, sets the tone for many of the stories, such as "La vita nuda" (1907, "Naked Truth"). The *vita,* or Life, in question is an allegorical statue to be sculpted for the tomb of the well-to-do Miss Consalvi's dead fiancé. Life will be represented embracing a skeleton, Death. Since the memorial designates her rejection of life after the terrible loss suffered and commemorates her eternal devotion to the dead, the bereaved woman wants Life to bear her features. As an upright lady, however, Miss Consalvi insists that the allegorical figure be clothed, against the sculptor's better judgment and counter to artistic convention. In the images of the tomb sculpture, Pirandello has symbolized the recurring dialectic of his fictional universe: the conflict between life and form. After repeated sittings for the artist, Miss Consalvi discovers that life is not immobile marble but fluid mutability. Having come to commemorate the dead and her own death in life, the young woman finds love again in the sculptor. In the end Life will be nude but deprived of Miss Consalvi's beautiful features; instead it will be fixed as a generic figure. It remains a paradoxical image, however, for the movement of life can never be stilled in the embrace of death, an absolute form.

Comic paradox is also the focus of Pirandello's second novel, whose plot is related to farce rather than drama. Like *The Outcast, Il Turno* (1902, *The Merry-Go-Round of Love*) is situated in the Sicily of small towns and little minds. The merry-go-round is set in motion by don Ravì, a well-meaning but authoritarian father who concocts an elaborate and somewhat amoral marital strategy for his pretty daughter Stellina. As the personification of paternal authority, don Ravì insists on marrying the girl to an elderly four-time widower who should soon leave her quite wealthy. Once she is free of the old spouse, the scheming father plans to see Stellina married to the attractive, noble, but not-so-prosperous Pepè Alletto, whose initial indolent attraction to the girl is flamed into ardor by don Ravì's machinations. In a typically Pirandellian fashion chance intervenes to spoil the best-laid plans of mice and fathers. Mooning over the unhappily married Stellina for months, the lovesick Pepè finally calls on his influential brother-in-law, the lawyer Ciro Coppa, a widower himself, to have the girl's abhorrent union dissolved. This aggressive attorney, in turn, falls in love with her, has the unconsummated marriage annulled, whisks her off to a convent, bullies her into submission, and weds Stellina in Pepè's place. However, the bilious Coppa dies suddenly, collapsing in a fit of rage after months of consuming jealousy. It can be assumed (or can it?) that the turn of the patient Pepè, who stands at Coppa's bedside, next to his young widow, has finally come. In the meantime the spry old widower contemplates taking a sixth bride, yet another opportunity to join the merry-go-round of love. In this succession of husbands and lovers, unpredictable events accompany the plot to an unanticipated resolution—making chance the real protagonist of the novel.

Beneath its amiable surface, *The Merry-Go-Round of Love* explores familiar Pirandellian topics. Readers are immediately struck by the capriciousness of life and the irrelevance of human attempts to manipulate it. Strong youthful men die while wizened oldsters survive; disconsolate lovers are betrayed by their chosen advocates; paternal affection is equal to tyranny; the most rational plans constructed by human logic are doomed to absurd failure, such as don Ravì's untenable marital schemes for Stellina. The novel implicitly levels an accusing finger at the institution of marriage and the structure of family life within the patriarchal environment of turn-of-the-century Sicily. Bullied twice into marriage, Stellina is no more than an object of the affections of a series of men who control her and subjugate her will. She submissively goes from the authority of her father to the authority of her husbands; she tries to accomodate them while being forever powerless to please herself. Although superficially comic the number of dead wives accumulated by Stellina's husbands is overwhelming: she has replaced five predecessors, seriously bringing into question the salubriousness of patriarchal marriage for women. Pirandello's vivid description of Sicilian courtship rituals, family life, and marital conventions places *The Merry-Go-Round of Love* in the naturalist tradition of social investigation and local color. But the institutions of marriage and family also function as a microcosm for society at large, where, effectively being coerced into conformity, the individual is trapped in roles by expectations, respectability, and custom.

The family is often the core of Pirandello's investigation of the human condition in the short stories as well as in the novels and plays. Nowhere is this clearer than in the stories set in a Sicilian locale, where issues of honor, religion, property, and position are played out in the "sacred" bosom of the family. This is a sun-scorched land of blood feuds and percolating emotions that is inhabited by primitive peasants, fishermen, and miners, provincial townspeople with their prejudices and quickness to judge, corrupt leaders, and indolent or overbearing aristocrats. Yet all share in the painful reality of living with the certainty of defeat. Some realistic tales describe the plight of the underclass with an intermingling of sympathy and bitter social commentary, as in "Il libretto rosso" (1911, "The Little Red Booklet"). The narrative concerns a poor family with numerous children which takes in foundlings to provide dowries for the older daughters. To insure the survival of her offspring, Rosa Marenga nurses foster children, but her milk is uncertain. Therefore she has trouble obtaining the red booklet which allocates her payments, allowing the family to subsist. Undernourished, the most recent baby in her care voraciously sucks his thumb, which grows monstrously while he withers. To underscore his point, Pirandello contrasts the wedding preparations of Rosa's fourth daugther to the infant's slow death: the woman is securing the future of her child at the expense of another being. The irony is that, after the baby's demise, Rosa applies for, and receives, yet another foundling and another red booklet. Also set among the impoverished Sicilian peasantry, "L'altro figlio" (1905, "The Other Son") is a poignant tale of frustrated familial loves. Having been widowed and raped during the war for Italian unification, the elderly Maragrazia despairs at the remoteness of her two older sons, who have emigrated and never communicate with their grieving mother. The other son, Rocco, is devoted but repeatedly rejected by Maragrazia, who sees only the image of her murdering rapist imprinted on this son's body and face. The good-hearted Rocco reaches out futilely to his mother. She, in turn, vainly seeks out her absent sons in letter after letter. But her words cannot reach them because they have never been written: the letters are no more than an undecipherable scrawl deceptively produced by a woman as illiterate as Maragrazia herself. Emblematic of the impossibility of rapport between parent and child(ren), the counterfeit letters signify the unanswered loves of both Maragrazia and Rocco, whose words and feelings cannot be interpreted by their intended recipients. On a basic, instinctive level, "The Other Son" demonstrates Pirandello's thesis that individuals, no matter how close their relationship, cannot achieve profound and effective communication.

The social indictment of poverty inherent in many of Pirandello's Sicilian-based tales is particularly potent in the story of the sulphur miners, "Ciàula scopre la luna" (1912, "Ciàula Discovers the Moon"). Ciàula, the crow, has been a miner's helper since childhood and has grown into a grotesque figure of a man. Filthy, more animal than human, and mentally deficient, the young man caws rather than speaks, smiling mindlessly. He inhabits the underground tunnels of the mine, which is his home and his prison. His world is the gloom of the shafts and the sun-scorched moonscape of the mining property seen only when he emerges from his labyrinth with his load; he is more beast of burden than worker. Ciàula, at home in the blackness of the mine, is afraid of the natural darkness of the night. A creature of man-made shadows, he cannot adjust to the mysterious world of unlit nature. Obviously Ciàula's fear and dehumanization are the consequences of the exploitation and brutalization received at the abusive hands of men. Yet a spark of humanity is left, even in such a creature. Fearfully emerging from his pit one night, he discovers the full moon in all its nocturnal splendor, illuminating the darkness. In ecstasy the youth bursts into tears of joy; he experiences an epiphany as the powerful beauty of nature heals and nurtures him, thus making the crow a man once again, if only for a moment "in the night now filled with his wonderment."[2]

Sulphur mines also figure prominently in Luigi Pirandello's only historical novel *I vecchi e i giovani* (1913, *The Old and the Young*). As Carlo Salinari has shown, Pirandello's developmental years in Sicily strongly influenced his political and moral attitudes. An heir to the idealistic, even heroic, view of man's ability to mold history, a view fostered by the Risorgimento, Pirandello soon joined the ranks of the disillusioned, who found concrete reality far less admirable or satisfactory. The young, in particular, felt defrauded by the mediocrity of their newly formed country, which had been established with glorious dreams of solidarity. Unlike Pirandello's other novels, which focus on a single individual or family, *The Old and the Young* returns to Sicily to present a sweeping picture of the social events which dominated the island in the 1890s. Pirandello himself defined it "a very bitter and populous novel" that enclosed the drama of his Sicilian generation. As a historical novel, various factual occurrences are depicted: the rise of the Sicilian middle class; the development of the socialist fasces, a revolt of long-suffering, enraged peasants and sulphur miners against the establishment; the atmosphere of social agitation leading to the proclamation of a state of siege—followed by military repression, the political victory of the Catholic forces, and the Banca Romana financial scandal which shook the peninsula. The author's brush is pessimistic, painting a tableau of collective and personal failures ranging from the betrayal of the romantic ideals of the struggle for unification to the fall of southern Italian socialism, not to mention madness and murder. Numerous characters weave in and out of a complex narrative of ambitions, class conflict, personal corruption, doomed loves, and human loss. Idealistic creators of the new state in the 1860s, the old are responsible in part for the demise of patriotic ideals and for the state of current ills. The young, in turn, are caught in crystallized social structures that suffocate them. It is a bitter vision without moderating illusions. Individuals give way to forces greater than themselves in a world filled with misfits and alienated souls. In this novel individual turmoil flows uneasily into historical chaos.

Set in Girgenti and Rome, the two poles of Pirandello's own life, the novel is a far-reaching portrayal of familiar environments and human types. Chronicling the events leading to the Sicilian fasces, the novel's lengthy cast of characters numbers cabinet ministers, sharecroppers, entrepreneurs, and nobles among the old generation who witnessed the promise born of the struggle for unification and its subsequent betrayal. Their children, the young generation, struggle to establish themselves in a changing society. The failed illusions of Pirandello's only historical novel are basically social—liberty, justice, equality, patriotism—but they are also experienced as individual losses by each of the novel's many protagonists. These are drawn primarily from two important extended families, their progeny, and dependents: the declining Laurentanos, an old aristocratic line, and the rising Salvos, ambitious and unscrupulous capitalists. Other, secondary characters are drawn from the peasant and working classes who come into contact with members of the Laurentano and Salvo clans. The actual protagonists number in the dozens in a loosely interwoven fabric of criss-crossing relationships. Throughout the novel public and private spheres repeatedly intersect each other, merging and separating. Involved in a number of historical events, the protagonists of *The Old and the Young* confront life's illusions and respond with varying degrees of awareness or wreckage as they pass through tragic loves, fatal ambitions, political idealism, social activism, inappropriate marriages, or doomed liaisons. Death and dementia follow in their wake. Often there is no logic to the events that shape or break the characters' lives. One such example is provided by the absurd death of the peasant Mauro Mortara, a decorated veteran of the Unification campaigns who dies needlessly at the hands of the army he supports while seeking peace. Mortara embodies the demise of his generation's profoundest ideal: a unified egalitarian country.

History, Pirandello suggests, is just as irrational as individual existence; without order or meaning it is inherently contradictory. In *The Old and the Young* the collective failure of history is reflected in a series of individual failures. In the words of Douglas Radcliff-Umstead: "throughout the apparently isolated cases of tortured individuals, the novelist attempted to demonstrate how history should be considered another of man's ideal constructions that no conscious or unconscious self-deception could prevent from crumbling in time."[3] It has been suggested that *The Old and the Young* depicts not just the failure of a specific period (Italy in the 1890s), a specific geographical area (Sicily), and a specific sociopolitical environment, but the far broader failure of an entire belief system and social structure: namely, the demise of the great credos of nineteenth-century bourgeois capitalist society. Taking this modernist argument one step further, the novel has been interpreted as a metaphor for the crisis of history itself—or, more precisely, for the crisis of the makers of history: men and women. Every character who seeks to act for change—no matter under which political banner—fails miserably. Every protagonist who gives in to his or her passions, whether amatory, sexual, ideological, or mercenary, fails just as miserably. There are no exits and no alternatives: the universe of *The Old and the Young* is unrelievedly pessimistic and nihilistic.[4]

What distinguishes this novel stylistically from Pirandello's other long fiction is the positioning of the narrative voice. Nino Borsellino has demonstrated that *The Old and the Young* follows the literary canon for historical novels that was established by Alessandro Manzoni (1785–1873) in *I Promessi Sposi* (1827/ 1840, *The Betrothed*), Italy's greatest and most influential nineteenth-century novel. Unlike the conventions fostered by naturalist theoreticians, Manzoni espoused the employment of an omniscient author who controls the interweaving of narrative threads, exposes character and historical motivations, and determines the mix of invention and fact in the novel—strategies used by Pirandello in his own work.[5] The third-person narration in *The Old and the Young* does not function in the same objectifying way as the naturalist style of *The Outcast* or *The Merry-Go-Round of Love* nor does it resemble the use of subjectively self-conscious interior monologues, occasionally bordering on stream of consciousness, found in *The Late Mattia Pascal, Shoot!,* and *One, No One, and One Hundred Thousand.* Pirandello's only historical novel projects a distinct authorial viewpoint of its own. Instead of centering on the analysis and musings of a single protagonist or narrator, *The Old and the Young* emphasizes a social perspective by describing an entire society in decay, enmeshed in its own paralysis, as presented by an omniscient narrator whose views are neither objective nor uninvolved.

Not all Pirandello's depictions of Sicilian life focus on dissolution or death, however. As in *The Merry-Go-Round of Love* and *Liolà,* several short stories employ comic elements to express the authorial voice and convey meaning. Both "La giara" (1909, "The Jar") and "Il capretto nero" (1913, "The Black Kid")[6] offer a Sicily of sunshine, countryside, song, and eccentrics. "The Jar" is one of Pirandello's best-known tales, as well as being the source for a play by the same title and for a popular ballet set to music by Alfredo Casella (1924). Don Lollò Zirafa is a wealthy landowner with a volatile temper and two compulsions: his attachment to *la roba,* or property, and his fondness for litigation. With his easily bruised ego and quickness to blame, don Lollò initiates repeated lawsuits which he regularly loses, squandering much of his considerable *roba.* His antagonist is Zi' Dima Licasi, one of Pirandello's most successful *macchiette.* A charmingly grotesque figure, Licasi is as gnarled as an olive branch and has an air of aloof sadness and contempt proper to misunderstood genius. Zi' Dima is the unheralded inventor of a magnificent glue that none of his conservative clients trusts him enough to use. Having acquired a large, round, and expensive amphora for storing olive oil—a "Mother Superior" of jars— don Lollò is obliged to hire Zi' Dima to repair a substantial crack. He demands, however, that rivets be added to Dima's wonder glue. Forced to wire the rivets from within, the offended Zi' Dima becomes trapped in the well-cemented jar, which must be broken to free him. Ever litigious, don Lollò, refusing to liberate the workman until he pays for the jar, consults his lawyer. A proud if poor man, Dima declares his innocence, cozily settles into his clay prison for the duration, and peacefully puffs away at his pipe. In the middle of the night, don Lollò is awakened by revelling farmhands. Drunk, they are dancing round the inhabited amphora, accompanied by Zi' Dima's loud singing. The furious Lollò Zirafa kicks the jar, which rolls away and splits open, freeing its prisoner. Zi' Dima has scored his victory. As this brief plot summary suggests, "The Jar" is one of Pirandello's more theatrical tales; it is filled with visual images, movement, dialogue, and physical farce. As in *Liolà* the serious implications of the plot—social distinctions, capitalist greed, self-serving egotism, oppression of the working class—are suppressed in favor of a comic development reminiscent of traditional folktales in which the "little guy" has the last laugh. Indeed, the final tableau of the story resembles a pagan celebration of Dionysus, god of wine and fertility. The image of inebriated peasants illuminated by a full moon and circling a make-shift altar of sorts (the jar) in a frenzy of song and dance brings the story to its culmination, functioning as a visual echo of the rites of ancient Magna Grecia.

Sicily's pagan past also figures prominently in "The Black Kid." Set in Pirandello's Girgenti, the *novella* focuses on two English protagonists: Mr. Charles Trockley, the British vice consul, and his vivacious guest, Miss Ethel Holloway, a young tourist. Trockley is the stereotypical English gentleman taken to extremes: exact, punctilious, pedantic, methodical, and unimaginative. Miss Holloway is his opposite: joyful, impetuous, uncontrolled, and emotional. As a pair the two personify familiar Pirandellian antitheses: youth/age, thought/emotion, male/female, mind/nature, life/form. These oppositional personalities clash in their differing perceptions of history and goats. On a visit to the splendid Greek ruins one fine spring day, Mr. Trockley arrives, Baedeker in hand and a substantial number of historical facts in mind, intent on properly educating the recalcitrant Miss Holloway on the local sights. The impetuous Miss is far more taken with living fauna than dead temples, however, which provides an amusing example of the conflict between life's fluidity and the deadening power of form. The goats, grazing in the shadows of the magnificent ruins, stir indignation in the gentleman, high spirits in the young lady. Miss Holloway is smitten with a mad, passionate affection for a graceful black kid that Trockley finds inherently repulsive. But ever the good host, the vice consul purchases the animal for his enamored guest and promises to care for it until Miss Holloway returns to England and sends for it. Months later, after several misadventures, the gentleman keeps his word and ships the fully grown goat to its anxious owner, only to receive a vituperative letter in reply. Miss Holloway declares the ugly beast an imposter, not her beloved black kid. Having done his duty to the letter, Mr. Trockley is taken aback, totally unable to comprehend the young woman's anger. It is up to a third character, the first-person narrator, a Sicilian (presumably Pirandello himself), to provide the interpretive keys to the tale. As the Sicilian suggests to Trockley, a substitution could have been made. A second sweet kid could have taken the place of the first, thereby bringing joy to Miss Holloway, who would never have doubted the little goat's identity. In her mind's eye the little black kid would never grow up. The reasonable Trockley, however, sees no point in such a ruse: it is illogical, unlikely, and dishonest. Reason (Trockley) cannot comprehend the positive nature of Illusion (Holloway). In Pirandello's universe the rational and the imaginative, facts and fictions, are destined to conflict. Only a humorist, like the Sicilian narrator, can merge opposites, thus creating a new perception of reality for himself and for others.

The stories of *Novelle per un anno* that treat self-aware protagonists caught in the vortex of their psyches often employ first-person narration as a means of entering consciousness itself, in order to directly experience the "I" being scrutinized. These characters are often psychologically traumatized, even mad. Their existence excludes them, yet they wrestle to find an identity and comfortable roles in a community bent on marginalizing them. At times violence is their response, directed either at others or themselves. Understandably suicide is a recurring topic. In the story "La carriola" (1916, "The Wheelbarrow"), the narrator is a respected professional, a success in business and family life. He is nevertheless ensnared in the Pirandellian tension of life's being constrained into forms. Each and every one of his multiple roles is "a death," as he puts it. The protagonist, mourning the infinite possibilities he will never know, yearns for other lives. His seemingly successful existence is a continuous series of masks that neither reflect nor fulfill the hungry inner self. The *novella*'s subject is alienation, from oneself and from others. Unlike Vitangelo Moscarda, however, this character does not seek to destroy the falseness of these "I's" but merely permits himself a daily dose of madness. Trapped by his self-consciousness, the narrator vindicates himself on a creature with no consciousness at all, with no sense of seeing itself living: the family dog. On a regular basis this apparently reasonable and satisfied man takes the pet by its hind legs, like a wheelbarrow, and walks it around his study, thereby giving vent to the controlled irrationality lying in wait within.

Late in his career as a storyteller, Pirandello was influenced by the literary experiments in European surrealism and Italian magic realism, popular literary trends of the 1920s and 1930s. Both movements specialized in planting the mysterious and diabolical within the seeming normalcy of everyday life and corresponded chronologically to Pirandello's examination of mythic structures and meanings in his drama. In some tales objective, knowable reality is put aside to make room for the fantastic. The exterior world crumbles, giving way to the bewildering dimensions of the irrational mind. In "Visita" (1935, "The Visit") the protagonist receives a formal call from a beautiful woman in white organdy with whom he had achieved a rare understanding during their one brief encounter three years earlier. The woman, however, is dead, killed by the same beautiful breasts that had initially drawn the narrator to her radiant flesh. Significantly, the visit takes place the day after her untimely death. Dream? Apparition? Wish fulfillment? All three possibilities are suggested by the perplexed narrator, whose personal mystification is transferred to the reader. In a similar story, "Soffio" (1931, Breath), the narrating protagonist discovers that he has attained the power to kill simply by blowing a particular type of breath in the direction of his victims. Soon the protagonist recognizes that he is death, impartial in his mortal dealings. In the end the narrator kills off his own double, his mirror image, emphasizing the human yearning for total dissolution and formlessness. Given the multiple significance of mirror images in Pirandello, the death of the reflected self also represents the destruction of self-awareness, personal fragmentation, and psychic distortion. It is the suicide of consciousness.

Drama

The contents of Pirandello's narrative universe are restated in the author's dramatic works, which are closely allied in theme and thought to his prose fiction. The critic E. Allen McCormick has pointed to this artistic fraternity by suggesting that novel, short story, and drama "derive their peculiar Pirandellian shape through the interplay of plot and commentary on plot" or, in dramatic terms, the fusion of "action and exposition of action."[7] Nor is it mere coincidence that half the plays were based on short stories or sections of novels. Fundamental Pirandellian themes are reworked in various genres, characterizations, and story lines throughout his long career, from the earliest poems to the final plays. To enumerate, these recurring motifs include the problem of identity and ontological being; the elusive, even illusory, nature of the personality; the unending mutability and fluidity of life; the lack of reliable fixed personal and social coordinates; the unattainability of absolute certainty; the indeterminancy of truth; the prevalence of relativity and flux; the occurrence of alienation and isolation within society; the imposition of masks and roles; the impossibility of authentic communication and the unreliability of words. These themes, employed with varying degrees of intensity and tone, are the conceptual framework for most of Luigi Pirandello's theater.

Like *Liolà* and *Cap and Bells,* Pirandello's early Sicilian plays stress the individual's relationship with his community, the construction of private and public masks, and the interplay of reality and illusion. Derived from previously published short stories, *Pensaci, Giacomino!* (1916, Think It Over, Giacomino!) and the one-acter *La patente* (1919, *The License*) are steeped in local color.[8] The first play depicts an elderly man, Professor Toti, who forments a great public scandal in his conservative Sicilian town. Unexpectedly taking a pregnant young wife, the professor sets up housekeeping with her lover as well, providing work for the young man, a name for the child, and happiness for himself. The crisis arises when the youth, Giacomino, is persuaded by his family and the local priest, the embodiment of public morality, to abandon mistress and child to marry a "proper" girl. Giacomino agrees, persuaded not only by their ethical arguments, but also by the social ridicule heaped upon him and the odd family he has joined. The weak youth cannot tolerate his difference and its social consequences. At the end, however, the old professor, hand in hand with "his" son, convinces Giacomino to return to their controversial ménage to await the day he can marry Lillina.

The principal in this sentimental play is the elderly Toti. After a frustrating life led in perfectly respectable drudgery, the professor rebels against the institutions and community that have suffocated him. The enemy of his newfound joy is the collective, which will not accept his choices. Initially Toti's marriage to Lillina is an act of passive rebellion against the many years of unappreciated labor for a community and government that exploited him by forcing him to live on meager wages. By leaving a young widow, he reckons the state will have to support her and the boy on his pension for many decades to come. Although it is clear Toti is not the biological father of Lillina's child, the community is willing to acknowledge this artificial construction as a reality. As in *Liolà* appearances, not facts, matter. However, the establishment of a ménage à trois is a public declaration of the fabricated nature of such a reality and is an unconventional act which will not be tolerated in this most conventional setting. Meek and gentle, Toti emerges as a revolutionary, an incendiary figure who challenges the validity of traditional institutions by defying conventional definitions of family, marriage, paternity, and love. Moreover, he is a corrupting influence, gradually leading the innately conventional Giacomino into accepting his odd logic, to await his turn at creating a socially acceptable life with Lillina. Like Toti the youth ceases to consider their situation indefensible and irrational. Unlike most Pirandellian characters the professor is a victor; he manages to sustain his constructed reality in the face of public censure. Finally, Toti is an embodiment of Pirandellian humor, a figure who appears ridiculous at first glance—an elderly husband who welcomes his wife's lover into the family. When the facts are known, this figure of comedy is transformed into a sympathetic character eliciting humor's understanding and pity.

Chiarchiaro, the protagonist of *The License,* is also a social outcast. This brief tragicomedy takes place in the office of a Sicilian judge who has undertaken a civil suit for defamation brought by the protagonist against an important man. Chiarchiaro, like Toti, is the victim of prejudice and ridicule. Unkempt, unpleasant, somewhat repulsive, he has gained the reputation of being a *iettatore,* the possessor of the evil eye. People avoid him on the street and make self-protective gestures as he passes. A few mock him. However unwarranted, this rumor has become Chiarchiaro's reality, bringing to mind the situation of Marta Ajala in *The Outcast.* Like her he has lost his position, and his suffering family is shunned. Total misery looms on the horizon because society accepts appearances over facts. Unable to deny the validity of the role inflicted upon him by local superstition, Chiarchiaro decides to don the mask as his reality, thus accepting the false identity imposed upon him. In an act of ferocious irony he is determined to transform his leprosy into an advantageous situation by turning the tables on the sadistic community. Rather than continue as society's victim, he will become its victimizer. Indeed, Chiarchiaro's rage for vengeance is so strong that it has been transformed into evil in his own mind.

To achieve his desired effect, the "bird of ill omen" has created a symbolic physical identity for himself, to "fit the role." His sallow face is hidden by an ugly beard, he wears huge round bone glasses that make him resemble a barn owl, his clothing is shiny and outsized, his teeth are yellowed, and he moves funereally, tapping the ground with his cane/wand. He is an actor offering a theatrical performance to an entire town, thereby validating their perception of his identity. Chiarchiaro's actions nevertheless declare for himself the inauthenticity of his being. The judge, a rational and sympathetic man, attempts to persuade the alleged spell caster to withdraw his complaint. But Chiarchiaro cannot be swayed. By losing the lawsuit, he will have "an official recognition of [his] power." Only this power, or the belief in it, is left him. By exercising it with a semiofficial license he will extort payment from local individuals and businesses who wish to avoid his evil presence. In this manner lies will become truth, and his poverty-stricken family will survive.

While Chiarchiaro and Toti, in different measure, elicit the humoristic feeling, or sense, of the opposite, evoking an empathetic reaction, the three protagonists of *L'uomo, la bestia e la virtú* (1919, *Man, Beast, and Virtue*) remain at the level of humoristic awareness, that is, of comedy. This risqué play is essentially farcical, based on the complications arising from a commonplace adulterous triangle: a tutor (man) loves the sweet but neglected wife (virtue) of a seafaring captain (beast). Like any standard farce the plot is characterized by visual humor and sudden complications. Nothing in the story line is presented very seriously, although the situation is serious indeed and could move toward tragic, as well as comic, resolution. The virtuous wife has been impregnated by the tutor, and the apathetic husband must be made to respond to her sexually before departing on another journey, so that the child will be considered his. The situation is further complicated by the captain's arrangements: a lecher, he keeps a concubine and second family elsewhere while pursuing available women in every port. His visits home have become a means of obtaining a welcome sexual lull. The tutor, as the brains of the operation, concocts a series of strategems: an aphrodisiac is baked into the cake; the wife is made up to re-semble a harlot, thus appealing to her husband's lower nature; flowerpots are to be placed on the balcony as signals of success. In one memorable scene at the end of act 2, the "presumed" identity of the main protagonists is captured in an ironic tableau: the wife assumes the pose of the Virgin Annunciate, her lover that of the archangel Gabriel holding out a potted lily. In visual language Pirandello has defined the lover's perception of his beloved: virginal in her maternity, pure in heart, Madonna-like. This contrasts sharply with the painted woman the tutor fabricates to seduce the captain. Of course, neither image is valid. What makes this tableau, and the whole play, Pirandellian is its dichoto-mous, even duplicitous, quality. The action is filled with deceptions and concealments as roles and poses are manufactured to hide the actual nature of things. Reality and appearance are once again the playwright's central issue. The virginal virtuous wife is unescapably pregnant by a man who is not her husband; the rational ethical lover lectures against hypocrisy but lives it; pre-ferring a chaste rapport with his spouse, the animalistic husband wants no part of sexuality. Nothing, Pirandello appears to be saying, is really what it seems—at least not on the evidence of mere appearance. As in all comedies the ending is a happy one. The baby will be legitimate for the world, including the duped husband, while the lovers can continue their liaison with discretion. But, as always in Pirandello's comic works, there is the hint of a bitter aftertaste. The difference between virtue and bestiality is not clearcut. For all his ethical pos-turing, the lover, as representative man, contains within himself more than a little of the beast.

The subject matter of Pirandello's Sicilian works are also present in his bourgeois dramas. Accompanying the need to maintain beneficial illusions to survive in an antagonistic world, masks are prominent features of the drawing-room plays. At times Pirandello's characters unexpectedly come face to face with their externally imposed identities—even discovering an entire lifetime built on illusory perceptions—with painful consequences. This is the case of Martino Lori, protagonist of *Tutto per bene* (1920, *All for the Best*). For years the widower Lori has held the belief that he had been happily married to an honest woman whose memory he venerates. For years he has not understood his only child's indifference, even antipathy, toward him. By chance all is unintentionally revealed by the young woman when she mistakes Lori for his friend and mentor, the rich Senator Manfroni, her biological father. Suddenly Lori comes face to face with his illusory images: a faithful wife, a beloved daughter, a great friend. He intuits that he has lived a fiction: he is the husband of another man's woman and the father of another man's child. His pain is heightened because he now perceives himself as society, even his own daughter, believes him to be. In their eyes he is a complaisant, if not conniving, cuckold and a self-serving sycophant. In short, Martino Lori's life has been a misunderstanding. Lori's identity comes crashing down around him, as it had for Vitangelo Moscarda once he looked into his mirror. Like Moscarda, Lori has found that the man he believed himself to be—the inner self—was not the self others knew, not even those closest to him. Therefore he must reassess his past and reevaluate his relationships while trying to reclaim an authentic self. Yet Lori's fate is not totally bleak. He comes to understand the sincerity of his wife's devotion in their final years together, regains the affectionate respect of a daughter who no longer believes he is a hypocritical pimp, and unmasks the gracious Manfroni as a dishonorable cad. Like many Pirandellian characters Lori has discovered the terrible power exerted on individuals by appearances and masks. He emerges a stronger man in the end, but he will continue in his roles, if consciously so. Paradoxically, all may be for the best.

Dual identity is also the guiding concept of *Come tu mi vuoi* (1930, *As You Desire Me*), which offers one of Pirandello's most powerful female protagonists. The woman in question is literally an enigma, designated only as *L'ignota* (the unknown woman) in the stage directions. Sensually beautiful, she is the object of multiple desires; undefined, she bends to the identities imposed upon her by others. The woman, called Elma in act 1, may be an amnesiac, although this is not perfectly clear. Her memory loss is one possible symbolic key to understanding the fluidity of identity, the absence of certainty, and the subjectivity of truth in the play. The first act is set in the decadent Berlin of the late 1920s, the environment Elma inhabits. She is a cabaret dancer with a series of past lovers and a drinking problem. Currently she is involved with Carl Salter, a writer whom she torments with fictions of her past by inventing situations and men to function as appropriate backdrops to the exotic and decadent woman she has become. When Bruno Pieri (re)enters her life, believing she is his long-lost wife, Cia, she takes the chance to start afresh, ready to assume another's life—a real past—to fill her inner voids. She wishes to empty her mind of all memories and become pure body, a body without a name waiting for someone to take it.

Traces of the actual Lucia Pieri were lost during the First World War, after the beautiful young wife was raped and dragged from her destroyed villa in northern Italy by a platoon of German soldiers. Notwithstanding the agonies endured by the "real" Cia or the corrupt, self-destructive lifestyle of Elma, the Unknown embodies Cia's youthful portrait, recalling the painting of Matilda brought to life in *Henry IV*. This undeniable physical resemblance does not satisfy the missing woman's family, however. They demand better proof, real documents, absolute certainty. As for Elma/Cia, history, documentation, and proof are all irrelevant. She is willing to assume Cia's identity, to be Cia to perfection, to construct her moment by moment. She models herself tirelessly to resemble every element of the lost bride: in her clothing, in her thoughts, in her inner being. She is giving a name to her body. Spiritual integrity emanates from the protagonist: the Unknown wishes to be accepted as Cia on faith, not proof, by those who say they love her. She says nothing to deceive them into believing she is Cia, nor does she deny it.

Desire defines the Unknown. In act 1 Elma is the object of the sexual affections of both Salter and his lesbian daughter, Mop, as they live together in un uneasy truce, each attempting to manipulate her through shows of morbid solicitude or contained threats. Her beauty is an exotic magnet, as demonstrated by her initial stage entrance; tipsy, she enters surrounded by four young drunks and a satanically masked protector. Once she loves Bruno, the Unknown willingly agrees to fill herself with his memories of Cia, to become the woman *he* desires, although his lingering doubts about her identity are never assuaged. The dramatic crisis explodes when she discovers that Bruno's desires also include Cia's inheritance. Added to the relatives' incorrect perception of her as a gold-digging imposter, the Unknown rejects her new situation for she is determined to find an identity of her own, neither borrowed from the past nor defined by external images. She will not lend her body any further. When Salter comes to fetch her back to Berlin, bringing a second, plausible Cia with him, she leaves. This second Cia is a demented creature who has spent many years in an asylum, yet she bears some resemblance to the missing wife. As the Unknown declares, the poor woman is a likely embodiment of the anguish and trauma suffered by the real Cia over the years.

The protagonist of *As You Desire Me* is an enigma to the end. She is Elma, Cia, no one: a multiplicity of selves and identities, none of which is absolute, all of which are constructs in their own way. As the Unknown states, Elma means water in Arabic; moving with the flow and mutability of life itself, she is as fluid as her adopted name. Her departure from Bruno's house is an intuitive recognition of an inner identity struggling to be articulated, seeking authenticity. It is an identity not founded on the past but constructed from the elements of her present, an identity subject to change but also to self-construction. The issue of the Unknown's factual identity is never resolved. The dialogue hints at multiple possibilities. She knows she is Lucia. She knows she is not. Or she may or may not know anything. If nothing is known, than everything or nothing can be possible. The character departs the stage as she entered it: a living symbol of ambiguity, a doubt to be answered according to each onlooker's perception, like Mrs. Ponza in *Right You Are*. As for herself, the Unknown has discovered that *essere è farsi*—being is making oneself.

Final Thoughts

Luigi Pirandello was one of the first writers to give voice to the dilemma of modern men and women, exhibiting what Carlo Salinari rightly calls "the awareness of crisis," a feeling for the inherent absurdity of life and a sense of human anguish when faced with chaos and nothingness. Signaling the end of a belief in a structured and well-ordered universe, Pirandello opened the doors to anarchy and angst; his works toll a death knell for nineteenth-century optimism with its faith in the human ability to shape reality and mold life. The author challenged the postulates of Western civilization by subverting their very existence. Denying the possibility of an objective reality, declaring the individual's fundamental unknowability and multiplicity, stressing the inherent fluidity of life and truth, and acknowledging the preponderance of chance, Pirandello created a tragicomic vision of the human condition. These concepts shaped future generations of Western artists and intellectuals, from Brecht to the Existentialists, from Ionesco to Sartre. Pirandello's characters are caught in uncertainties, trapped in masks, and unable to forge some measure of meaning in their existence without resorting to extreme actions. They are disoriented and anxious, struggling to establish a fragile inner balance to counteract the chaos surrounding them. Such attempts are illusory but necessary to survival. Using logic to signify the irrational, often the self-aware protagonist seeks to control his inner turmoil by rationalizing it. For this reason Pirandello has often been considered a cerebral writer, a philosopher of sorts, whose spokespeople are his heroes, eloquently arguing their points in a continuous dialectic with themselves, society, their audience, and life itself.

Luigi Pirandello continues to intrigue and challenge readers and audiences internationally. His legacy is vast. There is the sheer bulk of his work. There are the revolutionary theater plays, which altered the course of drama, so much so that the Nobel Prize Committee of 1934 singled out "his bold and brilliant renovation of the drama and the stage." For decades Pirandello's influence was felt in international theater and can be traced in playwrights such as Cocteau, Garcia Lorca, O'Neill, Anouilh, Camus, Yeats, Albee, Ionesco, Genet, and De Filippo. Pirandello's works continue to be rendered in today's most popular artistic medium—film—proving their universality and staying power in this new "form." The author is still read and produced across the world as the ever growing list of translations into foreign languages attest. And in his native land, Italy, he remains one of the luminaries of modern literature. Indeed, in 1985, the reputable newspaper *La Stampa* polled its readers on their favorite Italian novels: *The Late Mattia Pascal,* published in 1904, made the top ten. In the United States *Six Characters in Search of an Author* remains a staple in amateur and university productions.

As a modernist Pirandello captures the contradictory and disintegrating sense of the world surrounding humankind. It is a world where chaos, chance, and the irrational prevail, confronting individuals with absurd situations that challenge logic. Pirandello's fictional universe also challenges naturalist concepts of verisimilitude to express a universe without reason, certainty, or structures of belief. Moving from adherence to the objective world of verismo, the author became a symbol for the new subjective perception, or self-consciousness, that entered the cultural arena at the turn of the century. Having declared the relativity of truth and the inconsistency of the human personality in his uniquely humorous manner, Luigi Pirandello proposed some of the major themes of contemporary literature in his own works. The list is impressive: the individual's fractured sense of identity, the oppressive nature of society, the impossibility of words to communicate or interpret, the insufficiency of reason, the conflict between appearances and reality, the pain of living, the difficulty if not impossibility of authenticity, the categorization of the individual into socially determined roles, the fruitless search for absolutes, the existence of unconscious motivations, and the condemnation of traditional institutions as instruments of coercion. Pirandello's significance as a writer may well derive from his ability to give these concepts human form and individual names—the life of art—as the immortal characters of dramatic fiction and stirring theater.

Notes

Chapter 1: The International Provincial

1. From *Si gira! Quaderni di Serafino Gubbio, operatore* (*Shoot! The Notebooks of Serafino Gubbio, Cinematograph Operator,* 1915), Quaderno Quarto, 3 (Book Four, #3). My translation.

2. Titled "L'informazione sul mio involontario soggiorno sulla terra" (Information on my involuntary sojourn on earth), this autobiographical sketch was posthumously published in *Almanacco Letterario Bompiani* (Bompiani Literary Almanac) in 1938. The unfinished piece is generally quoted by Pirandello's biographers, such as Giudice (pp. 3–4).

3. This is one example of the serendipitous junctures occasionally found in mythological and literary allusion: Gaea, the divinity representing earth, is the offspring of Chaos.

4. These reflections are found in the letters written to Maria Antonietta Portulano during her brief engagement with Pirandello. The correspondence is dated December 1893 and January 1894. As is often the case with Pirandello, the demarcations between private and public writing, genres, and literary works are muddy. The private discussion of his two selves easily finds its way into the literary works "Dialoghi tra il Gran Me e il piccolo me" (Dialogues between the Big Me and the little me) of 1895 and 1897.

5. See especially Séailles's *Essai sur le Génie dans l'art* (Essay on Genius in Art). Paris: Alcon, 1883. For more information on these and other intellectual influences on Pirandello's ideas, consult Anthony Caputi. *Pirandello and the Crisis of Modern Consciousness.* Urbana and Chicago: University of Illinois Press, 1988, particularly chapters 1 and 5: "A World of Words" and "Relativity and the Fictions of the Spirit." Caputi has a substantial discussion of Pirandello's writings on art, consciousness, and science. Other informative sources are Olga Ragusa. *Luigi Pirandello: An Approach to His Theatre.* Edinburgh: Edinburgh University Press, 1980, and the section titled "Pirandello's World" in *A Companion to Pirandello Studies.* Ed. John Louis Di Gaetani. New York, Westport, Conn., and London: Greenwood Press, 1991, in which articles cover several related topics including Pirandello's use of philosophy and theosophy.

6. Leonardo Sciascia attributes Antonietta's mental fragility to environmental factors, citing the Sicilian tendency to conceive of family members as "roba," or exclusive possessions, which leads to the seclusion of women as well as to intemperate manifestations of jealousy. Antonietta Portulano had been raised in a restricted, conservative environment by a possessive father and never adapted to her husband's life choices and ambitions. Her extreme jealous possessiveness of her spouse was one of the main indicators of her disease.

7. Quoted by Eric Bentley in *The Pirandello Commentaries*. Evanston, Ill.: Northwestern University Press, 1986. P. 81.

8. See Antonio Gramsci. "Il Teatro di Pirandello." *Letteratura e Vita Nazionale.* 6th ed., Turin: Einaudi, 1966. P. 48. First published in 1950.

9. In Italy and elsewhere there is an established critical tendency to define Pirandello as a "Sicilian" writer. Leonardo Sciascia, for example, views the motif of the dissolution of individual identity as an aspect of Pirandello's Sicilianism rather than as a reflection of the vaster Western crisis of identity. Sciascia also categorizes Pirandellian dialectic as a Sicilian folk phenomenon. In addition to emphasizing the obvious Sicilian settings of many Pirandellian works and celebrating the writer's "roots," critics also point to specific regional attributes they contend distinguish Sicilians from Italians and other Westerners, such as an inclination to argumentation, philosophizing and mythmaking. The initiator of this Sicilian interpretation was Pier Maria Rosso di San Secondo, Pirandello's close friend and a fellow dramatist. In an essay dated 1916, Rosso writes about an innate tragic sense possessed by Sicilians which makes them transform any youthful enthusiasm into bitter silence as they hermetically imprison themselves in their disappointments. See "Luigi Pirandello," *Nuova Antologia,* I (1916): 390–403. Others see Sicilianism as a personality trait, inherently disposing the writer toward passionate impulsiveness, explosive intelligence, and general emotiveness. Critics from the Left, such as Sciascia, attribute the Pirandellian personality and worldview to the Sicilian sociohistorical context and often speak of social conditioning. In contrast to this insular dimension, Pirandello's Bonn experience is interpreted as a cultural and psychologocal awakening.

10. Paolucci compares *Liolà* to Machiavelli's Renaissance masterpiece *La Mandragola.* The two plays deal comically with the tricking of older wealthy husbands anxious for heirs. In both works virtuous wives succomb to the hero's persuasive discourse, in anticipation of the promised blessed event. Naturally differences in tone and characterization abound. See her *Pirandello's Theater: The Recovery of the Modern Stage for Dramatic Art.* Carbondale and Edwardsville: Southern Illinois University Press, 1974. Consult pp. 28–38.

11. Eric Bentley. "Liolà and Other Plays," *The Pirandello Commentaries,* p. 11. This article first appeared in 1952 as the introduction to the volume of Pirandello's translated plays, *Naked Masks.*

12. Susan Bassnett-McGuire. *Luigi Pirandello.* New York: Grove Press, 1984. P. 140.

13. *Cap and Bells* is drawn from the short story "La verità" (Truth), but major differences exist between the two works. The protagonist of the tale is Trararà, an ignorant peasant who did murder his wife and is on trial. In court he tells his truth to justify his actions. The peasant wife was unfaithful with a gentleman, Fiorica, whose own wife is responsible for the public announcement of the affair. To save face and satisfy the community's code of honor, Trararà, against his better judgment, had to act. The peasant blames neither himself nor his unfaithful spouse for the tragedy, but Mrs. Fiorica, who did not know when to remain silent and let things be.

14. The motif of the puppet relates to the play's title. *Cap and Bells* or, more literally, cap with bells, is a probable reference to the foolscap worn by medieval jesters and sometimes recycled in stock marionette characters derived from the Commedia dell'Arte, like Pulcinella. If the cap is part of Ciampa's "costume," as seems to be the case, it adds another dimension to his *pupo.*

15. One of the circumlocutions used to indicate a betrayed husband in Italian is *becco,* which translates as buck or billy goat. The reference is to the animal's horns, which are common Mediterranean symbols of cuckoldry that are often imitated in hand gestures.

16. Malcolm Bradbury. "Luigi Pirandello." *The Modern World: Ten Great Writers.* London: Secker & Warburg, 1988. P. 218.

17. Gobetti's review appeared in the Turin newspaper *L'ordine nuovo* on January 1, 1922.

18. The letter is addressed to Domenico Vittorini, a U.S. scholar whose study *The Drama of Luigi Pirandello* (Philadelphia: University of Pennsylvania Press, 1935) greatly pleased the playwright. The letter is reproduced as the foreward to Vittorini's monograph. It is dated "New York 30 VII 1935 XIII. "

19. Quoted in Gaspare Giudice. *Pirandello. A Biography.* Trans. Alastair Hamilton. London: Oxford University Press, 1975. P. 177 (dated 1926).

20. The best source for details about this relationship is the recently published volume of Pirandello's epistolary: *Pirandello's Love Letters to Marta Abba.* Ed. and trans. Benito Ortolani. Princeton, N.J.: Princeton University Press, 1994.

21. In Italian, the word *coscienza,* as used by Salinari, is a term loaded with two powerful and interrelated meanings. The first definition has psychological implications— consciousness; the second centers on issues of morality—conscience. Salinari clearly intends to attribute both meanings to Pirandello.

Chapter 2: *The Late Mattia Pascal* and Goddess Luck

1. A psychoanalytic approach to Marta Ajala's story emphasizes her identification with the father, exhibited in her attempts to take over the role of head of the Ajala household through her work and financial contribution. Such behavior has been interpreted as an obsessive need to recover her departed father by taking his place. Using this approach to the novel, Marta is seen as a parricide, who has killed off the male parent to take his place.

2. Carlo Salinari. "Luigi Pirandello fra Ottocento e Novecento." *Boccaccio Manzoni Pirandello.* Ed. Nino Borsellino and Enrico Ghidetti. Rome: Editori Riuniti, 1979. See pp. 171–184.

3. Olga Ragusa has a lengthy discussion of alternative terms Pirandello considered in lieu of *humor* which carry similar connotations. Among them: *ironismo* (ironism); *critica fantastica* (imaginative criticism), and *grottesco* (grotesque). See her *Luigi*

Pirandello: An Approach to His Theatre. Edinburgh: Edinburgh University Press, 1980. Pp. 30–42.

4. *On Humor.* Trans. Antonio Illiano and Daniel P. Testa. Chapel Hill: University of North Carolina Press, 1974. P. 112. Other quotations from this text will be cited in the chapter by page number in parentheses.

5. The episode of Mattia's seduction of Romilda, who is Malagna's niece, forms the basic plot outline for the play *Liolà,* written a dozen years after the novel.

6. Arcangelo Leone De Castris. "The Experimental Novel." *Pirandello: A Collection of Essays.* Ed. Glauco Cambon. Englewood Cliffs, N.J.: Prentice-Hall, 1967. P. 91. This is a translated section taken from the important study *Storia di Pirandello.*

7. Some critics believe that Mattia's tale represents an elaborate narrative joke. If this is the case, the validity of other Pirandellian themes in the novel, such as the difficulty of constructing a genuine identity and the weight of social definitions, are necessarily brought into question.

8. Enzo Lauretta. *Come leggere "Il fu Mattia Pascal" di Luigi Pirandello.* Milan: Mursia, 1976. Consult pp. 29–30; 57–68.

9. Gregory L. Lucente. "'Non conclude': Narrative Self-consciousness and the Voice of Creation in Pirandello's *Il fu Mattia Pascal* and *Uno, nessuno e centomila.*" *Beautiful Fables: Self-consciousness in Italian Narrative from Manzoni to Calvino.* Baltimore and London: Johns Hopkins University Press, 1986. See p. 121 on.

10. *The Late Mattia Pascal.* Trans. William Weaver. Hygiene, Colo.: Eridanos Press, 1987. P. 41. Original translation copyright, 1964. Quotations from this text will be cited in the chapter by page number in parentheses.

11. Pirandello himself was intrigued by the unknown and possessed a good working knowledge of key texts in theosophy. Olga Ragusa explores Pirandello's readings in the area, including works by scientists as well as mediums on issues ranging from spiritualism to astral planes, from the occult to abnormal psychology. See *Luigi Pirandello: An Approach to His Theatre.* Op. cit. Pp. 22–30.

Chapter 3: *Right You Are (If You Think So)* and the Crisis of Reality

1. Tom F. Driver. "Luigi Pirandello (1876–1936)." *Romantic Quest and Modern Query: A History of the Modern Theatre.* New York: Delacorte, 1970. P. 393.

2. One of the major figures in the Grottesco was Pirandello's close friend and protegé, Pier Maria Rosso di San Secondo (1887–1956), a fellow Sicilian. The two shared an intimate bond for many years. Rosso composed one of the monuments of the grotesque manner: *Marionette che passione!* (1918, Marionettes, What a Pity!). The play toys with the notion that individuals are pulled by invisible strings in their everyday lives, are reacting to stimuli that control them and condemn them to hopelessness, alienation, and despair. Rosso's debt to his confidante is obvious in both the guiding

metaphor of the play (marionettes, or puppets) and in the portrayal of the human condition. Another *grottesco,* Massimo Bontempelli (1878–1960), was one of the founders of the Teatro d'Arte. It was for the premiere of Bontempelli's play, *La nostra dea* (1925, Our Goddess), that Pirandello hired Marta Abba.

3. Eric Bentley. *"Right You Are."* In his *Theatre of War: Comments on 32 Occasions.* New York: Viking Press, 1972. P. 24.

4. *It Is So! (If You Think So).* Trans. Arthur Livingston. In *Naked Masks.* Ed. Eric Bentley. New York: E. P. Dutton, 1952. P. 102. Quotations from the play are taken from this text or are my own translation.

5. For Robert Brustein, critic and man of the theater, the "masks" of *Right You Are* resemble the comedic masks of ancient Greek theater which were later re-created in the Commedia dell'Arte. Using the Greek terms *alazones* (imposters or buffoons); *eirones* (self-deprecators), and *pharmakos* (scapegoats), Brustein divides all the characters of the Pirandellian play into the masks of ancient Greek comedy to define their functions: the *alazones* [buffoons] are the circle of local busybodies, the agents of organized society; the sufferers, or *pharmakos,* are the Ponzas and Mrs. Frola. But it is Laudisi, the *eiron* of the play, who has the richest potential of meanings and masks. Laudisi is a sufferer who hides his secret under a mask of appearances, that of a wise man, for he is well aware that he knows nothing. Brustein concludes that it is impossible to discover another's secret because the face beneath the mask is unknowable. As long as the masks, or illusions, remain in place, tragedy is averted, as is the case for the Ponza family triangle. See "Luigi Pirandello." In *The Theatre of Revolt.* Boston and Toronto: Little, Brown, 1964. P. 292 on.

6. Cited in Roger W. Oliver. *Dreams of Passion: The Theater of Luigi Pirandello.* New York: New York University Press, 1979. P. 8.

7. All three plays are drawn from earlier Pirandellian short stories. *The Rules of the Game* was inspired by the tale "Quando s'è capito il giuoco" (When the Game Has Been Understood), first published in 1913. *Right You Are* is derived from "La Signora Frola e il Signor Ponza, suo genero" (Mrs. Frola and Mr. Ponza, Her Son-in-Law), first published in 1915. *The Pleasure of Honesty* is drawn from "Tirocinio" (Trial Period), published in 1905. *A Companion to Pirandello Studies,* ed. John Louis Di Gaetani (New York, Westport, Conn., and London: Greenwood Press, 1991), contains an informative list of Pirandello's plays and the fictional sources from which they were drawn in "Appendix D: A Pirandello Bibliography. "

8. *The Pleasure of Honesty.* Trans. William Murray. In *Masterpieces of the Modern Italian Theatre.* Ed. Robert W. Corrigan. New York: Collier, 1967. P. 136. All quotations are taken from this edition and will be indicated by page number in the text.

9. *The Rules of the Game.* Trans. Robert Rietty and Noel Cregeen. In Luigi Pirandello, *Collected Plays.* Vol. III. Ed. Robert Rietty. New York: Riverrun Press, 1992. P. 12. All quotations are taken from this edition and will be indicated by page number in the text.

10. Cited in Walter Starkie. *Luigi Pirandello 1867–1936.* 3d revised ed. Berkeley and Los Angeles: University of California Press, 1965. p. 33. The interview took place in Barcelona, Spain.

11. The review first appeared in the newspaper *L'Idea nazionale* on February 27, 1920. Cited in Maurice Valency. "Pirandello." *The End of the World.* Oxford and New York: Oxford University Press, 1980. P. 96.

Chapter 4: Moscarda's Nose, or the Disintegration of the Individual

1. A new novel was being contemplated at the time of Pirandello's death: *Adamo e Eva* (Adam and Eve), dealing with the quest for inner peace. Of the seven of Pirandello's novels published, only *Suo marito* (1911, Her Husband) has not been translated into English.

2. Quoted in Richard Gilman. "Pirandello." *Luigi Pirandello.* Ed. Harold Bloom. New York and Philadelphia: Chelsea House, 1989. P. 39.

3. *One, No One, and One Hundred Thousand.* Trans. William Weaver. Boston: Eridanos Press, 1990. P. 13. All quotations taken from this translation will be indicated in the text by page number.

4. The phrase comes from Oscar Büdel. *Pirandello.* 2d ed. London: Bowes and Bowes, 1969. P. 52.

5. The cinematographic environment of *Shoot!* recalls other episodes and directions in Pirandello's artistic life. When the novel was written, Italian cinema was in its infancy, and films were silent, wordless, commercial ventures. However, talkies appeared at the time of Pirandello's international celebrity, and, not surprisingly, the author became involved in the booming world of the movies. In *Shoot!* the camera is an abhored mechanical "black spider," reflecting Pirandello's profound distaste for the cinema. But in later years he arrived at a form of compromise with the world of film. The first talkie produced in Italy, titled *La canzone dell'amore* (1930, The Song of Love), was drawn from the Pirandellian short story "In silenzio" (In silence, 1905/1923). In 1932 the author, son Stefano, and other writers produced a movie script based on another story, "Gioca, Pietro!" (Play, Peter), filmed as *Acciaio* (Steel) by the director Walter Ruttmann. Several film versions of Pirandello's plays, including *Six Characters in Search of an Author,* were proposed to the writer. A few years after *Acciaio,* Hollywood and MGM beckoned, purchasing the rights to *Come tu mi vuoi* (1930, *As You Desire Me*) as a suitable vehicle for the talents of studio stars Greta Garbo and Erich von Stroheim. In Pirandello's opinion the artistic potential of "talking" pictures did not resemble filmed theater: he envisioned successful film as a fusion of music and images, rather like Disney's film *Fantasia,* in which animation is set to classical music.

6. Pirandello reused this section of *Shoot!*'s plot to form the main action of his play within a play, *Ciascuno a suo modo* (1924, *Each in His Own Way*). See chapter 6 of this study for more information on this drama.

7. *Shoot! The Notebooks of Serafino Gubbio Cinematograph Operator*. Trans. C. K. Scott-Moncrieff. 2d ed. London: Chatto & Windus, 1927. P. 225. All quotations taken from this translation will be indicated in the text by page number.

8. From a letter dated "10/10/1921," addressed to Ugo Ojetti. Quoted in Pirandello's *Carteggi inediti* (Unpublished Papers). Ed. Sarah Zappulla Muscara. Rome: Bulzoni, 1980. P. 82. My translation.

9. See Umberto Bosco. "Luigi Pirandello." *I Contemporanei*. Vol. I. Roma: Lucarini, 1979. Pp. 91–125.

10. From Douglas Radcliff-Umstead. *The Mirror of Our Anguish: A Study of Luigi Pirandello's Narrative Writings*. Rutherford N.J.: Farleigh Dickinson University Press, 1978; London: Associated University Presses, 1978. P. 251.

Chapter 5: Henry IV's Sane Madness

1. *Henry IV*. Trans. Edward Storer. *Naked Masks*. Ed. Eric Bentley. New York: E. P. Dutton, 1952. P. 192. All excerpts from the play are from this edition and will be quoted in the text by page number.

2. June Schlueter. "Pirandello's Henry IV." *Metafictional Characters in Modern Drama*. New York: Columbia University Press, 1979. P. 22.

3. In their "Psychoanalysis in Search of Pirandello: *Six Characters* and *Henry IV*." *Psychoanalysis, Creativity, and Literature: A French-American Inquiry*. Ed. Alan Roland. New York: Columbia University Press, 1978. P. 341.

4. John L. Styan. "Towards Tragic Inversion: Pirandello." *The Dark Comedy: The Development of Modern Comic Tragedy*. 2d ed. London: Cambridge Universtiy Press, 1968. P. 144.

5. According to Eric Bentley, the modern Henry always failed at the Pirandellian task of constructing himself, succeeding only in play-acting and masquerading. Even the choice of the German Henry IV as his new identity is morally dubious. In Bentley's opinion the historical emperor is not a heroic or tragic figure but a monarch remembered for a single act of ignoble self-abasement. Rather than denoting true humility, Henry's prostration before the pope at Canossa is an act of pure political expediency. The critic connects the emperor's cunning hypocrisy with Henry's murder of Belcredi, a shabby act against an undefended man. In point of fact both actions are in keeping with the personalities involved. Above the laws of God and man, the absolute ruler of an empire is indeed capable of murder for political and emotional reasons. Henry's humility—his sackcloth and ashes—is a front for a man whose choices place him outside the norms of legal, moral, and social behavior. Belcredi's murder is an act of violence involving no real fear of accountability; it also merges Henry and his role as a powerful man of superior will and mental arrogance. See Eric Bentley. "Enrico IV." In his *Theatre of War: Comments on 32 Occasions*. New York: Viking Press, 1972. P. 33 on.

6. See Anthony Caputi. *Pirandello and the Crisis of Modern Consciousness*. Urbana

and Chicago: University of Illinois Press, 1988. Pp. 93–99. Caputi goes on to discuss Pirandello's choice of the Holy Roman Emperor Henry IV as a rich analogy for the protagonist's condition as scapegoat. Both a rebel against papal authority and a self-effacing penitent in the snows of Canossa, the emperor foreshadows the modern Henry, who tends to reject the structures of his world in addition to his ambivalent need for security. In Caputi's interpretation both men are torn apart by similar existential tensions.

7. A. Richard Sogliuzzo. *Luigi Pirandello Director: The Playwright in the Theatre.* Metuchen, N.J.: Scarecrow Press, 1982. P. 183.

8. Bentley 38.

9. *Henry IV* was specifically written for Ruggero Ruggeri, one of Italy's greatest and most versatile leading men. Pirandello greatly admired the actor's expressive capabilities and vast range. Ruggeri often performed in Pirandello's works, but he was not a permanent member of the Teatro d'Arte's repertory troupe.

10. Roland and Rizzo view Matilda Spina's rejection of the young Henry as a repetition of an earlier maternal rejection, which would explain the young man's lack of feeling (as described by Belcredi in act 2) in terms of the lack of a warm maternal internalization or presence, leading to masochistic relationships with unresponsive love objects such as Matilda.

11. Tilgher's formula was first applied to *Henry IV* in a review of the play published on October 20, 1922, in *Il mondo,* a newspaper.

12. *On Humor.* Trans. Antonio Illiano and Daniel P. Testa. Chapel Hill: University of North Carolina Press, 1974. P. 137. Roger W. Oliver points out that Pirandello's ideas of life opposing form are far from original but have strong links to Henri Bergson's concept of the élan vital, Friedrich Nietzsche's "life force," and W. F. Hegel's "levels of consciousness." Pirandello transfers these theoretical concepts to an original level of artistic creation. See *Dreams of Passion: The Theater of Luigi Pirandello.* New York: New York University Press, 1979. Pp. 5–7.

13. See Adriano Tilgher. "Il teatro di Luigi Pirandello." *Studi sul teatro contemporaneo.* 3d ed. Rome: Libreria di Scienze e Lettere, 1928. (First edition 1923). Glauco Cambon translated the central portion of this essay for his *Pirandello: A Collection of Critical Essays.* Englewood Cliffs, N.J.: Prentice-Hall, 1967. Pp. 19–34.

14. Sogliuzzo 218.

15. Robert Brustein. "Luigi Pirandello." *The Theatre of Revolt: An Approach to the Modern Drama.* Boston and Toronto: Little, Brown, 1964. P. 303.

16. *Diana and Tuda* is one of several plays specifically composed for Marta Abba. In fact, Tuda's physical appearance as described in the stage directions forms a verbal portrait of the leading lady of the Teatro d'Arte. Critics often see a Pirandellian self-portrait in the sculptor Giuncano, who, like the author himself, expresses profound concern over issues of aging and the impropriety of loving a young, vital woman. The playwright, nevertheless, began writing stronger female roles for his talented protegée. A. Richard Sogliuzzo finds some of these plays somewhat incongruous: their "commercial exploitation of bourgeois chic" contrasts with the author's extensive employment of

psychological and metaphysical questions. "However, bourgeois chic and pathetic heroines never mixed well with Pirandello's humorous attitude" (Sogliuzzo 216).

17. *When Somebody Is Somebody*. Trans. Marta Abba. In Luigi Pirandello, *The Mountain Giants, and Other Plays*. New York: Crown Publishers, 1958. P. 277. All excerpts from the play are from this edition and will be quoted in the text by page number.

18. Susan Bassnett-McGuire interprets Donata Genzi's ideal of art as a metaphysical concept, so that her masks elevate the actress to "an almost mystical state." The critic believes this view of art shifts Donata's experience of the life/form antithesis to a higher level than found in either *Henry IV* or *Diana and Tuda*. Consequently, rather than viewing Donata's choice of form over motion as an act of rejection of life's uncertainties and pain, Bassnett-McGuire sees it as "a strong statement about a woman's need for personal freedom." See her *Luigi Pirandello*. New York: Grove Press, 1984. Pp. 123–126.

19. Quoted in Maurice Valency. "Pirandello." *The End of the World*. Oxford and New York: Oxford University Press, 1980. P. 132.

20. William Herman. "Pirandello and Possibility." In Cambon, op. cit. p. 171. As Herman notes, the title *To Clothe the Naked* derives from Roman Catholic devotional exercises: the seven Corporeal Works of Mercy. In the play "these works are done on stage in symbolic form: feeding the hungry, giving drink to the thirsty, clothing the naked, harboring the stranger, visiting the sick, ministering to prisoners, burying the dead."

Chapter 6: The Theater Plays

1. Quoted in Gaspare Giudice. *Luigi Pirandello*. Turin: UTET, 1963. P. 337. My translation.

2. Quoted in James V. Biundo. *Moments of Selfhood: Three Plays by Luigi Pirandello*. New York: Lang, 1990. P. 145.

3. Both tales appear in the *Novelle per un anno* (Short Stories for a Year), a collection and reworking of Pirandello's numerous published volumes of short fiction. Frederick May translated "The Tragedy of a Character" for his selection of Pirandello's *Short Stories*. London and New York: Oxford University Press, 1965. This book is also a valuable resource instrument, thanks to May's extensive addenda, which include bibliographies, a chronological list of stories by year of composition, and a bibliography of translated stories that appear in multiauthored collections or are published singly in books and periodicals. May's volume concludes with a brief discussion of the rapport between Pirandello's stories or longer fiction and the plays; this section lists by title and year(s) the fictional sources from which the dramas are drawn. The quotations from the story "The Tragedy of a Character" are from May's translation and will be indicated in the text by page number. To my knowledge the "Colloqui" have not been translated.

4. "Pirandello's Introduction to *Six Characters in Search of an Author*." Trans. Felicity Firth. In Luigi Pirandello, *Collected Plays*. Vol. II. Ed. Robert Rietty. New

York: Riverrun Press, 1988. P. xiv. All quotations are taken from this text and Firth's translation of the play and will be cited in the essay by page number.

5. Robert Brustein. *The Theatre of Revolt: An Approach to the Modern Drama.* Boston and Toronto: Little, Brown, 1964. P. 285.

6. Some critics have compared the multiple layers of *Six Characters* to a contemporary movement in art: cubism. Constance A. Pedoto, for one, notes parallelisms between the collage techniques and multifacetedness of some Picasso paintings, which create a series of new realities while self-consciously exposing the ingredients of the pictorial product, and Pirandello's employment of fragmentation, particularly in *Six Characters,* termed "a process-oriented" or "kaledioscopic" play. "Like subjects in a Cubist painting, [the protagonists] are fragmented or incomplete and they are caught part in a world of fiction and part in the womb of Pirandello's conception" (56). See her "Luigi Pirandello's *Six Characters in Search of an Author* through Incollato and Picasso's Cubism." In *Painting Literature: Dostoesvsky, Kafka, Pirandello, and Garcia Marquez in Living Color.* Lanham: University Press of America, 1993. For a more literary perspective on the topic, consult Wylie Sypher's "Cubist Drama." *Pirandello: A Collection of Essays.* Ed. Glauco Cambon. Englewood Cliffs, N.J.: Prentice-Hall, 1967.

7. The play rehearsed is *The Rules of the Game.* The particular scene used describes Leone Gala's beating an egg while wearing his chef's apparel. The Producer is explaining the scene to the Actors, suggesting that the eggshell is reason and the yolk is blind instinct being beaten into submission. This explanation prefigures the mind/nature division of the Characters themselves. One critic parallels Gala's shaping of life into a game with the Author's shaping of the story into an artwork: both are metaphors for the attempt to mold the flux surrounding the individual into controllable forms.

8. In his own productions of *Six Characters* for the Teatro d'Arte, Pirandello never employed the masks suggested in the stage directions; he preferred to rely on makeup and the expressive capability of his gifted actors, such as Marta Abba, who was a superb Stepdaughter by all accounts. But the masks provide powerful allusions to classical Greek theater, in which all protagonists wore large cumbersome masks to conceal the actor behind the character; these ancient masks also symbolized roles and traits. By employing them, Pirandello is defining himself as a continuator and innovator of the long tradition of Western drama. Since Pirandello himself called his plays "Naked Masks," the logical presumption is that characters, as products of art, are permanent masks, unlike humans who assume masks to hide their nakedness.

9. In translations of *Six Characters,* this protagonist is given various names, including Manager and Director. In the history of Italian theater, the *Capocomico* was the leader of a company or troupe of actors, with a variety of artistic and administrative functions.

10. Martin Esslin. "Pirandello: Master of the Naked Masks." In *Reflections: Essays on Modern Theatre.* New York: Doubleday, 1969. P. 53.

11. Richard Gilman. "Luigi Pirandello." In *The Making of Modern Drama.* New York: Da Capo Press, 1987. P. 174.

12. As a play about constructing plays, *Six Characters* has ties to the theatrical environment in which it was conceived. In a suggestive and thought-provoking article, European scholar Peter Szondi analyzes the theatrical referentiality of *Six Characters,* which he believes reprises important dramatic voices and movements in its formulation of a new type of play. Szondi points out that the Stepdaughter's repeated protests of misrepresentation and her insistence on accuracy in details indicate a naturalist perspective. By demanding the exact replica of her experience, from the color of objects to the ordering of events, the Stepdaughter is defining theater as the imitation of reality, a point of view inevitably bound to fail because of the innate differences between theatrical reality and life. The Stepdaughter's ego, Szondi goes on to declare, makes her a Strindbergian protagonist: an "I" that insists on ruling the scene, thus resulting in the Producer's rejection of her subjective dramaturgy. Ibsen, Szondi continues, is the inspiration for the story line. The logical conclusion to Szondi's critical appraisal must be that Pirandello, by rejecting the Characters' drama and proposing a new one based on his own rejection, is also setting aside former forms of dramaturgy.

13. *Each in His Own Way.* Trans. Felicity Firth. In Luigi Pirandello, *Collected Plays.* Vol. III. Ed. Robert Rietty. New York: Riverrun Press, 1992. P. 53. All quotations are taken from this text and will be cited in the chapter by page number.

14. Oscar Büdel. *Pirandello.* 2d ed. London: Bowes and Bowes, 1969. P. 95.

15. *Tonight We Improvise* was written during Pirandello's long residence in Berlin, where he came into frequent contact with the great innovators of the German stage. During that period avant-garde European theater was dominated by superdirectors, such as Reinhardt and Piscator, who emphasized the vision of the director as key to interpreting the meaning of dramatic works. Reinhardt, in particular, was fond of using technology and special effects at the expense of the written text. Hinkfuss is often interpreted as a parody of these legendary superstar directors.

16. Olga Ragusa. *"Tonight We Improvise:* Spectacle and Tragedy." In *A Companion to Pirandello Studies.* Ed. John Louis Di Gaetani. New York, Westport, Conn., and London: Greenwood Press, 1991. P. 247.

17. Brustein 306.

18. Eric Bentley. *Theatre of War: Comments on 32 Occasions.* New York: Viking Press, 1972. P. 56.

19. Binion goes on to explain other elements of the Characters' melodrama in terms of Pirandello's personal experiences, although some interpretations could be considered an imaginative stretch. For example, Binion believes that Lietta Pirandello's suicide attempt, first by shooting herself, then by looking for the Tiber River to drown herself, is embodied in the silent children of the play who die by drowning and shooting. In his analysis of the "play within the play" of *Six Characters,* Albert Bermel purports that the family relationships as presented are incorrect: the Son is actually a stepson of the Father while the Stepdaughter is his real daughter and the Little Girl their child. Such interpretations of *Six Characters* were popular after the appearance of an article by the psychoanalyst Charles Kligermann: "A Psychoanalytic Study of Pirandello's *Six*

Characters in Search of an Author," *Journal of American Psychoanalytic Association,* X (1962). The psychoanalyst suggests that the play offers a series of Freudian fantasies: father/daugher incest, Oedipal triangle, sibling rivalry, wishful fantasy of murder; guilty suicide. Kligerman too refers his interpretations to biographical evidence in Pirandello's life. Finally, according to Alan Roland and Gino Rizzo, "the inner drama of the six characters is ultimately concerned with the most primal form of repudiation a human being can experience, the repudiation of a child by his mother and all the pain attendant upon such a rejection" (336).

20. In Bentley's view Madama Pace represents "a mother who sells sex," thus degrading both maternity and sexuality. The psychoanalyst Kligermann defines her as the "giantess of the nursery," a castrating nanny (see Bentley, *Theatre of War,* 53). In keeping with this Freudian interpretation, Bentley defines the deaths of the Boy and Child as "sibling murder," the elimination of unwanted contenders for the Mother's affections.

Chapter 7: The Myths

1. Quoted in Ferdinando Virdia. *Invito alla lettura di Pirandello.* Milan: Mursia, 1975. P. 137. My translation.

2. *The New Colony.* Trans. Marta Abba. In Luigi Pirandello, *The Mountain Giants, and Other Plays.* New York: Crown Publishers, 1958. P. 201. All quotations are taken from this translation and will be cited by page number in the text.

3. See Susan Bassnett-McGuire. *Luigi Pirandello.* New York: Grove Press, 1984. P. 148.

4. Robert S. Dombroski. "Pirandello's Modernity: Epistemology and the Existential of Theater." In *Pirandello and Modern Theater.* Eds. Antonio Alessio, Domenico Pietropaolo, and Giuliana Katz. Ottawa: Canadian Society for Italian Studies, 1992. P. 33.

5. A. Richard Sogliuzzo. *Luigi Pirandello Director: The Playwright in the Theatre.* Metuchen, N.J.: Scarecrow Press, 1982. P. 211.

6. *Lazarus.* Trans. Frederick May. In Luigi Pirandello, *Collected Plays.* Vol. I. Ed. Robert Rietty. New York: Riverrun Press, 1987. P. 172. The statement is made by a secondary character. The bold face is in the original. All quotations are taken from this translation and will be cited by page number in the text.

7. A variation on this perception, without the emphatic Christian context of *Lazarus,* is found in the conclusion of Vitangelo Moscarda's travails as he searches for his identity in *One, No One, and One Hundred Thousand.* In the novel, however, immanentism is equivalent to self-denial, to being no one.

8. Anne Paolucci. *Pirandello's Theater: The Recovery of the Modern Stage for Dramatic Art.* Carbondale and Edwardsville: Southern Illinois University Press, 1974. P. 112.

9. Quoted in Bassnett-McGuire 154.

10. Sogliuzzo offers a hypothetical sociohistorical reading of the Giants, the tyrannical rulers of the mountain, as an allegory of Fascists and Nazis, who suppressed and censured artists. In his reading the critic suggests that Pirandello foresaw the spiritual disintegration of Italy and Germany. On a more personal level, the fate of the play's troupe recalls Pirandello's own Teatro d'Arte, which, like Ilse's wandering players, attempted to bring theater to the masses, only to be curtailed by the Fascist establishment, threatened by the playwright's independence and devotion to art rather than ideology. See p. 39.

11. Renate Matthaei. *Luigi Pirandello.* Trans. S. and E. Young. New York: Ungar, 1973. P. 159.

12. *The Mountain Giants.* Trans. Marta Abba. In Luigi Pirandello, *The Mountain Giants, and Other Plays.* Op. cit. p. 97. All quotations are taken from this translation and will be cited by page number in the text.

13. See her "Woman or Mother? Feminine Conditions in Pirandello's Theater." In *A Companion to Pirandello Studies.* Ed. John Louis Di Gaetani. New York, Westport, Conn., and London: Greenwood Press, 1991. Consult pp. 57–72.

14. Leonardo Sciascia. *Pirandello e la Sicilia.* Caltanisetta-Roma: Sciascia, 1961. 2d ed. 1968. Pp. 24–25.

Chapter 8: Other Works

1. See May's appendix, "Translations of the Short Stories," to Luigi Pirandello. *Short Stories.* Trans. Frederick May. London and New York: Oxford University Press, 1965.

2. This is the only Pirandellian tale published in *Stories of Sicily.* Ed. and trans. Alfred Alexander. London: Paul Elek, 1975. P. 122.

3. Douglas Radcliff-Umstead. *The Mirror of Our Anguish: A Study of Luigi Pirandello's Narrative Writings.* Rutherford N.J.: Farleigh Dickinson University Press, 1978; London: Associated University Presses, 1978. P. 202.

4. Critics have looked to *The Old and the Young* to develop an understanding of Pirandello's sociopolitical views and motivations, particularly to justify his adherence to Fascism. In the author's discussion of the Sicilian Fasces, for example, the reasons behind the populist movement are explained in terms of poverty, dehumanizing labor, and negative living conditions. But, in the meditations of key characters in the novel, revolutionary zeal is indicated as an inappropriate response to poor conditions; Pirandello clearly favors cooperation between the classes to achieve reform. Like other middle-class intellectuals, Pirandello was initially taken aback by the bitterness of class struggle and the virulence of the nationalist groups that would eventually lead Italy into colonialist expansionism and war. Yet, as Francesco Nicolosi has pointed out, Pirandello probably saw his own youthful social and nationalistic tendencies reflected in the dynamic Fascist

ideology, which shared his harsh criticism of the failures of parliamentary democracy in Italy. See Francesco Nicolosi. "Pirandello e il fascismo: da una breve riflessione su *I vecchi e i giovani.*" In *Il "Romanzo" di Pirandello.* Ed. Enzo Lauretta. Palermo: Palumbo, 1976. Pp. 267–269).

5. Nino Borsellino. "L'illusione storica: *I vecchi e i giovani.*" *Ritratto di Pirandello.* Bari: Laterza, 1983. Pp. 49–52.

6. This story has also been translated as "Miss Holloway's Goat" and "The Beauty and the Beast."

7. E. Allen McCormick. "Luigi Pirandello: Major Writer, Minor Novelist." In *From Verismo to Experimentalism.* Ed. Sergio Pacifici. Bloomington: Indiana University Press, 1969. P. 78.

8. *Pensaci, Giacomino!* has been produced in English although the translated versions have not been published. Manlio Lo Vecchio-Musti lists two such productions from a translation by Robert Rietty in his excellent bibliography on Pirandello. Although the translation seems to be the same, the play was performed under two separate titles in the 1950s: *Think It Over, Giacomino* and *The Shameless Professor.* The original short story (1910) is more accessible to readers and titled "Better Think Twice about It!" *The License* was drawn from a story by the same title, dated 1911.

Selected Bibliography

Comprehensive Italian Editions

The most complete Italian editions of Pirandello's works were published by Mondadori as *Opere di Luigi Pirandello* in six volumes first issued between 1956 and 1960 in the series I Classici Contemporanei Italiani (Contemporary Italian Classics). Since their original publication these volumes have been repeatedly reprinted and updated. Mondadori is currently publishing revised critical editions in the series I Meridiani. These recent Mondadori editions include manuscript and publication variants as appendixes, an important factor in Pirandello's production, for he often revised extensively for new editions and anthological collections of his works, making the Meridiani series the most accurate and complete editions available of Pirandello's works in the original language.

I Classici Contemporanei Italiani

Novelle per un anno [the collected short stories]. Ed. Corrado Alvaro. Vols. I & II. Milan: Mondadori, 1956, 1957.

Tutti i romanzi [novels]. Ed. Corrado Alvaro. Vol. III. Milan: Mondadori, 1957.

Maschere nude [plays]. Vols. IV & V. Ed. Silivo D'Amico. Milan: Mondadori, 1958.

Saggi, poesie e scritti vari [essays, poetry, miscellaneous pieces]. Vol. VI. Ed. Manlio Lo Vecchio-Musti. Milan: Mondadori, 1960. This volume contains an excellent bibliographical section which extensively lists translations of Pirandello's works into other languages.

I Meridiani

Maschere nude (Naked Masks). Ed. Alessandro d'Amico. Vols. I & II. Milan: Mondadori, 1986, 1993. Vol. I contains 12 plays; vol. II contains 8. Further volumes pending.

Novelle per un anno. (Short Stories for a Year). Ed. Mario Costanzo. 3 vols. Milan: Mondadori, 1985, 1987, 1990. Nuova ed. Each volume comes in two books.

Tutti i Romanzi (All the Novels). Ed. Mario Costanzo and Giovanni Macchia. 2 vols. Milano: Mondadori, 1986. Vol. I contains 4 novels; vol. II contains 3.

Works

Many dates for the first editions of Pirandello's works are deceptive. Most of his short stories were first published in newspapers and periodicals, as were the serialized novels. Nor do publication dates necessarily reflect the dates of composition. Pirandello often reworked his texts from one publication or edition to the next, just as he altered titles of both fiction and drama. For comprehensive bibliographical data on secondary sources consult Alfredo Barbina and Corrado Donati, listed below. For a bibliographical listing of criticism in English, see Antonio Illiano's article cited below. Illiano's book on Pirandello criticism, written in Italian, covers in essay form the major trends in Italy and abroad to the 1960s.

Poetry, Italian First Editions

Mal giocondo (Joyful Ill). Palermo: Libreria Internazionale Clausen, 1889.
Pasqua di Gea (The Easter of Gaea, or Earth). Milan: Libreria Editrice Galli, 1891.
Pier Gudrò. Rome: Voghera, 1894.
Elegie renane (Rhenish Elegies). Rome: Unione Cooperativa Editrice, 1895.
Elegie romane (Roman Elegies). Livorno: Giusti, 1896. (Translations from Goethe's *Römische Elegien)*
Zampogna (Bagpipes). Rome: Società Editrice Dante Alighieri, 1901.
Fuori di chiave (Off Key). Genoa: Formiggini, 1912.

Fiction, Italian First Editions

Amori senza amore (Loves without Love). Rome: Bontempelli, 1894.
Beffe della morte e della vita (Jests of Life and Death). Florence: Lumachi, 1902.
Quand'ero matto . . . (When I Was Mad . . .). Turin: Streglio, 1902.
Il turno [trans. as *The Merry-Go-Round of Love*]. Catania: Giannotta, 1902.
Beffe della morte e della vita (Jests of Life and Death II). Seconda serie. Florence: Lumachi, 1903.
Bianche e nere (Black and White). Turin: Streglio, 1904.

Il fu Mattia Pascal (*The Late Mattia Pascal*). Rome: Nuova Antologia, 1904.

Erma bifronte (Two-faced Herm). Milan: Treves, 1906.

L'esclusa (*The Outcast*). Milan: Treves, 1908. (First serialized in *La Tribuna,* June–August, 1901.)

La vita nuda (Naked Life). Milan: Treves, 1910.

Suo marito (Her Husband). Florence: Quattrini, 1911. (Later retitled *Giustino Roncella nato Boggiòlo* [Giustino Roncella Born Boggiolo].)

Terzetti (Tercets). Milan: Treves, 1912.

I vecchi e i giovani (*The Old and the Young*). Milan: Treves, 1913. (First serialized in *Rassegna Contemporanea,* January–November, 1909.)

Le due maschere (The Two Masks). Florence: Quattrini, 1914.

La trappola (The Trap). Milan: Treves, 1915.

Erba del nostro orto (Grass from Our Own Yard). Milan: Studio Editoriale Lombardo, 1915.

Si gira . . . (Shoot . . .) Milan: Treves, 1916. (Later titled *Quaderni di Serafino Gubbio operatore* [*Shoot! The Notebooks of Serafino Gubbio, Cinematograph Operator*])

E domani, lunedì . . . (Tomorrow, Monday . . .). Milan: Treves, 1917.

Un cavallo nella luna (Horse in the Moon). Milan: Treves, 1918.

Berecche e la guerra (Berecche and War). Milan: Facchi, 1919.

Il carnevale dei morti (The Carnival of the Dead). Florence: Battistelli, 1919.

Novelle per un anno (Short Stories for a Year). Florence: Bemporad, 1922.

Uno, nessuno e centomila. (*One, No One, and One Hundred Thousand*). Florence: Bemporad, 1926. (First serialized in *La fiera letteraria,* 1925–1926.)

Drama, Theatrical Premieres

La Morsa (*The Vise*). Rome; December 9, 1910. (First pub. as *L'epilogo*)

Lumie di Sicilia (*Sicilian Limes*). Rome; December 9, 1910. Pub. 1911.

Il Dovere del Medico (*The Doctor's Duty*). Rome; June 20, 1913. Pub. 1912.

Se Non Cosí (If Not So). Milan; April 19, 1915. Pub. 1916. (Later retitled *La ragione degli altri* [Other People's Reasons].)

Cecè (*Chee-Chee*). Rome; December 14, 1915. Pub. 1913.

Pensaci, Giacomino! (Think It Over, Giacomino!). Rome; July 10, 1916. Pub. 1917.

Liolà (*Liolà*). Rome; November 4, 1916. Pub. 1917.

Cosí è (se vi pare) (*Right You Are [If You Think So]*). Milan; June 18, 1917. Pub. 1918.

Il berretto a sonagli (*Cap and Bells*). Rome; June 27, 1917. (Sicilian title: *'A birritta cu' i ciancianeddi*.) Pub. 1918.

La Giara (*The Jar*). Rome; July 9, 1917. (Sicilian title: *'A giarra*.) Pub. 1925.

Il piacere dell'onestà (*The Pleasure of Honesty*). Turin; November 27, 1917. Pub. 1918.

Ma non è una cosa seria (It's Nothing Serious). Leghorn; November 22, 1918. Pub. 1919.

Il giuoco delle parti (*The Rules of the Game*). Rome; December 6, 1918. Pub. 1919.

L'innesto (*Grafted*). Milan; January 29, 1919. Pub. 1921.

La patente (*The License*). Rome; February 19, 1919. (Sicilian title: '*A patenti.*) Pub. 1918.

L'uomo, la bestia e la virtú (*Man, Beast, and Virtue*). Milan: May 2, 1919.

Tutto per bene (*All for the Best*). Rome; March 2, 1920.

Come prima, meglio di prima (As Before, Better Than Before). Venice; March 24, 1920. Pub. 1921.

La signora Morli, una e due (Mrs. Morli, One and Two). Rome; November 12, 1921. Pub. 1922.

Sei personaggi in cerca d'autore (*Six Characters in Search of an Author*). Rome; May 10, 1921.

Enrico IV (*Henry IV*). Milan; February 24, 1922.

All'uscita (*At the Exit*). Rome; September 29, 1922. Pub. 1916.

L'imbecille (*The Imbecile*). Rome; October 10, 1922. Pub. 1926.

Vestire gli ignudi (*To Clothe the Naked*). Rome; November 14, 1922. Pub. 1923.

L'uomo dal fiore in bocca (*The Man with the Flower in His Mouth*). Rome; February 21, 1923. Pub. 1926.

La vita che ti diedi (*The Life I Gave You*). Rome; October 12, 1923. Pub. 1924.

L'altro figlio (*The Other Son*). Rome; November 23, 1923. Pub. 1925.

Ciascuno a suo modo (*Each in His Own Way*). Milan; May 22, 1924.

Sagra del Signore della nave (*The Festival of Our Lord of the Ship*). Rome; April 4, 1925. Pub. 1924.

Diana e la Tuda (*Diana and Tuda*). Zurich, Switzerland; November 20, 1926. Pub. 1927.

L'amica delle mogli (*The Wives' Friend*). Rome; April 28, 1927.

Bellavita (*Bellavita*). Milan; May 27, 1927. Pub. 1928.

Scamandro (Scamandro). Florence; February 19, 1928. (In verse with music by Fernando Liuzzi.) Pub. 1909.

La nuova colonia (*The New Colony*). Rome; March 24, 1928.

O di uno o di nessuno (Belonging to One or None). Turin; November 4, 1929.

Lazzaro (*Lazarus*). Huddersfield, England; July 9, 1929.

Questa sera si recita a soggetto (*Tonight We Improvise*). Königsberg, Germany (now Kaliningrad, Russia); January 25, 1930.

Come tu mi vuoi (*As You Desire Me*). Milan; February 18, 1930.

Sogno (ma forse no) (*I'm Dreaming, but Am I?*). Lisbon, Portugal; September 22, 1931. Pub. 1929.

Trovarsi (*To Find Oneself*). Naples; November 4, 1932.

Quando si è qualcuno (*When Somebody Is Somebody*). Buenos Aires, Argentina; September 20, 1933.

La favola del figlio cambiato (*The Fable of the Changeling*). Brunswick, Germany; January 13, 1934. (Music by Gian Francesco Malipiero.) Pub. 1933.

Non si sa come (*No One Knows How*). Prague, Czechoslovakia; December 19, 1934. Pub. 1935.

I giganti della montagna (*The Mountain Giants*). Florence; June 5, 1937. Pub. 1938.

English Editions

All for the Best. Trans. Henry Reed. Harmondsworth: Penguin Books, 1960.
As You Desire Me. Trans. Samuel Putnam. New York: E. P. Dutton, 1931.

Better Think Twice About It! and Twelve Other Stories. Trans. Arthur and Henrie Mayne. London: J. Lane, 1933; New York: E. P. Dutton, 1934. Rpt. 1976. Comprises "The Other Son," "Better Think Twice about It," "The Jar," "The Madonna's Gift," "A Call to Duty," "The Captive," "Chants the Epistle," "The Wet-Nurse," "The King Set Free," "The Crow of Mizzaro," "It's Nothing Serious," "The Quick and the Dead," "Black Horses."

Cap and Bells. Salt Lake City: Manyland Books, 1974.
Collected Plays. Ed. Robert Rietty. Vol. I. London: John Calder, 1987; New York: Riverrun Press, 1987. Comprises *Henry IV*, trans. Robert Rietty and John Wardle; *The Man with the Flower in His Mouth*, trans. Gigi Gatti and Terry Doyle. *Right You Are (If You Think You Are)*, trans. Bruce Penman; *Lazarus*, trans. Frederick May. Vol. II. London: John Calder, 1988; New York: Riverrun Press, 1988. Comprises *Six Characters in Search of an Author*, trans. Felicity Firth; *All for the Best*, trans. Henry Reed; *Clothe the Naked*, trans. Diane Cilento; *Limes from Sicily*, trans. Robert Rietty. Vol. III. London: John Calder, 1992; New York: Riverrun Press, 1992. Comprises *The Rules of the Game*, trans. Robert Rietty and Noel Cregeen; *Each in His Own Way*, trans. Felicity Firth; *Grafted*, trans. Robert Rietty; *The Other Son*, trans. Bruce Penman.
Contemporary Italian Fiction: Pomilio, Pirandello, Bonaviri. Trans. Giovanni Bussino. Whitestone, N.Y.: Griffon House, 1988. Contains three short stories: "Equal"; "The First Night"; "The Fish Trap."

Diana and Tuda. Trans. Marta Abba. New York: Samuel French, 1950.

Each in His Own Way and Two Other Plays. Trans. Arthur Livingston. New York: E. P. Dutton, 1923; London: Dent, 1924. Also contains *The Pleasure of Honesty* and *Naked*.
The Emperor (Enrico IV). Trans. Eric Bentley. *The Genius of the Italian Theatre*. Ed. Eric Bentley. New York: New American Library, 1964.

Four Tales. Trans. V. M. Jeffrey. London: Harrap, 1939.

Henry IV. Trans. Frederick May. Harmondsworth: Penguin Books, 1960.
Henry IV. Trans. Julian Mitchell. London: Eyre Methuen, 1979.
Horse in the Moon: Twelve Short Stories. Trans. Samuel Putnam. New York: E. P. Dutton,

1932. Comprises "Horse in the Moon," "Adriana Takes a Trip," "The Cat, a Gold-finch and the Stars," "The Schoolmistress's Romance," "A Dinner Guest," "Sunlight and Shadow," "Gay," "The Imbecile," " Miss Holloway's Goat," "The Light Across the Way," "A Wee Sma' Drop," "Sicilian Limes."

The Late Mattia Pascal. Trans. Arthur Livingston. London: Dent, 1923; New York: E. P. Dutton, 1923; 3d ed. 1934.
The Late Mattia Pascal. Ed. Nicoletta Simborowski. London and New York: Dedalus and Hippocrene, 1987.
The Late Mattia Pascal. Trans. William Weaver. Garden City, N.Y.: Doubleday, 1964; Hygiene, Colo.: Eridanos Press, 1987.
Lazarus, Ed. E. Martin Browne. Trans. Frederick May. Harmondsworth: Penguin, 1959.
Lazarus. Trans. Phyllis H. Raymond. Sydney, Australia: Dante Alighieri, 1952.
The Life I Gave You. Trans. Frederick May. Harmondsworth: Penguin Books, 1959.
Luigi Pirandello in the Theatre: A Documentary Record. Ed. Susan Bassnett. University of Warwick, Great Britain: Harwood Academic, 1993. Collection of essays, letters, reviews.

Man, Beast and Virtue. Trans. Charles Wood. Bath, England: Absolute Press, 1989.
The Man with the Flower in His Mouth. Trans. Eric Bentley. In *One Act.* Ed. Samuel Moon. New York: Grove Press, 1961; rpt. 1994.
The Man with the Flower in His Mouth. Trans. Frederick May. Leeds, England: Pirandello Society, 1959.
The Medals and Other Stories. Trans. Michele Pettinati. New York: E. P. Dutton, 1939; U.S. version of *A Character in Distress.* London: Duckworth, 1938. Comprises "A Character in Distress," "The Beauty and the Beast," "The Haunted House," "An Oversight," "The Husband's Revenge," "A Wronged Husband," "Sicilian Hour," "Mother," "A Widow's Dilemma," "A Mother-In-Law," "War," "Sicilian Tanger-ines," "Professor Lamis' Vengeance," "The Medals," "Bitter Waters," "A Cat, a Finch and the Stars," "When a Bear Went to Church," "Tortoises . . . for Luck," "My Last Journey."
The Merry-Go-Round of Love and Selected Stories. Trans. Frances Keene and Lily Duplaix. New York: New American Library, 1964.
The Mountain Giants. Trans. Charles Wood. Bath, England: Absolute Classics, 1993.
The Mountain Giants, and Other Plays. Trans. Marta Abba. New York: Crown Publish-ers, 1958. Also contains *The New Colony* and *When Somebody Is Somebody.*

Naked Masks. Ed. Eric Bentley. New York: E. P. Dutton, 1952; in print. Comprises *Liolà,* trans. Eric Bentley and Gerardo Guerrieri; *It Is So! (If You Think So)* and *Each in His Own Way,* trans. Arthur Livingston; *Henry IV* and *Six Characters in Search of an Author,* trans. Edward Storer.
The Naked Truth and Eleven Other Stories. Trans. Arthur and Henrie Mayne. New York: E. P. Dutton, 1934; London: John Lane, 1934. Comprises "The Annuity," "The Na-

ked Truth," "The Wayside Shrine," "The Spirit of Service," "The Rivers of Lapland," "Va Bene," "The Wax Madonna," "The Red Booklet," "The Fly," "The Benediction," "The Evil Spirit," "The Changeling."
No One Knows How. Trans. Marta Abba. London: S. French, 1949, 1963.

The Old and the Young. Trans. C. K. Scott-Moncrieff. 2 vols. New York: E. P. Dutton, 1928; London: Chatto and Windus, 1927. Rpt. announced by Dedalus Ltd.
On Humor. Trans. Antonio Illiano and Daniel P. Testa. Chapel Hill: University of North Carolina Press, 1974.
The One-Act Plays of Luigi Pirandello. Ed. Arthur Livingston. Trans. Elisabeth Abbott, Arthur Livingston, and Blanche Valentine Mitchell. New York: E. P. Dutton, 1928. Comprises eleven plays: *The Imbecile, By Judgment of Court, Our Lord of the Ship, The Doctor's Duty, Chee-Chee, The Man with the Flower in His Mouth, At the Gate, The Vise, The House with the Column, Sicilian Limes, The Jar.*
One, None and a Hundred-Thousand. Trans. Samuel Putnam. New York: Dutton, 1933.
One, No One, and One Hundred Thousand. Trans. William Weaver. Boston: Eridanos Press, 1990.
The Outcast. Trans. Leo Ongley. New York: Dutton, 1925; new ed. 1935.

Pirandello's Love Letters to Marta Abba. Ed. and trans. Benito Ortolani. Princeton, N.J.: Princeton University Press, 1994. Contains translations of 164 of 552 letters written by Pirandello to his ideal actress and platonic love, Marta Abba, between 1926 and 1936, the year of his death. Excellent documentary source. Private, previously unpublished correspondence.
Pirandello's Major Plays. Trans. Eric Bentley. Evanston, Ill.: Northwestern University Press, 1991. Comprises four plays: *Right You Are, Six Characters in Search of an Author, Emperor Henry, The Man with the Flower in His Mouth.*
Pirandello's One-Act Plays. Trans. William Murrary. Garden City, N.Y.: Doubleday Anchor Books, 1964; New York: Samuel French, 1970; New York: Funk & Wagnalls, 1970. Comprises thirteen plays: *The Vise, Sicilian Limes, The Doctor's Duty, The Jar, The License, Chee-Chee, At the Exit, The Imbecile, The Man with the Flower in His Mouth, The Other Son, The Festival of Our Lord of the Ship, Bellavita, I'm Dreaming, but Am I?*
The Pleasure of Honesty. Trans. William Murray. *Masterpieces of the Modern Italian Theatre.* Ed. Robert W. Corrigan. New York: Macmillan/Collier Books, 1967.

Right You Are. Ed. and trans. Eric Bentley. New York: Columbia University Press, 1954; rpt. in *The Great Playwrights.* Ed. Eric Bentley. New York: Doubleday, 1970.
Right You Are (If You Think So). Trans. Frederick May. Harmondsworth: Penguin, 1960.
The Rules of the Game. Trans. and adapted David Hare. Bath, England: Absolute Classics, 1993.
The Rules of the Game, The Life I Gave You, Lazarus. Ed. E. Martin Browne. Trans. Robert Rietty and Frederick May. Harmondsworth: Penguin Books, 1959/1960.

Shoot! The Notebooks of Serafino Gubbio, Cinematograph Operator. Trans. C. K. Scott Moncrieff. New York: E. P. Dutton, 1926; London: Chatto & Windus, 1927; 2d ed. 1934. Rpt. as *The Notebooks of Serafino Gubbio, or, Shoot!*. Ed. Nicoletta Simborowski. Sawtry, England: Dedalus, 1990.

Short Stories. Trans. Lily Duplaix. New York: Simon & Schuster, 1959. Comprises "Lost and Found," "Fumes," "Bombolo," "Who Pays the Piper . . .," "A Mere Formality," "Watch and Ward," "The Examination," "Man's Best Friend," "A Breath of Air," "Yesterday and Today," "Escape," "The Footwarmer," "The Soft Touch of Grass," "Gingi," "The Umbrella," "The New Suit," "The Rose," "Candelora," "The Black Shawl," "Such Is Life," "The Wreath."

Short Stories. Trans. Frederick May. London and New York: Oxford University Press, 1965; 1975; Rpt. London, England: Quartet Encounters, 1987. Comprises "The Little Hut," "The Cooper's Cockerels," "A Dream of Christmas," "Twelve Letters," "Fear," "The Best of Friends," "Bitter Waters," "The Jar," "The Tragedy of a Character," "A Call to Duty," "In the Abyss," "The Black Kid," "Signora Frola and Her Son-In-Law, Signor Ponza," "The Man with the Flower in His Mouth," "Destruction of the Man," "Puberty," "Cinci," "All Passion Spent," "The Visit," "The Tortoise," "A Day Goes By."

Sicilian Comedies. Cap and Bells and Man, Beast and Virtue. Trans. Norman A. Bailey and Roger W. Oliver. New York: Performing Arts Journal Publications, 1983.

Sicilian Limes. Trans. Issac Goldberg. In *Plays of the Italian Theatre.* Boston: J. W. Luce, 1921.

Six Characters in Search of an Author. Trans. Eric Bentley. In *The Great Playwrights.* New York: Doubleday, 1970.

Six Characters in Search of an Author. Trans. John Linstrum. London: Eyre Methuen, 1979.

Six Characters in Search of an Author. Trans. Frederick May. London: Heinemann Educational Books, 1954–1978.

Six Characters in Search of an Author. Trans. Paul Avila Mayer. In *Masterpieces of the Modern Italian Theatre.* Ed. Robert W. Corrigan. New York: Macmillan/Collier Books, 1967.

Six Characters in Search of an Author: A Comedy in the Making. Trans. Edward Storer. In *Sixteen Famous European Plays.* New York: Modern Library, 1943.

Six Characters in Search of an Author and Other Plays. Trans. Mark Musa. New York: Penguin, 1996. Also comprises *Henry IV* and *So It Is (If You Think So).*

The Sounds of the Girgenti Dialect and Their Development. Trans. Giovanni Bussino. American University Series: Linguistics, XIII (1992). New York: Peter Lang. Pirandello's doctoral thesis.

Tales of Madness: A Selection from Luigi Pirandello's "Short Stories for a Year." Ed. and trans. Giovanni R. Bussino. Brookline Village, Mass.: Dante University of America Press, 1984. Comprises sixteen stories: "Who Did It?," "If . . .," "When I Was Crazy,"

"The Shrine," "Pitagora's Misfortune," "Set Fire to the Straw," "A Horse in the Moon," "Fear of Being Happy," "In the Whirlpool," "The Reality of the Dream," "The Train Whistled . . .," "Mrs. Frola and Mr. Ponza, Her Son-in-Law," "The Wheelbarrow," "Escape," "Puberty," "Victory of the Ants."

Tales of Suicide: A Selection from Luigi Pirandello's "Short Stories for a Year." Ed. and trans. Giovanni R. Bussino. Boston: Dante University of America Press, 1988. Comprises twenty stories: "Sun and Shade," "Sunrise," "The Black Shawl," "This Makes Two!," "Into the Sketch," "In Silence," "The Trip," "The Stuffed Bird," "The Lonely Man," "The Trap," "The Imbecile," "The Fish Trap," "By Himself," "The Long Dress," "Candelora," "While the Heart Suffered," "Aunt Michelina," "Nothing," "An Idea," "A Challenge."

Three Plays by Pirandello. Trans. Arthur Livingston and Edward Storer. New York: E. P. Dutton, 1922; London: Dent, 1923; 3d ed. 1929. Comprises *Right You Are (If You Think So), Henry IV, Six Characters in Search of an Author.*

To Clothe the Naked, and Two Other Plays. Trans. William Murrary. New York: Dutton, 1962. Also contains *The Pleasure of Honesty* and *The Rules of the Game.*

To Find Oneself. Trans. Marta Abba. New York: Samuel French, 1959.

Tonight We Improvise. Trans. Samuel Putnam. New York: Dutton: 1932.

Tonight We Improvise; and, "Leonora Addio!" Trans. J. Douglas Campbell and Leonard G. Sbrocchi. Ottawa: Canadian Society for Italian Studies, 1987. Biblioteca di Quaderni d'Italianistica No. 3. Rpt. in *Twentieth-Century Italian Drama: An Anthology of the First Fifty Years.* Ed. Jane House and Antonio Attisani. New York: Columbia University Press, 1995. This volume also includes "Why?" ("Perché?" 1892), a sketch. Trans. Jane House.

The Wives' Friend: A Drama in Three Acts. Trans. Marta Abba. New York: French, 1949/1960.

Critical Works

Books and Issues of Journals Dedicated to Pirandello

Alessio, Antonio, Domenico Pietropaolo, and Giuliana Katz, eds. *Pirandello and the Modern Theatre.* Ottawa: Canadian Society for Italian Studies, 1992. Biblioteca di Quaderni d'italianistica, No. 10. A dozen articles on drama, theatrical innovations, and influence on Italian dramatists.

Barbina, Alfredo. *Bibliografia della critica pirandelliana 1889–1961.* Firenze: Le Monnier, 1967. Covering a seventy-year span, this is an international compilation of critical works on Pirandello. A valuable bibliographical source.

Bassnett-McGuire, Susan. *Luigi Pirandello.* New York: Grove Press, 1984. An overview stressing contemporary interpretations of the major plays.

Bentley, Eric. *The Pirandello Commentaries.* Evanston, Ill.: Northwestern University Press, 1986. An excellent collection of many of Bentley's previously published articles, dated 1946 to 1986.

Biasin, Gian Paolo, and Nicolas J. Perella, eds. *Pirandello 1986: Atti del Simposio internazionale (Università di California, Berkeley, 13–15 marzo 1986).* Roma: Bulzoni, 1987. The published proceedings of an international scholarly conference; fifteen articles, eight in English.

Bishop, Thomas. *Pirandello and the French Theater.* New York: New York University Press, 1960. Focuses on Pirandello's influence on French theater from the 1920s to the 1950s.

Biundo, James V. *Moments of Selfhood: Three Plays by Luigi Pirandello.* New York: Peter Lang, 1990. An overview followed by a close analysis of *Six Characters in Search of an Author, Right You Are,* and *Henry IV.*

Bloom, Harold ed. *Luigi Pirandello.* New York and Philadelphia: Chelsea House, 1989. A fine representative selection of previously published and reprinted English-language scholarship on Pirandello.

Büdel, Oscar. *Pirandello.* London: Bowes and Bowes, 1966. 2d ed. 1969. Four essays explore Pirandello's relativism, position in modern theater, and humour. Presupposes some familiarity with Pirandello's life and works.

Cambon, Glauco, ed. *Pirandello: A Collection of Essays.* Englewood Cliffs, N.J.: Prentice-Hall, 1967. An anthology of important international critical essays, some abridged, published between 1923 and 1966.

Canadian Journal of Italian Studies, VI, 2–3 (1983). *Special Issue: Pirandello.* Scholarly articles on such topics as theater as memory, Pirandello and Sicily, the artist's role, filming of *The New Colony.*

Canadian Journal of Italian Studies, XII, 38–39 (1989), & XIII, 40–41 (1990). *Special Issues: Pirandello I & II.* Ed. Douglas Radcliff-Umstead. Scholarly articles in both English and Italian. Topics include Pirandello's notions of time, his philosophy, the themes of individual limits, incest, play within the play, sources, influences, and so forth.

Caputi, Anthony. *Pirandello and the Crisis of Modern Consciousness.* Urbana and Chicago: University of Illinois Press, 1988. An engaging, thought-provoking study of Pirandello's work as a long, multifaceted meditation on consciousness.

Da Vinci Nichols, Nina, and Jana O'Keefe Bazzoni. *Pirandello and Film.* Lincoln and London: University of Nebraska Press, 1995.

Di Gaetani, John Louis, ed. *A Companion to Pirandello Studies.* New York, Westport, Conn., and London: Greenwood Press, 1991. An excellent compendium of articles that is divided in thematic units. Includes several useful bibliographical and informational appendixes.

Donati, Corrado. *Bibliografia della critica pirandelliana 1962–1981.* Florence: Editrice

La Ginestra, 1986. An extensive international listing (more than 1,200 titles) of secondary sources covering a twenty-year span. Accompanied by a lengthy article on critical tendencies and a concordance. A valuable bibliographical tool.

Firth, Felicity. *Pirandello in Performance.* Cambridge, England, and Alexandria, Va.: Chadwyck-Healey, 1990. Accompanied by fifty slides.

Forum Italicum. I, 4 (1967) *Special Issue: A Hommage to Pirandello in the First Centennial of His Birth.* Thirteen scholarly articles, four in English, on topics ranging from the absurd to Zen.

Giudice, Gaspare. *Luigi Pirandello.* Turin: UTET, 1963. The best and most extensive biography of the writer. Trans. as *Pirandello: A Biography* by Alastair Hamilton. London, New York, and Toronto: Oxford University Press, 1975. The translation is also an abridgment with some reorganization of chapter materials. Hamilton has been criticized for distorting or diminishing some of Giudice's careful discussions.

Günsberg, Maggie. *Patriarchal Representations: Gender and Discourse in Pirandello's Theatre.* Oxford and Providence: Berg, 1993. A feminist approach to sex roles.

Illiano, Antonio. *Introduzione alla critica Pirandelliana.* Verona: Fiorini, 1976. Discussion of international secondary sources.

Italica, XLIV, 1 (1967). *Special Issue: Pirandello Centenary Number.* Four scholarly articles, three in English. Topics include *Six Characters* as a comedy in the making and the puppet world.

Leone De Castris, Arcangelo. *Storia di Pirandello.* 2d ed. Biblioteca di cultura moderna, 571 (Bari: Laterza, 1962); rpt. Bari: Laterza, 1966. A key text.

MacClintock, Lander. *The Age of Pirandello.* Bloomington: Indiana University Press, 1951. Pirandellian drama in the context of the theater of his day, including the *Grottesco* and the French.

Matthaei, Renate. *Luigi Pirandello.* Trans. S. and E. Young. New York: Ungar, 1973. Translated from the German 1967 original. A general overview followed by analyses, with a Euro-German perspective, of nine plays .

Mignone, Mario, ed. *Pirandello in America: Atti del Simposio Internazionale (Università Statale di New York, Stony Brook, 30 ottobre–1 novembre1986).* Rome: Bulzoni, 1988. The published proceedings of an international scholarly conference, the volume contains nineteen articles, eleven in English.

Modern Drama, VI, 4 (1964). *Special Issue: Pirandello.* Five scholarly articles on such subjects as symbolism, use of mirror and masks.

Modern Drama, XX, 4 (1977). *Special issue: Pirandello.* Seven scholarly articles on such topics as use of comedy and paradox, metaphysical dimensions, rapport with theosophy, and a Derridean analysis of *Six Characters in Search of an Author.*

Modern Drama, XXX, 3 (1987). *Special Issue: Pirandello.* Includes several scholarly articles.

Moestrup, Jorn. *The Structural Patterns of Pirandello's Work.* Odense: Odense University Press, 1972.

Nardelli, Federico Vittore. *L'Uomo segreto: Vita e croci di Luigi Pirandello.* Milan: Mondadori, 1932. A somewhat rhetorical, embellished biography authorized by Pirandello. Encomiastic, therefore not always accurate or objective. Expanded edition titled *Vita segreta di Pirandello.* Rome: Bianco, 1962.

Newberry, W. *The Pirandellian Mode in Spanish Literature from Cervantes to Sastre.* Albany: State University of New York Press, 1973.

Oliver, Roger W. *Dreams of Passion: The Theater of Luigi Pirandello.* New York: New York University Press, 1979. Humor as the underlying concept in Pirandellian drama. Close analyses of five plays.

Paolucci, Anne. *Pirandello's Theater: The Recovery of the Modern Stage for Dramatic Art.* Carbondale and Edwardsville: Southern Illinois University Press, 1974; London and Amsterdam: Feffer & Simons, 1974. Valid analyses of several plays to define the development of Pirandello's theatrical art.

Pirandellian Studies (Winter 1985–now). A scholarly journal published at irregular intervals.

PSA: The Official Publication of the Pirandello Society of America. (1985–now). An annual scholarly journal.

Radcliff-Umstead, Douglas. *The Mirror of Our Anguish: A Study of Luigi Pirandello's Narrative Writings.* Rutherford N.J.: Farleigh Dickinson University Press, 1978; London: Associated University Presses, 1978. In-depth analysis of Pirandello's seven novels and the short stories.

Ragusa, Olga. *Luigi Pirandello.* New York and London: Columbia University Press, 1968. An informative monograph.

———. *Luigi Pirandello: An Approach to His Theatre.* Edinburgh: Edinburgh University Press, 1980. Stresses drama but includes critical essays and other writings. Detailed.

Review of National Literatures 14 (1987). *Special Issue: Pirandello.* Ed. Anne Paolucci. Nine scholarly articles, eight in English, on topics ranging from naturalism to the playwright's rapport with his audience, and comparative studies.

Sciascia, Leonardo. *Pirandello e la Sicilia.* Caltanisetta-Roma: Sciascia, 1961. 2d ed. 1968. Major text on Sicilianism.

Sogliuzzo, A. Richard. *Luigi Pirandello Director: The Playwright in the Theatre.* Metuchen, N.J.: Scarecrow Press, 1982. In-depth analysis of several plays accompanied by discussion of their original performance and reception. Discussion of aesthetic theories on theater.

Starkie, Walter. *Luigi Pirandello*. London: Dent, 1926; 2d ed. London: John Murray, 1937; 3d ed. as *Luigi Pirandello 1867–1936*. 3d revised ed. Berkeley and Los Angeles: University of California Press, 1965. A fine early study, influenced by Tilgher's life/form duality and emphasis on cerebralism. Explores Pirandello's place in modern drama.

Stocchi-Perucchio, Donatella. *Pirandello and the Vagaries of Knowledge: A Reading of "Il fu Mattia Pascal."* Stanford French and Italian Studies, v. 64. Saratoga, Calif.: ANIMA Libri, 1991.

Stone, Jennifer. *Pirandello's Naked Prompt: The Structure of Repitition in Modernism*. Ravenna, Italy: Longo, 1989. A critical study, the approach includes semiotics and Freudian analysis.

Tulane Drama Review. X, 3 (Spring 1966). *Special Issue: Pirandello*. Five articles on topics such as the passage of time, possibility, and directing Pirandello for the stage.

Vittorini, Domenico. *The Drama of Luigi Pirandello*. Philadelphia: University of Pennsylvania Press, 1935; 2d ed. New York: Dover, 1957; rpt. New York: Russell & Russell, 1969. One of the first organic studies in English devoted to the theater works. Valid points, a bit dated.

Yearbook of the British Pirandello Society (1981–now). An annual publication containing scholarly articles and reviews.

Chapters and Sections in Books

Abbott, Anthony S. "Luigi Pirandello." *The Vital Lie: Reality and Illusion in Modern Drama*. Tuscaloosa and London: University of Alabama Press, 1989. Pp. 71–86. The interrelationship of reality and illusion and the presence of human suffering in five plays.

Bassnett-McGuire, Susan. "Art and Life in Luigi Pirandello's *Questa sera si recita a soggetto*." *Drama and Mimesis*. Ed. James Redmond. Cambridge and New York: Cambridge University Press, 1980. Pp. 81–102. This play as representative of Pirandellian theater.

Bentley, Eric. *The Life of the Drama*. New York: Atheneum, 1967. See Pp. 132–36. A discussion of the pathological nature of some Pirandellian characters that explores schizophrenia and neurosis.

———. *"Right You Are," "Enrico IV," "Six Characters in Search of an Author." Theatre of War: Comments on 32 Occasions*. New York: Viking Press, 1972. Pp. 22–63. In-depth analyses, including staging.

————. "Pirandello's Joy and Torment." *In Search of Theater.* New York: Knopf, 1953. Rpt. New York: Vintage Books, 1959. Pp. 279–95. Rpt. New York: Atheneum, 1975. Pp. 296–314. A critique of the formal aspects of Pirandellian theater followed by a psychological analysis.

Bermel, Albert. "The Living Statues: *Six Characters in Search of an Author.*" *Contradictory Characters: An Interpretation of the Modern Theatre.* New York: Dutton, 1973. Pp. 122–43. A psychoanalytical interpretation of family story in *Six Characters.*

Biasin, Gian-Paolo. "Moscarda's Mirror." *Literary Diseases: Theme and Metaphor in the Italian Novel.* Austin and London: University of Texas Press, 1975. Pp. 100–126. An analysis of image, mirror, and madness in *One, No One, and One Hundred Thousand.*

————. "Strategies of the Anti-hero: Svevo, Pirandello, and Montale." *Italian Literature: Roots and Branches. Essays in Honor of Thomas Goddard Bergin.* Ed. Giosè Rimanelli and Kenneth John Atchity. New Haven and London: Yale University Press, 1976. Pp. 363–81. Vitangelo Moscarda of *One, No One, and One Hundred Thousand* as antihero.

Binion, Rudolph. "The Play as Replay or The Key to Pirandello's *Six Characters in Search of an Author, Henry IV,* and *Clothe the Naked.*" *Soundings: Psychohistorical and Psycholiterary.* New York: Psychohistory Press, 1981. Pp. 127–55. A psychoanalytical reading based on biographical data.

Bradbury, Malcolm. "Luigi Pirandello." *The Modern World: Ten Great Writers.* London: Secker & Warburg, 1988. Pp. 203–27. Pirandello the dramatist as a seminal modern writer.

Brustein, Robert. "Luigi Pirandello." *The Theatre of Revolt: An Approach to the Modern Drama.* Boston and Toronto: Little, Brown, 1964. Pp. 279–317. Rpt. Chicago: Elephant Paperbacks, 1991. Excellent piece on Pirandello as an existential, social, and messianic rebel and founder of modern drama.

Chandler, Frank W. "The Philosophic Pirandello." *Modern Continental Playwrights.* New York and London: Harper, 1931. Pp. 573–95. Somewhat dated overview.

Chiaromonte, Nicola. "Pirandello and Humor." *The Worm of Consciousness and Other Essays.* Ed. Miriam Chiaromonte. New York: Harcourt Brace Jovanovich, 1976. Pp. 80–93. Discussion of *On Humor.*

Dashwood, J. R. "Pirandello and Dream Theatre." *Writers and Performers in Italian Drama from the Time of Dante to Pirandello: Essays in Honor of G. H. McWilliam.* Lewiston, N.Y., Queenston, Ontario, and Lampeter, Wales: Edward Mellen Press, 1991. Pp. 145–64. Emphasis on the one-act *Sogno (ma forse no)* in the context of Freudian displacement.

Della Terza, Dante. "On Pirandello's Humorism." *Veins of Humor.* Ed. H. Levin. Cambridge: Harvard University Press, 1972. Pp. 17–33.

Dombroski, Robert S. "Luigi Pirandello: Epistemology and Pure Subjectivity."

Properties of Writing: Ideological Discourse in Modern Italian Fiction. Baltimore and London: Johns Hopkins University Press, 1994. Pp. 69–92. Excellent study of *One, No One, and One Hundred Thousand* from the perspective of ideological criticism.

Driver, Tom F. "Luigi Pirandello (1867–1936)." *Romantic Quest and Modern Query: A History of the Modern Theatre.* New York: Delacorte, 1970. Pp. 391–414. Good thematic overview of drama.

Esslin, Martin. "Pirandello: Master of the Naked Masks." *Reflections: Essays on Modern Theatre.* New York: Doubleday, 1969. Pp. 49–57. Discusses relativity, personality, and reality.

Fergusson, Francis. "Action as Theatrical: *Six Characters in Search of an Author.*" *The Idea of a Theatre.* Garden City, N.Y.: Doubleday, 1953. Pp. 198–206.

Freedman, Morris. "Moral Perspective in Pirandello." *The Moral Impulse: Modern Drama from Ibsen to the Present.* Carbondale and Edwardsville: Southern Illinois University Press, 1967; London: Feiffer, 1967. Pp. 74–88.

Ganz, Arthur. "Ibsen, Pirandello, Pinter." *Realms of The Self: Variations on a Theme in Modern Drama.* New York and London: New York University Press, 1980. Pp.170–90. Discussion of the "imprisoned self."

Garzilli, Enrico. "Between the Circle and the Labyrinth: Mask, Personality and Identity—Luigi Pirandello." *Circles without Center: Paths to the Discovery and Creation of Self in Modern Literature.* Cambridge: Harvard University Press, 1972. Pp. 75–88. Self-consiousness and the fragmentation of identity.

Gascoigne, Bamber. "Luigi Pirandello (1867–1936)." *Twentieth-Century Drama.* London: Hutchinson & Co., 1962. Pp. 98–108; New York: Barnes & Noble, 1966. An overview.

Gaskell, Ronald. "Pirandello: *Six Characters in Search of An Author.*" *Drama and Reality: The European Theatre since Ibsen.* London: Routledge & Kegan Paul, 1972. Pp. 117–27. General overview.

Gassner, John. "Pirandello and the Illusionism of the Italian Stage." *Masters of the Drama.* New York: Random House, 1940; 3d expanded ed. New York: Dover Publications, 1954. Pp. 431–45. General overview of Italian theater and Pirandello.

———. "Pirandello and the Six Characters." *The Theatre in Our Times.* New York: Crown, 1954. Pp. 193–99. Discussion of theatricality.

Gilman, Richard. "Luigi Pirandello." *The Making of Modern Drama. A Study of Büchner, Ibsen, Strindberg, Chekhov, Pirandello, Brecht, Beckett, Handke.* New York: Farrar, Strauss and Giroux, 1974. Pp. 157–79. Paperback rpt. New York: Da Capo Press, 1987. Pp. 157–89. An overview, stressing *Right You Are, Six Characters,* and *Henry IV.*

Harrison, Thomas. "Luigi Pirandello: The Mechanical Phantasmagoria" and "Luigi Pirandello: Cheating the Image." *Essayism: Conrad Musil & Pirandello.* Baltimore

185

and London: Johns Hopkins University Press, 1992. Pp. 87–120; 189–215. A somewhat philosophically oriented approach to issues of creativity and consciousness.

Heffner, Hubert C. "Pirandello and the Nature of Man." *Modern Drama: Essays in Criticism.* Ed. Travis Bogard and William I. Oliver. London and New York: Oxford University Press, 1965. Pp. 255–75. Issues of personality, consciousness, and characterization.

Hodgson, Terry. "Pirandello: Creativity, Pessimism and the Limits of Naturalism." *Modern Drama: From Ibsen to Fugard.* London: B. T. Batsford, 1992. Pp. 36–43. Analysis of *Six Characters.*

Illiano, Antonio. "Pirandello in England and the United States: A Chronological List of Criticism." *Bulletin of the New York Public Library,* LXXI, 2 (1967): 105–30. An excellent resource tool for earlier English-language criticism.

Knapp, Bettina L. "Luigi Pirandello's *Tonight We Improvise*—Machine, Magus, and Matriarchate." *Machine, Metaphor, and the Writer: A Jungian View.* University Park and London: Pennsylvania State University Press, 1989. Pp. 59–76. Theater as a machine hungry for poetry.

Krutch, Joseph Wood. "Pirandello and the Dissolution of the Age." *Modernism in Modern Drama.* Ithaca: Cornell University Press, 1953. Pp. 77–87. Rpt. 1966. Pp. 65–87. Considers Pirandello and Proust major exponents of the dissolution of the self, resulting from Marxism, Darwinism, and Freud.

Lepschy, Anna Laura. "The Treatment of Antefact in Pirandello's Theatre in the Theatre Trilogy." *Writers and Performers in Italian Drama from the Time of Dante to Pirandello: Essays in Honor of G. H. McWilliam.* Lewiston, N.Y., Queenston, Ontario, and Lampeter, Wales: Edward Mellen Press, 1991. Pp. 129–43. Treatment of the "play within a play" structure.

Lewis, Allan. "The Relativity of Truth: Pirandello, *Henry IV.*" *The Contemporary Theatre.* New York: Crown, 1971. Pp. 127–43. A thematic overview emphasizing *Henry IV.*

Lorch, Jennifer. "Pirandello, Commedia dell'Arte and Improvisation." *The Commedia dell'Arte: From the Renaissance to Dario Fo.* Ed. Christopher Cairns. Lewiston, N.Y., Queenston, Ontario, and Lampeter, Wales: Edward Mellen Press, 1989. Pp. 297–313. Pirandello's views on improvisation, emphasizing *Tonight We Improvise.*

Lucas, Frank Laurence. "Luigi Pirandello." *The Drama of Chekhov, Synge, Yeats and Pirandello.* London: Cassel, 1963. Pp. 133–69. Rpt: New York: Phaeton Press, 1976. Pp. 359–422. General biographical and thematic overview.

Lucente, Gregory L. "'Non conclude': Narrative Self-consciousness and the Voice of Creation in Pirandello's *Il fu Mattia Pascal* and *Uno, nessuno e centomila.*" *Beautiful Fables: Self-consciouness in Italian Narrative from Manzoni to Calvino.* Baltimore and London: Johns Hopkins University Press, 1986. Pp. 116–55.

Lumley, Frederick. "The Mask and Face of Luigi Pirandello." *Trends in 20th Century Drama: a Survey Since Ibsen and Shaw.* London: Barrie and Rockliff, 1956, 2d ed. 1960. Pp. 19–35. New eds.: *New Trends in 20th Century Drama.* London and New York: Oxford University Press, 1967, 1972. Pp. 18–34. Struggle between the real and the illusory, and between the absolute and the relative, and the function of characters.

McCormick, E. Allen. "Luigi Pirandello: Major Writer, Minor Novelist." *From Verismo to Experimentalism: Essays on the Modern Italian Novel.* Ed. Sergio Pacifici. Bloomington: Indiana University Press, 1969. Pp. 61–80. Analysis of the major novels.

McFarlane, James. "Neo-Modernist Drama: Yeats and Pirandello." *Modernism 1890–1930.* Ed. Malcolm Bradbury and James McFarlane. New York: Viking Penguin, 1976; rpt. Hassocks, England: Harvester, 1978; Atlantic Highlands, N.J.: Humanities Press, 1978/1986. Pp. 561–70. Pirandello as a principal representative of modernism.

Nelson, Robert J. "Schnitzler and Pirandello." *Play within a Play: The Dramatist's Conception of His Art: Shakespeare to Anouilh.* New Haven: Yale University Press, 1958. Pp. 115–33. Drama as life in the theater plays and *Right You Are.*

Nicoll, Allardyce. "The Extension of the Realistic: Luigi Pirandello." *World Drama from Aeschylus to Anouilh.* London: Harrap, 1949; New York: Harcourt, Brace, 1950. Pp. 707–18. 2d ed: London: Harrap, 1976. General overview of major and minor plays.

Pacifici, Sergio. "Luigi Pirandello: Man and His Masks." *The Modern Italian Novel from Capuana to Tozzi.* Carbondale: Southern Illinois University Press, 1973; London: Feffer & Simons, 1973. Pp. 108–35. A general overview with specific analyses of three novels.

Pedoto, Constance A. "Luigi Pirandello's *Six Characters in Search of an Author* through *Incollato* and Picasso's Cubism." *Painting Literature: Dostoevsky, Kafka, Pirandello, and Garcia Marquez in Living Color.* Lanham: University Press of America, 1993. Pp. 49–71. Links between Cubist collage techniques and painting and Pirandellian fragmentation and multiplicity of individuals.

Roland, Alan, and Gino Rizzo. "Psychoanalysis in Search of Pirandello: Six Characters and Henry IV." *Psychoanalysis, Creativity, and Literature: A French-American Inquiry.* Ed. Alan Roland. New York: Columbia University Press, 1978. Pp. 323–51. A variation on psychoanalytic literary criticism as applied to Pirandello.

Rolfs, Daniel. "Beyond Sin and Glory: Pirandello." *The Last Cross: A History of the Suicide Theme in Italian Literture.* Ravenna: Longo, 1981. Pp. 115–21. Suicide theme in the short stories.

Salinari, Carlo. "La coscienza della crisi." *Miti e coscienza del decadentismo italiano (D'Annunzio, Pascoli, Fogazzaro e Pirandello).* Milan: Feltrinelli, 1960. Pp. 249–84. Pirandello as the principle Italian literary exponent of the existential crisis facing the modern individual.

Schlueter, June. "Pirandello's Henry IV." *Metafictional Characters in Modern Drama.* New York: Columbia University Press, 1979. Pp. 19–34. Henry IV as embodiment of reality and illusion.

Stein, Walter. "Drama." *The Twentieth-Century Mind: History, Ideas and Literature in Britain.* Vol. II: "1918–1945." Ed. C. B. Cox and A. E. Dyson. London and New York: Oxford University Press, 1972. See pp. 427–32. Pirandello as modernist playwright.

Styan, John L. "Pirandello and the *teatro grottesco.*" *Modern Drama in Theory and Practice.* Vol. II. Cambridge and New York: Cambridge University Press, 1981. Pp. 76–84. Brief general overview emphasizing *Six Characters in Search of an Author.*

————. "Towards Tragic Inversion: Pirandello." *The Dark Comedy: The Development of Modern Comic Tragedy.* 2d ed. London: Cambridge University Press, 1968. Pp. 137–57. An in-depth analysis of *Henry IV.*

Szondi, Peter. "Enacting the Impossibility of the Drama: Pirandello." *Theory of the Modern Drama.* Trans. Michael Hays. Minneapolis: University of Minnesota Press, 1987. Pp. 77–81. Original: *Theorie des modernen Dramas,* Suhrkamp Verlag, 1965. *Six Characters* and the drama genre.

Tilgher, Adriano. *Studi del teatro contemporaneo.* 3d ed. Rome: Libreria di Scienze e Lettere, 1928. The formulation of life/form antithesis.

Valency, Maurice. "Pirandello." *The End of the World: An Introduction to Contemporary Drama.* Oxford and New York: Oxford University Press, 1980. Pp. 84–205. Excellent presentation of Pirandellian themes and major dramatic works.

Vittorini, Domenico. "Pirandello's Philosophy of Life." *Essays in the Modern Drama.* Ed. Morris Freedman. Boston: D. C. Heath, 1964. Pp. 80–90. Reprinted section from Vittorini's book, cited above.

Wellwarth, George E. *Modern Drama and the Death of God.* Madison: University of Wisconsin Press, 1986. See pp. 32–45. A discussion of philosophical subjectivism and fragmentation.

Index

Abba, Marta, 19, 20–21, 125, 129, 136, 159n. 20, 160n. 2, 164n. 16, 166n. 8
Acciaio (film) 162n. 5
Adultery, 12–16, 25–28, 44–45, 55–62, 94–95, 100–101, 119–20, 126–29, 151–53
Albee, Edward, 156
Alienation, 6–7, 26–27, 35–36, 38–39, 48, 55–62, 65–68, 70–75, 77, 81, 83, 86, 91–92, 94–96, 104–5, 117–20, 122–23, 126–29, 143–45, 148, 150–51
Almanacco letterario Bompiani, 157n. 2
Alvaro, Corrado, 138
Anouilh, Jean, 156
Appearances. *See* reality and illusion
Ark of the Covenant, 128
Art as myth, 121–22, 129–33
Authenticity, 27–28, 31–41, 63–70, 72, 93–94, 107, 125, 134, 151–55

Banca Romana scandal, 144
Bassnett-McGuire, Susan, 11, 124, 165n. 18
Beffa (tricking story), 12
Bentley, Eric, 11, 48, 50, 51, 87, 88, 118, 163n. 5, 170n. 20
Bergson, Henri, 4, 8, 61, 84, 164n. 12
Bermel, Albert, 167n. 19
Bildungsroman, 32
Binet, Alfred, 7–8; *Les Altérations de la Personnalité,* 7
Binion, Rudolph, 88, 118, 167n. 19; "The Play as Replay," 118
Bishop, Thomas, 88
Bontempelli, Massimo, 160n. 2; *La nostra dea,* 161n. 2
Borsellino, Nino, 145–46

Bosco, Umberto, 74
Bourgeois drama 10, 17, 43–46, 55–57, 61, 108–11, 152–55
Bradbury, Malcolm 17, 105
Brecht, Bertolt, 155
Brustein, Robert, 90–91, 100, 116, 161n. 5
Büdel, Oscar, 109, 115

Camus, Albert, 156
Canzone dell'amore, La (film), 162n. 5
Capuana, Luigi, 5, 9, 22–23, 24, 25, 139; *Il Marchese di Roccaverdina,* 25; *Ribrezzo,* 25
Caputi, Anthony, 87, 157n. 5, 165n. 6
Carducci, Giosuè, 137
Casella, Alfredo, 146
Chance, 2, 30–41, 84, 139, 141–42, 153
Character, Pirandello's concept of, 20, 40–41, 92–93, 97–100, 102–7, 109–10, 113–17, 133, 166nn. 6 & 8
Chiarelli, Luigi, 45; *La maschera e il volto,* 45
Chaos, 2, 21, 157n. 3
Chekhov, Anton, 42
Cinema in Italy, 70–75, 162n. 5
Classical theater, 42, 86, 122, 161n. 5, 166n. 8
Clown figure, 52. *See also* Commedia dell'Arte
Cocteau, Jean, 156
Collage technique in art, 74–75, 166n. 6
Comédie humaine, 138–39
Commedia dell'Arte, 52, 87, 159n.14, 161n. 5
Consciousness, 7–8, 15–16, 18, 21, 24, 26–

189

Consciousness *(continued)*
41, 44–45, 53–87, 89, 92–93, 104–5, 107, 117–18, 133, 143, 146, 148–49, 153–55
Corporeal Works of Mercy, 166n. 20
Creative imagination, 98–99, 102–4, 106, 116, 121, 129–32
Creative process, 97–100, 102–4, 106, 118, 120, 131, 167n. 6
Crisis of identity, 1, 4–5, 16, 21, 26–28, 31–41, 45, 50–89, 91–96, 111–12, 118–20, 127–29, 134, 152–55
Croce, Benedetto, 8–9
Cubism, 75, 166n. 6

D'Annunzio, Gabriele, 7, 17, 23, 44
Darwin, Charles, 23
De Filippo, Edoardo, 156
De Roberto, Luigi, 25; *I Viceré* (*The Viceroys*), 25
Determinism. *See* Positivism and Naturalism
Deus ex machina, 124
Dialectic, Pirandellian, 18, 50–51, 60–61, 88, 109–10, 117, 137, 147–48, 158n. 9
Dionysus, 132, 147
Disney, Walt, 162n. 5
Dissociation, 35–36, 38–40, 67–68, 70–75, 81, 92–96, 107, 127, 153–55
Dombroski, Robert S., 168n. 4
Don Juan, 11
Dostoyevsky, Fyodor, 33
Doubling of the self, 5–6, 35–39, 53–54, 64, 78–80, 83–85, 88, 107–10, 149, 153–55
Drama of ideas. *See* Theater of ideas
Driver, Tom F., 44
Dualism, Pirandellian, 18–19, 74, 76–96, 99–110, 114–117, 120, 140–41, 164n. 12, 167n. 12

Edenic world, 70, 122, 128
Einstein, Albert, 75

Esslin, Martin, 106
Eurydice, 132
Existentialism, 155

Fantasia (film), 162n. 5
Fascism, 5, 19, 20, 23, 168n. 10, 169n. 4
Fiera Letteraria, La, 68
Form and flux, 8, 40, 67–68, 70, 74, 76–85, 88–93, 95–96, 101–2, 112–14, 117, 140–41, 147–48, 153–55, 164n. 12, 166n. 7. *See also* dualism
Fortune. *See* chance
Fourth wall, 99–100, 107–108, 117
Fragmentation of identity and reality, 21, 33–41, 53–54, 63–75, 79–80, 82, 88, 92–96, 107, 110–12, 119–20, 138, 153–55, 166n. 6. *See also* consciousness; crisis of identity
Fragmentation of time, 80–81, 83–86
Frankenstein story, 38, 127
Frese Witt, Mary Ann, 133
Freudian psychoanalysis 75. *See also* psychoanalytical interpretations

Garbo, Greta, 162n. 5
Garcia Lorca, Federico, 156
Garibaldi, Giuseppe, 2
Genet, Jean, 156
Giacosa, Giuseppe, 44
Gilman, Richard, 107
Giudice, Gaspare 97, 157n. 2
Gobetti, Piero, 18, 159n. 17
Goethe, Johann Wolfgang von, 3, 136; *Römische Elegien* (*Roman Elegies*), 3, 136
Graf, Arturo, 137
Gramsci, Antonio 10–11
Grottesco, 45–46, 61–62, 160n. 2

Hamlet, 37
Hegel, W. F., 164n. 12
Henri IV, king of France, 80

Henry IV, Holy Roman Emperor, 77, 78, 82, 85, 163n. 5, 164n. 6
Herman, William, 166n. 20
Historical novel, 2, 137, 143–46
History, 67, 73, 76–90, 96, 143–45, 147
Hollywood, 162n. 5
Human condition, 1, 4–5, 10, 36–37, 44–45, 59, 73, 85, 87, 93, 106–7, 117–20, 122–25, 134–35, 138–39, 142–45. *See also* alienation; reality and illusion; societal imposition
Human document, 10, 22–24, 26, 46, 70, 74. *See also* naturalism
Humor, 7–9, 21, 25, 28–32, 36, 45, 61–62, 86, 126, 137, 139–41, 148, 150–51, 159n. 3

Ibsen, Henrik, 10, 42, 167n. 12
Illusion of theater, 98–120, 129–32
Illusions, 37, 47–51, 86, 94–96, 110, 129–33, 140, 143–45, 147–48, 150–53
Immanentism, 129, 168n. 7
Impersonality, authorial. *See* naturalism
Improvisational theater, 112–116
Incongruity. *See* chance; irony; paradox
Industrial revolution and society, 73, 121, 130
Intellect vs. instinct or emotion, 57–62, 104–5, 133, 147–48, 168n. 7. *See also* dualism
Interiority, 30–41, 51–62, 63–75, 91–92. *See also* consciousness; spirituality
Ionesco, Eugène, 155, 156
Irony, 24–25, 27–29, 56–57, 151–52. *See also* humor; paradox
Italian Academy 20, 23
Italian theater, history of, 42–45, 168n. 9
Jesus Christ, 126, 128, 129

Kligermann, Charles, 167n. 19, 168n. 20; "A Psychoanalytic Study of Pirandello's *Six Characters in Search of an Author*," 167n. 19
Knapp, Bettina L., 114

Landi, Stefano. *See* Stefano Pirandello
Laughter, 16, 29–30, 34–35, 47–48, 51, 61–62. *See also* consciousness
Lauretta, Enzo, 32–33
Lazarus, 126, 127, 129
Leone De Castris, Arcangelo, 32, 72
Life and art. *See* dualism; form and flux
Life and form. *See* dualism; form and flux
Life as theater, 76, 78–84, 113, 151
Local color. *See* naturalism
Love triangle, 44–48, 50–51, 55–62, 71, 78, 111, 150–52. *See also* adultery
Lo Vecchio-Musti, Manlio, 170n. 8
Lucas, Frank Laurence, 59
Lucente, Gregory L., 34, 160n. 9

Machiavelli, Niccolò, 158n. 10; *La Mandragola*, 158n. 10
Madness, 9, 14–16, 30, 47–49, 65–68, 70, 76–88, 140, 148
Magic Realism, 148–49
Magna Grecia, 11, 147
Magus, 114
Malipiero, Gian Francesco, 132
Man and machine, 70–75, 130
Manzoni, Alessandro, 145–46; *I promessi sposi* (*The Betrothed*), 145
Martoglio, Nino, 9, 42, 43
Mary Magdalene, 125
Masks and masquerades, 14–16, 20–21, 32, 38–39, 45, 52, 54, 56–57, 59–62, 64–65, 67, 70, 76–88, 91–93, 95–96, 100, 103–5, 117–19, 124, 148, 151–53, 161n. 5, 163n. 5. *See also* alienation; crisis of identity; societal impositions
Maternity and maternal archetypes, 11–13, 119, 125, 128, 132–35, 170n. 20; Mater dolorosa, 103; Mother Earth or Great

Maternity *(continued)*
Mother archetype 67–68, 119, 125, 128, 137–38; Virgin Annunciate, 152
Matilda of Tuscany, 77, 78, 80, 82, 85
Matteotti affair, 19
Matthei, Renate, 16, 130–31
May, Frederick, 136, 165n. 3
McCormick, E. Allen, 149
MGM, 162n. 5
Mind vs. nature. *See* intellect vs. instinct
Mirrors, 21, 34–36, 38, 53–54, 59, 63–65, 81, 85, 92, 106, 110–11, 127, 149, 153. *See also* consciousness; crisis of identity
Modernism, 21, 39, 41, 68, 75, 99–100, 145, 155–56
Mondadori Publishers, 138
Mortier, Alfred, 97
Multiplicity of human personality, 9, 18, 33, 52–54, 63–70, 79–80, 92–93, 103–4, 110, 148, 152–55. *See also* consciousness; crisis of identity
Musco, Angelo, 9–10, 43
Mussolini, Benito, 19, 20
Myths and archetypes, 121–22, 124–26, 128–35, 137–8, 148, 157n. 3; Don Juan archetype, 11; femme fatale archetype, 71, 73, 111; Mary Magdalene archetype, 125; Orphic myth, 132–33; Pygmalion myth, 91; Ulysses archetype, 32. *See also* maternity and maternal archetypes
Myth Trilogy, 19, 119, 121–135

Narcissism, 63–67, 88
Nardelli, Federico Vittore, 97
Naturalism, 5, 10, 17, 22–26, 30–31, 40–46, 54–55, 60–61, 74–75, 89, 99–100, 102, 108–10, 119, 126, 139, 142, 145–46, 156, 168n. 12. *See also* bourgeois drama; human document
Nature, 66–70, 73, 104, 121, 123–25, 128, 133–34, 137–38, 143

Nelson, Robert J., 110
Nicolosi, Francesco, 169n. 4
Nietzsche, Friedrich, 4, 44, 165n. 12
Noah and the Flood story, 124, 128
Nobel Prize for Literature, 20, 156
Nouveau roman, 75
Nuova Antologia, La, 30–31

Oedipal triangle, 117–18, 169n. 19. *See also* psychoanalytical interpretations
Ojetti, Ugo, 163n. 8
Oliver, Roger W., 164n. 12
O'Neill, Eugene, 156
Orestes, 37, 38
Orpheus, 132–33

Paolucci, Anne 11, 13, 50, 129, 158n. 10
Paradox, 10, 12–13, 16, 24–25, 27–28, 30–41, 50, 57–60, 79, 141–42, 147–48, 151–55. *See also* dualism; humor; irony
Pascal, Blaise, 40
Pascal, Theophile, 40
Pedoto, Constance A., 166n. 6
Picasso, Lamberto, 19, 87
Picasso, Pablo, 166n. 6
Pirandellismo, 17–18, 51, 60–61, 93, 117–18
Pirandello, Fausto, 9
Pirandello, Lietta, 9, 17, 97, 169n.19
Pirandello, Luigi
Biographical information, 1–21, 42, 45, 87–88, 97, 163n. 5, 166n.16, 168n. 8, 169n.15, 169n.19

Works

Adamo e Eva, 162n. 1
All for the Best (Tutto per bene), 153
"Arte e Scienza," 7
As You Desire Me (Come tu mi vuoi), 153–55, 162n. 5

Works *(continued)*
  L'epilogo, 42. See also *The Vise*
  Barbaro, 42
  "Black Kid, The" ("Il capretto nero"),
  146–48
  Cap and Bells (Il berretto a sonagli),
  10, 13–16, 149
  "Capannetta," 5
  Carteggi Inediti, 163n. 8
  *Changeling, The (La favola del figlio
  cambiato),* 132–33
  "Ciàula Discovers the Moon" ("Ciàula
  scopre la luna"), 143
  "Colloqui coi personaggi 1 & II," 97,
  165n. 3
  Come prima, meglio di prima, 134
  "Dialoghi tra il Gran Me e il piccolo
  me," 157n. 4
  Diana and Tuda (Diana e la Tuda), 18,
  89–91, 96, 164n. 16, 165n. 18
  *Each in His Own Way (Ciascuno a suo
  modo),* 17, 99, 100–101, 107–112, 116–
  17, 119, 162n. 6
  Elegie renane, 3, 137–38
  *Festival of Our Lord of the Ship, The
  (Sagra del Signore della nave),* 19–20,
  43
  "First Night, The" ("Prima Notte"),
  139
  Fuori di chiave, 138
  "Gioca, Pietro!," 162n. 5
  Grafted (L'innesto), 134
  Henry IV (Enrico IV), 29–30, 76–89,
  90, 96, 118, 154, 165n. 18; as trag-
  edy 86–87; life as theater 76, 78–84
  "In silenzio," 162n. 5
  "Jar, The" ("La giara"), 146–47
  Jar, The (La giara), 10
  *Late Mattia Pascal, The (Il fu Mattia
  Pascal),* 6–8, 11, 30–41, 69, 74, 83,
  140, 156, 160n. 8
  Lazarus (Lazzaro), 121–22, 126–29,
  134

License, The (La patente), 150–51,
  170n. 8
Liolà, 10–13, 16, 146–47, 149–50
"Little Red Booklet, The" ("Il libretto
  rosso"), 142
"Long Dress, The" ("La veste lunga"),
  140
Mal giocondo, 3, 137
*Man, Beast, and Virtue (L'uomo, la
  bestia e la virtú),* 151–52
Maschere nude, 16, 54, 136, 166n. 8
*Merry-Go-Round of Love, The (Il
  turno),* 141–42, 146
*Mountain Giants, The (I giganti della
  montagna),* 19, 121–22, 129–33
Naked Masks. See *Maschere Nude.*
"Naked Truth" ("La vita nuda"), 140–
  41
New Colony, The (La nuova colonia),
  121–26, 128–29, 133
No One Knows How (Non si sa come),
  44
Novelle per un anno, 136, 138–39, 148,
  165n. 3
*Old and the Young, The (I vecchi e i
  giovani),* 2, 137, 143–46, 169n. 4
*One, No One ,and One Hundred Thou-
  sand (Uno, nessuno e centomila),* 52,
  63–70, 73–75, 89, 146, 148, 153, 168n.
  7
On Humor (L'umorismo), 7–9, 24, 28–
  30, 40, 89, 136
"Other Son, The" ("L'altro figlio"), 143
Outcast, The (L'esclusa), 25–28, 39, 41,
  141, 146, 151
Pasqua di Gea, 4, 137–38, 157n. 3
Pensaci, Giacomino!, 10, 150–51,
  170n. 8
Pier Gudrò, 137
*Pleasure of Honesty, The (Il piacere
  dell'onestà),* 54–59, 61–62
"Quando si è capito il giuoco," 161n. 7
Ragione degli altri, La, 133–34

Works *(continued)*
 Right You Are (If You Think So) (Cosí è [se vi pare]), 10, 45–54, 61–62, 110–11, 155
 Rules of the Game, The (Il giuoco delle parti), 54–55, 57–62, 118–19, 166n. 7
 Shoot! The Notebooks of Serafino Gubbio, Cinematograph Operator (Quaderni di Serafino Gubbio operatore), 70–75, 101, 146, 157n. 1
 Short Stories (trans. F. May), 165n. 3
 Sicilian Limes (Lumie di Sicilia), 9
 "Signora Frola e il Signor Ponza, suo genero, La," 161n. 7
 Six Characters in Search of an Author (Sei personaggi in cerca d'autore), 16–17, 42, 87, 98–99, 100–107, 114, 116–19, 133, 156, 167n. 19, 168n. 20
 "Soffio," 149
 Suo marito, 136, 162n. 1
 "Tirocinio," 161n. 7
 To Clothe the Naked (Vestire gli ignudi), 93–96, 165n. 20
 To Find Oneself (Trovarsi), 90, 92–93, 96
 Tonight We Improvise (Questa sera si recita a soggetto), 17, 43, 99–101, 112–16, 119–20, 167n. 15
 "Tragedy of a Character, The" ("La tragedia di un personaggio"), 97–98, 105, 165n. 3
 "Train Whistled, The" ("Il treno ha fischiato"), 139–40
 "Verità, La," 158n. 13
 Vise, The (La morsa), 9, 42–44
 "Visit, The" ("La visita"), 148–49
 "Wheelbarrow, The" ("La carriola"), 148
 When Somebody Is Somebody (Quando si è qualcuno), 90–92, 96
Pirandello, Stefano (Pirandello's father), 2–3
Pirandello, Stefano (Pirandello's son), 9, 19, 68, 129, 131, 162n. 5
Piscator, Erwin, 167n. 15
Pitoïff, George and Ludmilla, 17, 103–4
Play within a play, 17, 100–102, 106–17, 119, 131–33, 167n. 19
Portulano, Maria Antonietta Pirandello, 5–6, 9, 88, 118, 157n. 4, 157n. 6
Positivism, 5, 22–23, 30, 46. *See also* naturalism
Praga, Marco, 44
Psychoanalytic interpretations, 85, 87–88, 118–20, 159n. 1, 164n. 10, 167n. 19, 168n. 20
Pupo. See puppets.
Puppets and puppet shows, 3, 15–16, 37–38, 52, 81, 88, 130, 132, 159n. 14, 161n. 2
Pygmalion, 91

Radcliff-Umstead, Douglas, 68, 74, 145
Ragusa, Olga, 115, 157n. 5, 159n. 3, 160n. 11
Raisonneur characters 18, 51–62, 111, 114, 117–18
Rapport between drama and fiction, 9–11, 42, 146, 149–50, 158n. 13, 161n. 7, 165n. 3, 170n. 8
Realism. *See* naturalism
Reality and illusion. 11–15, 26–28, 40–41, 46–62, 82–83, 85, 88, 94–95, 107, 109–12, 117, 119–20, 134, 144–45, 150–55. *See also* masks and masquerades; truth
Regionalism. *See* naturalism; positivism
Reinhardt, Max, 17, 167n. 15
Relativity of reality or perception, 46–54, 63–75, 88, 95, 105, 107, 110–12, 147–48, 152–55. *See also* consciousness; masks and masquerades; reality and illusion
Religious faith, 121–22, 125–29
Ricci-Gramitto, Caterina Pirandello, 2

Risorgimento (Italian Unification), 2–3, 137, 143–45
Rizzo, Gino, 85, 88, 164n. 10, 167n. 19
Roaring '20s, 43
Roland, Alan, 85, 88, 164n. 10, 167n. 19
Rosso di San Secondo, Pier Maria, 158n. 9; *Marionette che passione!*, 161n. 2
Rovetta, Gerolamo, 44
Ruggieri, Ruggero, 19, 164n. 9
Ruttmann, Walter, 162n. 5

St. Francis of Assisi, 68
Salinari, Carlo, 21, 28, 73, 143, 155, 159n. 21; *Miti e coscienza del Decadentismo italiano*, 21
Sara, wife of Abraham, 128
Sartre, Jean-Paul, 155
Schlueter, June, 79
Schulz-Lander, Jenny, 4, 137
Sciascia, Leonardo, 133, 157n. 6, 158n. 9
Science and faith, 121, 126–27, 129
Séailles, Gabriel, 7, 157n. 5; *Essai sur le Génie dans l'Art*, 157n. 5
Seduction, 11–13, 71, 94–95, 110–12
Self-awareness. *See* consciousness; crisis of identity
Shakespeare, William, 86
Shock therapy, 78
Sicilian Fasces, 144, 169n. 4
Sicilianism, 133, 138, 158n. 9
Sicilian Plays, 9–16, 19–20, 42–43, 45, 132–33, 149–52
Sicily, Pirandello and, 1–5, 10–17, 21, 43, 101, 112, 119–20, 141–48, 158n. 6
Snow White story, 64
Societal impositions and interference, 13, 26–27, 31–32, 34, 46–52, 65–67, 83, 94–95, 119–20, 123–25, 140, 142–45, 150–53. *See also* alienation
Sodom and Gomorrah, 124
Sogliuzzo, A. Richard, 87, 126, 164n. 16, 169n. 10

Spiritualism, 36–40, 160n. 11
Spirituality, 67–68, 125, 126–29, 165n. 18. *See also* interiority; religious faith
Stagecraft, 99, 102–10, 113, 116, 152
Stampa, La, 156
Starkie, Walter, 11
Strehler, Giorgio, 130
Strindberg, August, 42, 167n. 12
Styan, John L., 50, 86; *The Dark Comedy*, 86
Subconscious, 44, 60, 87–88, 114, 118–20, 130–33, 167n. 19. *See also* psychoanalytical interpretations
Subjectivity. *See* consciousness; interiority
Suicide, 9, 31, 35, 39, 50, 67–68, 71, 94–95, 100–101, 131, 140, 148, 169n. 19
Surrealism, 148–49
Sypher, Wylie, 166n. 6
Szondi, Peter, 167n. 12

Teatro d'Arte di Roma, 19–20, 43, 87, 97, 160n. 2, 164n. 9, 164n. 16, 166n. 8, 169n. 10
Theater, nature of, 99–120, 129–132
Theater of ideas, 10, 42–43, 51
Theater of consciousness, 60
Theater plays, 17, 20, 97–120, 131, 156
Theory of evolution, 23
Theory of relativity, 75
Theosophy, 36–40, 160n. 11
Tilgher, Adriano, 18, 19, 88–93, 164n. 11; Life/Form formula, 88–93, 165n. 18; *Studi del teatro contemporaneo*, 89
Transgression, 12–13, 27–28, 66–67, 71, 94–95, 150–51
Treves Publishers, 8, 25
Truth, 14, 22–23, 47–52, 62, 70, 83, 94–95, 105–7, 110–12, 117, 151, 153–55. *See also* consciousness; masks and masquerades; multiplicity of human personality; relativity of reality or perception; reality and illusion

Ulysses, 32
Utopian ideal, 121–24, 129

Verdi, Giuseppe, 100, 101, 113; *Il Trovatore,* 101
Verga, Giovanni, 5, 23–26, 126, 139; theory of the vanquished, 23–24, 26, 126, 139; *I Malavoglia* (*The House by the Medlar Tree*), 25, 126; *Mastro Don Gesualdo,* 25
Verisimilitude, 41, 102, 167n. 12. *See also* naturalism

Verismo (Italian naturalism). *See* naturalism
Views on literature, Pirandellian, 7–8, 18–20, 23–25, 28–30, 40–41, 89–91, 93, 97–100, 102–3, 159n. 3, 164n. 12
Vittorini, Domenico, 159n. 18
von Stroheim, Erich, 162n. 5

Wellwarth, George E., 115
World War I, 9, 44, 61, 154

Yeats, William Butler, 156